W9-AQS-749

JX
1904.5
. T415
1995

# TEACHING
# ABOUT INTERNATIONAL
# CONFLICT AND PEACE

SUNY Series, Theory, Research, and Practice in Social Education
Peter H. Martorella, Editor

BELL LIBRARY
TEXAS A&M UNIVERSITY
CORPUS CHRISTI

# TEACHING ABOUT INTERNATIONAL CONFLICT AND PEACE

*edited by*

## MERRY M. MERRYFIELD
### and
## RICHARD C. REMY

State University
of New York
Press

YAAABIL LIAB
TEXAS A&M UNIVERSITY
CORPUS CHRISTI

This publication was developed through a grant from the United States Institute of Peace. Additional support for this publication was provided by The Ohio State University's College of Education and the Mershon Center. The ideas expressed here do not necessarily reflect the opinions or policies of these organizations.

Published by
State University of New York Press, Albany

© 1995 State University of New York

All rights reserved

Production by Susan Geraghty
Marketing by Nancy Farrell

Printed in the United States of America

No part of this book may be used or reproduced in any manner whatsoever without written permission. No part of this book may be stored in a retrieval system or transmitted in any form or by any means including electronic, electrostatic, magnetic tape, mechanical, photocopying, recording, or otherwise without the prior permission in writing of the publisher.

For information, address State University of New York Press, State University Plaza, Albany, N.Y., 12246

**Library of Congress Cataloging-in-Publication Data**

Teaching about international conflict and peace / editors, Merry M.
    Merryfield & Richard C. Remy.
        p.     cm. — (SUNY series, theory, research, and practice in
    social education)
        Includes bibliographical references and index.
        ISBN 0-7914-2373-5 (hardcover : acid-free paper). — ISBN 0-7914-2374-3
    (pbk. : acid-free paper)
        1. Peace—Study and teaching—United States.  2. Pacific
    settlement of international disputes—Study and teaching—United
    States.  I. Merryfield, Merry M., 1945–  .  II. Remy, Richard C.
    III. Series.
    JX1904.5.T415   1995
    327.1'071'273—dc20
                                                                    94-13643
                                                                    CIP

10  9  8  7  6  5  4  3  2  1

# CONTENTS

# REVIEWERS

## FIELD TESTED AND REVIEWED ENTIRE BOOK

Carole Hahn
Emory University

Steven Lamy
University Southern California

Howard Mehlinger
Indiana University

Murry Nelson
Pennsylvania State University

Jan Tucker
Florida International University

### *Reviewed Book*

Marie Blake
Upper Arlington High School
Upper Arlington, OH

Keith Bossard
Columbus Alternative High School
Columbus, OH

Craig Brelsford
Eastland Career Center
Groveport, OH

Susan Chase
Hilliard High School
Hilliard OH

Tim Dove
McCord Middle School
Worthington OH

Pat Forward
McCord Middle School
Worthington OH

Shirley Hoover
Upper Arlington High School
Upper Arlington, OH

Richard Lackey
Hilliard High School
Hilliard, OH

David Loynachan
Columbus Alternative High School
Columbus, OH

Dan Ludlum
Upper Arlington High School
Upper Arlington, OH

James Norris
Linden McKinley High School
Columbus OH

Robert Rayburn
Eastland Career Center
Groveport, OH

Scott Reeves
Independence High School
Columbus, OH

Steven Shapiro
Reynoldsburg High School
Reynoldsburg, OH

Michelle Stasa
Linden McKinley High School
Columbus, OH

Jay Wise
Eastland Career Center
Groveport, OH

Barbara Wainer
Independence High School
Columbus, OH

Connie White
Linden McKinley High School
Columbus, OH

Robert Wightman
McCord Middle School
Worthington, OH

Bruce Wythe
Hilliard High School
Hilliard, OH

## REVIEWED ONE OR MORE ESSAYS

Chadwick Alger
The Ohio State University

Robert C. Johansen
Harvard University

Richard Pierre Claude
University of Maryland

Louis Kriesberg
Syracuse University

Vicki L. Golich
California State University
  at San Marcos

Joe Kruzel
The Ohio State University

Elizabeth C. Hanson
University of Connecticut

Timothy J. Lomperis
Duke University

Barry B. Hughes
University of Denver

Claude E. Welch
State University of New York at Buffalo

# INTRODUCTION

Today people in our nation and the world are increasingly connected to international conflict through dynamic global change. Although conflict has been a characteristic of the human condition throughout history, the scientific revolution and global dissemination of modern technologies have accelerated the sharing of knowledge of human conflict so that the majority of the world's peoples are cognizant of and involved in international conflicts at home and abroad. Headlines and television news remind us daily of the many kinds of conflicts that characterize life on planet Earth in the last decade of the twentieth century. International conflicts are not only wars of weapons or words. Terrorism, arms races, economic rivalries, competitions for power and prestige, and the violence done by widespread pollution and poverty are part of international conflict in today's world. International conflict touches all our lives.

The spread of human conflict to the global level has been accompanied throughout history by the persistent effort of thoughtful people to find ways to limit, manage, or resolve international conflicts. Over time, nations and other international actors have evolved a variety of practices and ideas for managing conflict such as diplomacy, international law, treaties, alliances, and other means of negotiation and settlement. Scholars have studied the management and resolution of international conflict and developed a base of knowledge about such critical issues as the use and control of military power, diplomacy, human rights, self-determination, economic cooperation, and the global environment. Given the interconnected nature of today's world, knowledge of such practices and issues is critical for citizenship in a global age.

Yet over the last two decades there has been a growing concern that American schools are not preparing young people to understand or participate effectively in today's increasingly interdependent, conflictual world. In the past many teacher education programs have not prepared teachers to teach about any international topics, and this remains the case even today. The American Association for Colleges of Teacher Education has estimated that only about 5 percent of the nation's K–12 teachers have had any academic preparation in international studies. Other scholars have noted that few preservice teachers study world history, international relations, or the dynamic changes of globalization in the twentieth century. College students in teacher education programs take fewer courses with international content than do all other college majors. It is no wonder that the National Governor's Association has pointed to inadequate teacher preparation in global education as a major obstacle in the United States' ability to meet the economic, political, and social challenges of the twenty-first century.

This lack of attention to international content in college and university teacher education programs is especially worrisome as more and more states and school districts mandate courses in world cultures, local-global connections, and global history in secondary social studies. Teachers need to be prepared to teach about global interconnectedness and international conflict, yet few instructional materials on these topics have been developed for beginning teachers or preservice teacher education programs.

*Teaching about International Conflict and Peace* was designed to help social studies educators better understand international conflict management as they learn about instructional methods and begin to teach. The book brings together current scholarship on major topics in the management of international conflict and methods for teaching that are especially important in globally oriented social studies education. We have selected international topics and instructional methods that are critical for preparing secondary social studies teachers for globally oriented curriculum innovations in an era of school reform and restructuring.

*Teaching about International Conflict and Peace* also benefits from our own long-term research and instruction in civic and global education and our school-university collaboration in restructuring preservice teacher education. Over the last four years we have developed a Professional Development School (PDS) Network in Social Studies and Global Education at the Ohio State University. Outstanding social studies teachers and university professors have worked together in developing new program goals and rubrics (assessment tools for assignments), team-teaching methods courses, mentoring and supervising preservice teachers, and providing ongoing inservice education and professional presentations in global education. Twenty of these teachers field-tested and reviewed this book as a part of our new field-based methods courses. Many of its issues, insights, and illustrations have been influenced by the long-term collaboration of preservice teachers, inservice teachers, and university professors.

The book is divided into two parts. It is the purpose of the part 1 (chapters 1 and 2) to explain relationships between substantive content about international conflict management and exemplary teaching practice in secondary social studies classrooms. In the first chapter, Merry M. Merryfield and Richard C. Remy discuss ways in which such content fits into secondary social studies and how some instructional methods are especially appropriate. Through vignettes of actual classroom practice, the reader learns from experienced teachers how they have integrated these instructional methods to achieve content goals. In the second chapter, Steve Shapiro and Merry M. Merryfield provide a case study of an experienced teacher and student teacher working together to develop and teach a unit on international conflict management in a school that is undergoing some fundamental restructuring as a member of the Coalition of Essential Schools. They capture the planning process from selecting content, assessment, and teaching methods to developing the scope and sequence of lessons. They also provide insights into the implementation of such ideas as backwards-building curriculum, interdisciplinary connections, and authentic assessment.

In part 2, eminent scholars provide substantive essays on major themes in international conflict management. Chadwick F. Alger provides a conceptual map to elements in the management and resolution of international conflict. David P. Barash focuses on the roles of diplomacy and negotiation in bringing about peaceful settlements. Peter D. Feaver describes how the use and control of the military contribute to the management of international disputes. Karen Mingst analyzes the role of economic cooperation in reducing international conflict. David P. Forsythe examines issues of human rights in the context of international disagreements. Dov Ronen explores how the search for self-determination relates to the management of international conflict. Finally, Marvin S. Soroos looks at emerging environmental issues related to the seas, air, and land shared by the peoples of the world. At the end of the book, an appendix on resources developed by Yasemin Alptekin-Oguzertem provides additional insights into organizations, instructional materials, computer networks, and other scholarly work that can help teachers improve their instruction on international conflict management.

We believe that *Teaching About International Conflict and Peace* can make a significant difference in preparing social studies teachers to help their students acquire knowledge and understanding of how the peoples of the world have dealt with international conflict in the past and how increasing global interconnections provide new alternatives for the management of international conflict in the present and future.

PART 1

# Linking Content, Methods, and Educational Goals

# CHAPTER 1

# *Choosing Content and Methods for Teaching About International Conflict and Peace*

## Merry M. Merryfield and Richard C. Remy

Social studies is about people and their interactions in groups ranging from the family to the global community. Ever since people have lived in groups conflict has been an inevitable characteristic of the human condition. The rise of modern nation-states, the scientific revolution, and the global dissemination of modern technology have made human conflict a fact of contemporary international life as well as a continuing feature of people's face-to-face relations.

The spread of human conflict to the global level has been accompanied throughout history by the persistent effort of thoughtful people to find ways to limit, manage or resolve international conflicts. Over time nations and other international actors have evolved a variety of practices and ideas for managing conflict such as diplomacy, international law, treaties, alliances, and other means of negotiation and settlement.

Scholars have studied the management and resolution of international conflict and developed a base of knowledge about such critical issues as the use and control of military power, diplomacy, human rights, self-determination, economic cooperation, and the global environment. Knowledge of such practices and issues is a key for competent citizenship in a global age.

In recognition of this fact more and more states and school districts are mandating courses in world cultures, local-global connections, and global history in secondary social studies. Beginning teachers need to be prepared to teach about global interconnectedness and international conflict and peace, yet there are few instructional materials on these topics developed for beginning teachers or preservice teacher education programs.

This book was designed to help you better understand international conflict and peace as you learn about instructional methods and begin to teach. The book brings together current scholarship on major topics in the management of international conflict and methods for teaching that are especially important in globally-oriented social studies education. We have selected international topics and instructional methods that are critical for preparing secondary social studies teachers for globally-oriented curriculum innovations in an era of school reform and restructuring.

The book is divided into two parts. Part One (Chapters 1 and 2) explains the relationships between content about international conflict and peace, and exemplary teaching practice in secondary social studies classrooms. In Part Two, eminent scholars provide essays on major themes in international conflict management relevant to the social studies curriculum.

## THE CHALLENGE OF SELECTING CONTENT AND METHODS

Most beginning teachers struggle with choosing content and appropriate instructional methods. Matt, a preservice teacher in his second social studies methods course, and Barb, his cooperating teacher, are discussing a unit Matt is planning to teach in Barb's global history class.

> BARB: We should be ready to start teaching about independence movements and self-determination next week. How have you decided how to begin the unit?
> MATT: First the students need to understand the effects of World War II on colonized peoples. Then we'll examine steps in gaining indepen-

dence and compare independence movements and reactions of colonial powers in different countries. Finally we will come up with what the concept of 'self-determination' meant then and what it means today. Here are my ideas.

Matt pulls out his tentative plans for sequencing the unit and shares it with Barb.

BARB: So you want to begin with outcomes of the war for colonial peoples in Africa and Asia. How are you going to teach about what it meant to those people? What would be appropriate methods to use given your goals and content?

MATT: I could have them examine some primary sources where people are explaining their views. Perhaps they could read some speeches or letters or even stories that were written about that time? They could use that information to role-play discussions that could have taken place in Algeria or Kenya or India . . . And France or Britain. Or I could lecture on the relationship between the war and independence movements over the last fifty years? They do well in cooperative groups, so I could have them work in small groups and use those books in your collection to construct a time-line of independence movements from the 1940s to today. There's that video on the independence movement in Indonesia. I could use that as the beginning of a case study. There are so many ways to teach. How do I decide?

As Matt indicates, there are many choices. What methods of teaching will be most effective in helping his students understand self-determination? How can his instructional methods support his content goals? By choosing methods that are appropriate for his students and congruent with his content, Matt can provide a cohesive and powerful learning experience.

In this chapter we share our assumptions about teaching and learning, discuss steps involved in making decisions on choosing content and methods, and then describe methods that are particularly appropriate for teaching about how people throughout history and today have found ways to deal with, manage, or resolve international conflicts. By *methods* we mean the ways a teacher may structure teaching and learning experiences for students. The chapter concludes with vignettes of actual classroom practice that illustrate how experienced teachers have integrated these instructional methods to achieve content goals.

## ASSUMPTIONS ABOUT TEACHING AND LEARNING

This book is grounded in several assumptions about the teaching and learning of social studies. These assumptions, in effect, form criteria by which one can make judgements about the quality of instruction. Research on teaching and learning indicates that instruction that embodies these assumptions will be more effective than instruction that fails to do so.

### *Planning Begins with Knowledge of One's Students*

Although American secondary school students share many similarities, it is the complexity of their differences that challenges every teacher. We must understand our students before we can effectively help them learn. Knowledge of students' backgrounds and lifestyles (for example, a student's Muslim upbringing, a father's job at General Motors), developmental levels (an eighth grader's attention span of twelve minutes), cognitive styles (a visual learner), special needs (a ninth grader reading at a fifth-grade level), and personal interests or experiences (a fascination with computers) help teachers make appropriate instructional decisions. Good teachers use knowledge of their students to sequence content, choose methods and materials, connect them to the topic under study, create interest, build on previous knowledge and skills, and individualize the process of learning so that all students can and will succeed.

### *Content Is Basic*

We believe that good teaching in the social studies is based on the conceptual understandings and knowledge available from the social sciences, history, the humanities, and occasionally other disciplines. Findings from more than twenty-five years of research in cognitive science—the study of how we think, remember, and learn —clearly indicate that attempting to teach problem solving and higher-level thinking skills in the absence of solid content is not effective. Put another way, trying to teach students inquiry and thinking skills without simultaneously teaching domain specific knowledge —knowledge, for instance, about world history or American foreign policy—will not work, because such "strategies can help us process knowledge, but first we have to have the knowledge to process."[1]

Not just any historical or social science knowledge will prepare young people for citizenship in the twenty-first century. The ever increasing political, economic, social, technological, and environmental connections between the United States and the rest of the world demand that American students develop an understanding of why international conflicts arise and how such conflicts can be managed, resolved, or possibly avoided.

## Active, Reflective Learning is Essential

Students master content not only by being exposed to information through readings and lectures or by learning to recall facts for a test but also by engaging in a reflective process in which they make the information their own by evaluating and using it. Teaching and learning are likely to be most effective when the teacher serves as coach and reflective practitioner and when the students are active learners who take responsibility for their own learning. In this process the student learns to be a researcher, thinker, decision maker, and meaning maker.

Survey approaches that skim the surface of large bodies of discrete facts do not give students the time for reflection or the depth of knowledge they need to apply the content to new situations. Used judiciously, the less-is-more or depth-over-coverage approach in planning curriculum and selecting content can provide students the time and in-depth knowledge they need for mastery learning, reflection, and practice in using knowledge. Although teachers may employ a variety of tools and methods to evaluate student learning, there should be some assessment where students demonstrate their mastery of learning through meaningful tasks, performances, or exhibitions that are authentic for their adult life as citizens in a democracy.

## Attention to Values Is Necessary

By the nature of its content, social studies instruction is value laden and deals with controversial issues. One cannot understand the human condition without considering the role of individual and

---

[1]John T. Bruer, "The Mind's Journey From Novice to Expert," *American Educator* 17, no. 2 (summer 1993): 15.

societal values in the evolution of human history and without paying some attention to past and present perspectives on injustice, inequality, and inhumanity. If the study of international conflict management is to be addressed effectively in the classroom, students must understand how human differences in values, gender, race, ethnicity, religion, national origin, or economic development have been and continue to be the basis for conflict, discrimination, and aggression.

## Instruction Must Have Variety

A central feature of good teaching is instructional variety. We have all known social studies teachers who rely heavily on one method as *the* way they teach day after day. In some schools students know that Mr. Davis will lecture on history, in economics Ms. Casper will have them answer questions out of the textbook, and geography means watching videos with Mr. Page. Not only is the use of the same instructional method unstimulating to students and teacher alike, but such teaching does not address diverse student needs and learning styles. Some students learn effectively by reading, writing, or listening, but many students need visuals, cooperative learning, active learning, or hands-on experiences. Instructional variety gives all students opportunity to demonstrate their strengths and work on their weaknesses.

Teachers who seek out and incorporate a variety of teaching methods learn to improve their effectiveness as facilitators of learning as they grow professionally from one year to the next. Every time we try a new method or experiment with new materials, we have the opportunity to examine and reflect upon the eternal questions of teaching and learning—what involves the students in the learning process and excites them about the subject? What helps them master content and learn to synthesize and make use of knowledge? How do students learn *how* to learn? Such reflective practice is central to becoming a good teacher. In the vignettes that conclude this chapter you will meet experienced teachers who continue to improve their teaching by finding new materials and integrating new methods into their practice year after year.

## Content, Methods and Educational Goals Are Connected

Finally, there should be a direct relationship between teaching methods and knowledge, skill, and attitudinal objectives. How we teach should support what we teach. The lecture method, for instance, can be an excellent means to convey a large amount of factual information to students but is ill suited to helping students learn to develop thinking skills. Teachers who take account of the relationship among content, educational goals, and methods plan instruction so that *how* they teach maximizes their educational goals. Some teaching methods are more appropriate than others for teaching about major dimensions of international conflict management, such as diplomacy, negotiation, peaceful settlement, military power, economic cooperation, human rights, self-determination, and the global environment. These methods can help students better understand and reflect upon the complexity and interconnectedness of international conflict management and encourage them to apply what they are learning to their own decisions, actions, and worldviews.

## INTEGRATING CONTENT
## ON INTERNATIONAL CONFLICT AND PEACE
## WITH THE SOCIAL STUDIES CURRICULUM

A key theme of this book is that if our students are to make informed judgments and decisions in today's world, they must develop some fundamental understanding of the management, resolution, and avoidance of international conflict. For this to happen, social studies educators need to be prepared to teach about themes in international conflict and peace in basic social studies courses.

What is the process of planning instruction that will bring topics in international conflict and peace into your social studies curriculum? Matt, the preservice teacher we met earlier, has just finished his first day of teaching and sits down to discuss it with Barb, his cooperating teacher.

MATT: I'm not sure what went wrong. They certainly got confused over my instructions on developing cases. They just sat and looked at the print and video materials I had brought in for them to use. Was it because they don't understand self-determination? Or was it a mistake to think they could construct case studies? Maybe I should have first shown them how I developed that case study of self-determination in India.

BARB: Sounds like you aren't sure whether they understood the content or whether you should have used another method.

MATT: You make it look so easy. I guess I thought I could just chose a topic and a way to teach from the ones I've seen you use. It's so complicated. I have to decide what to teach and how to teach it, find resources, and get it all organized—and then they say they don't understand, and I have to change it as I teach. How can I do better tomorrow?

Good teachers do make planning look easy, but most beginning teachers find it difficult and confusing at first. Where do you begin? An important first step is to to recognize that there is no one right way to plan social studies instruction in the United States. In fact most teachers modify the way they plan through years of practice as they learn, experiment, and incorporate ideas from colleagues, inservice education, and professional journals or meetings. Experienced teachers have developed many approaches to planning courses. In some school districts or specific schools, teachers are required to write formal plans that meet criteria such as those embodied in state frameworks or proficiency tests or are consistent with a school district's graded course of study. In other districts or schools without such criteria teachers often develop their own individual approach to sequencing content, organizing instructional units, and writing lesson plans.

### Planning Instruction: Forward or Backward?

Many teachers begin the planning process by making decisions on the scope and sequence for the entire course of study (for example, the breadth and depth of a year-long world history course) and then allocating time periods for specific topics (the first nine-week grading period on ancient and classical civilizations) or questions (three weeks for, How has technology changed the environment?). Most teachers use unit planning to develop instruction on a single topic or theme for one to several weeks (for example, a three-week unit on conflict in the medieval world). Daily lesson plans are usually sequenced within the unit plan and modified as they are taught (a lesson of map work and small group discussion on the spread of diffusion of Islam may end up taking two days instead of one).

Traditionally teachers have built their curriculum forward

from setting goals or objectives to developing lesson one, two, three, four, and so forth. The major assessment for student learning (such as a unit test) has been usually developed last, perhaps even after much of the unit has been taught. Working with new educational reforms such as Ted Sizer's Coalition of Essential Schools, some social studies teachers are now planning backward. They first develop essential questions that are the targets for student learning, and then they plan how they can assess the students' performance in answering those questions. After the assessment is developed, the teachers plan backwards to identify the knowledge and skills students need in order to achieve success in the assessment. The vignette of Steve Shapiro's planning at the end of this chapter and his unit in chapter 2 illustrate interdisciplinary teaming and backwards building curriculum in high school social studies.

At each step in the planning process, teachers make decisions on educational outcomes (what students should know, be able to do, and be like), on the scope and sequence of knowledge, skills, and attitudes, and on the instructional methods that help students to learn. Teachers often alter instructional plans in the process of teaching to meet the needs of students and the many interruptions they usually encounter during the school day.

## Identifying Content for Basic Social Studies Courses

Although there is no national curriculum in social studies per se, the typical secondary school curriculum includes courses in world and U.S. history and geography, U.S. government, and economics. How do topics in international conflict and peace relate to such courses? While we cannot answer that question in detail here, we can give some examples of how the topics and issues presented by the international relations scholars in part 2 of this book fit with these courses. As you study the essays in part 2 you will readily see how systematic attention to such topics can enrich your social studies courses by helping your students:

1. view the world from multicultural and global perspectives and appreciate the views of people different and similar to themselves;

2. make connections over time (past, present and future) and space (local, national, regional, and global) as they examine events, ideas, and issues;

3. apply the knowledge and skills they have already mastered to interests, issues, or concerns in their own lives so that they can better meet the challenges and realities posed by an interdependent world.

**World/Global History.** Whether social studies teachers use a chronological approach or a thematic one, most teach about the rise and fall of great kingdoms, civilizations, nations, and their alliances. Having used their military to subdue new peoples and take new lands, many rulers throughout history enforced peace through conquest and direct or indirect rule. Students can compare the use of the military to bring about peace in the time of the Pax Romana with its use to bring about peace in India during colonialization or its use to bring about peace in Bosnia in the 1990s. Issues such as human rights and self determination can serve as major themes in the study of the world's history, as slavery, genocide, use of torture, suppression of people's rights and people's search for self-government have gone hand in hand with conquest, imperialism, colonialization, and liberation.

Throughout history people have found ways to maintain peaceful contact and interaction through diplomacy, negotiation, alliances, and the trade of products and services. At the same time, the search for trade routes, products, and markets has often precipitated conflict and raised issues of human rights, ethics, and fairness. Students could compare the effects of trade on conflict and peace from the Phoenicians and early Arab traders to the Spanish globalization of trade, the integration of the European Community, the 1990 conflict in the Persian Gulf, and the recent round of the General Agreement on Tariffs and Trade (GATT). Over the course of history, what have been the relationships between trade and the use of the military? What have been the benefits of economic alliances? What have been the connections between economic development and peace? Can economic boycotts bring about political change? What roles have diplomacy, negotiation, and alliances played in shaping the world of today?

The history of the world is one of increasing globalization through technological changes in transportation, communications, energy, agriculture, industry, health, and engineering. These innovations have brought peoples closer together and, in general, improved the quality of life for people on the planet. New technologies have also given rise to new environmental issues and conflicts about our global commons of land, air, and water. From the study of early terracing of rice patties and building of dikes to today's pollution and urbanization, history is also the study of humans modifying their physical environment. How have people worked together to manage conflicts over the use of the oceans, the atmosphere, Antarctica, and outer space? What roles have the United Nations, regional alliances such as Rarotonga Treaty's South Pacific Nuclear-Free Zone, or people's organizations such as Greenpeace played in management or resolution of environmental conflicts?

**World Cultures/World Geography.**    Contemporary world cultures and the planet's changing physical environment are often major topics of study in secondary geography courses. Themes in international conflict and peace can serve to unify these courses and help students develop a global perspective on the world's cultures, regions, and ecological systems. For example, in many world geography courses students study regional units such as North America, Europe, Africa, Asia, and so on. Focusing on unifying themes such as dealing with conflict or managing the global environment, teachers can help students synthesize and connect what they have learned about each region's experiences with environmental issues and conflict management and apply these generalizations to current regional or global issues.

Self-determination, the use of the military, and economic cooperation are three critically important themes if students are to understand world cultures and world maps today. What are the relationships between cultures and nations? Why are there Chinese subcultures in Malaysia and Indonesia? What are the effects on other cultures and nations around the globe of the Jewish diaspora? Why do most African nations trade more with Europeans than with other Africans? Why has Slovenia recently become a new nation? Why do some cultures within nations or regions (such as the Lebanese in West Africa) have such different economic development from other cultures in the same country or region? If students are to understand cultural conflicts of today's world, teachers must help students make connections across regions and think critically about peoples' desires for freedom and self determination, security, and economic development and the effects of alliances, nationalism, and military power.

**United States History.**    Placed in the context of world history and globalization, U.S. history provides invaluable insights into relationships between international and domestic conflict and peace. The roots of what we have come to call "the American experience" are found in the world's political and cultural conflicts, human rights abuses, and economic tribulations. Given our increasing interconnectedness with other peoples and nations, the future of the U.S. depends upon its citizens' abilities to understand and interact with people beyond our borders.

Social studies teachers have usually addressed diplomacy and the use of the military and military alliances in bringing about conflict management or resolution in the study of our wars and military entanglements at home and overseas. Self-determination is often taught in the context of the American Revolution and the plight of Native Americans during the European settlement of North America. All of these concepts can be enriched by linking them historically to other world events (such as self determination of other peoples under British rule) and by asking students to compare the American experience with that of other peoples today (as in issues of self-determination of French Canadians, Armenians, or indigenous peoples in East Timor).

In both U.S. History and American Government students learn the history of American foreign policy and the issues that we face today. What should be the role of the United States in international conflicts? Should we work through the United Nations and alliances such as the North Atlantic Treaty Organization (NATO)? Should Americans intercede where people are suffering because of regional conflicts, governmental persecution, poverty, or environmental catastrophes? How do Americans work through peoples' organizations such as Amnesty International, CARE, the Red Cross or Catholic Relief Services to influence international conflict and peace? How do foreign policy and economic alliances affect American businesses, jobs, and peoples' standard of living?

U.S. History is also a history of land use and environmental decisions that increasingly deal with shrinking resources and complex ecological, economic and political issues. How do American decisions reflected in acts such as promulgating the Clean Air Act or joining the North American Free Trade Association (NAFTA) affect the global environment? How does nuclear proliferation in North Korea or drift net fishing in the Pacific affect the future of the United States? Do Americans debating clear-cutting of forests need to understand forest-related issues and experiences in Germany or Brazil?

**United States Government.**    Concepts such as 'democracy,' 'constitutional law,' 'individual rights and liberties,' and 'political participation' are central to U.S. Government courses. Actions based on interpretations of these concepts play a central role in international conflict and peace. By learning about such topics as the development of political parties or civil rights within the context of other countries' experiences, students can begin to see their own government in a global framework and recognize how their actions can affect the management of international conflict.

Certainly a U.S. Government course is the ideal place to examine the role of government (local, state, national, or international) in resolving conflicts between people at home and those abroad. How have Americans used their government to resolve economic conflicts with other countries (or their businesses)? How does political participation affect the government's decision to send in troops or begin a economic boycott or sign an alliance?

**Economics.**    'Economic cooperation,' 'economic development,' and 'economic exchanges' are key concepts in secondary economics courses. By examining these in the contexts of international conflict and peace, students can understand the critical role that economics plays in global security and issues such as self-determination, the use of the military, and the global environment. In their study of benefits and costs, students can explore the ramifications of an expansion of off-shore drilling or an oil spill both on a multinational oil corporation (e.g., its employment and profits) and on the oil-rich region's environment (e.g., tourist industries, regional fisheries, endangered species, or the fishing rights of indigenous peoples. How can economic cooperation bring about peace and justice in such conflicts?

World trade, tariffs, international economic organizations and economic alliances affect all our lives. Students need to understand conflicts growing out of the global assembly-line, long-term effects of regional economic unions, such as the European Community and NAFTA, or the work of international organizations, such as the World Bank and the International Monetary Fund. What is the relationship between economic cooperation and peace? What are the effects on global security of North-South economic differences or demands for a new international economic order? How will the restructuring of the former Soviet Union and Eastern

Europe into market economies effect international conflict and peace?

Although history, geography, government, and economics courses may be the most obvious places for studying international conflict and peace, a psychology course could include a unit on interpersonal conflict resolution, or a sociology class could include global perspectives on the role of socioeconomic differences in international conflict and peace. In fact it is very difficult to teach a social studies course without paying considerable attention to how people deal with conflicts.

Topics related to international conflict and peace are ideal for interdisciplinary integration or parallel teaching across social studies and other subjects. The global environment and technology issues from links with science courses; literature, biography, research, and writing skills fit well with language arts or a humanities course. As you read the essays in the second half of the book you will find many other ways to strengthen student understanding of how individuals, organizations, and governments have addressed, managed, or resolved international conflicts.

*Strategies for Weaving Content into Courses and Units*

As teachers begin to sketch out their course plan at the beginning of the school year or semester, they may consider a variety of strategies for integrating content in international conflict and peace throughout the entire course as well as within specific units. Sometimes teachers find it appropriate to develop strands or themes for an entire course such as "conflict and cooperation" or "human rights." These strands become a facet of every unit and provide cognitive links across units. Another approach is through *thematic units* such as "self determination in the twentieth century" (in a world history course), "conflict resolution and democracy" (government), or "global environmental issues" (geography). Such units can help students generalize and draw conclusions across time periods in history, levels of governance, or geographic regions in a world cultures course.

Teachers may organize *units to synthesize and apply content* at the end of a term or year-long course, as Shirley Hoover did in her unit on "international conflicts and the state of the world" in global history (see vignettes at the end of chapter 1). An economics course could end with a two-week unit on "alternatives in resolving global economic conflicts," or a U.S. History might conclude with "the role of the United States in global peace and security." Such units require students to use the knowledge and skills they have worked with in several units in drawing generalizations or analyzing a major contemporary issue or problem.

Many teachers use an *infusion approach* which integrates concepts (e.g., intervention), issues (e.g., human rights, the role of United Nations), or strategies in conflict management (e.g., the use of the military, negotiation, diplomacy) units such as in Connie White's unit (described in the vignettes in chapter 1) on "Arab Achievements and the Middle East." The major topics in chapters 3–9 can be restated as a unit's *essential questions* such as, How do people resolve conflicts over the environment? (in a geography unit on North America) or, Does third-party negotiation work? (in a world history unit on twentieth-century conflicts). Steve Shapiro describes such a unit in chapter 2.

International conflict and peace can also serve as a *unifying structure throughout a social studies course* by linking ideas, concepts, and factual information. A teacher introduces students to the conceptualization of peace tools (see chapter 3) the first time the topic of diplomacy arises in a history or government class. In later units the teacher builds on those concepts to incorporate new approaches and later developments as the class studies other events, issues, and decisions. Such interconnections within a course create cohesion for mastery learning and reward students for linking content across months of study.

Another approach in planning topics in international conflict management is *assigning long-term projects or news reporting* so that students collect information and report on it to the class over a term or even a year. Each student reads a biography of a peacemaker during a course and presents an individual report at the appropriate chronological time, for example, a report on Martin Luther King when studying the Civil Rights Movement in a U.S. History course. Or perhaps students prepare all year to be a country representative at a simulated United Nations held in May. In their "General Assembly" the students discuss a number of issues, such as where peacekeeping or peace enforcement troops should be sent and ways to finance such operations. Some teachers assign students roles as "reporters" on regional conflicts (the Middle East) or global issues (human rights, conflicts over the environment) over a school term or course. They "report" on their regions or issues when they are pertinent to topics under study or when current events demand in-depth examination and discussion. Teachers may want to consider all of these approaches as they develop their course goals and plan units.

## TEACHING METHODS FOR INTERNATIONAL CONFLICT AND PEACE

Another critical step in planning instruction is selecting teaching methods appropriate for the content to be taught. In the remainder of this chapter we describe six categories of teaching methods that are particularly useful for teaching about international conflict and peace. For each category we provide:

1. a rationale for why the methods are especially appropriate for teaching about international conflict and peace,
2. sample methods in the category with examples of how they can be used in a lesson or activity,
3. some advice on planning instruction with these methods.

As you study the categories of methods below, think about the relationship between teaching methods and content as embodied in educational goals. How can methods support educational goals? How can methods increase learning of knowledge, skills, and values in teaching about international conflict management? What are roles of the teacher in these instructional methods? What is expected from the students?

### Methods That Help Students Experience Cultural Differences and Similarities

**Rationale.**    If students are to understand international conflict and the intricacies of cross-cultural communication and understanding, they must have some first-hand knowledge, experience, and practice in working with people from different cultures within the United States and in other parts of the world. Methods that provide cross-cultural learning can contribute to students' academic and psychological readiness for understanding and appreciating people whose views or experiences differ from their own.

Students should be encouraged to apply their own cross-cultural learning experiences to understand other peoples' historical and contemporary experiences with conflict, negotiation, cooperation, and other key themes.

Experiential learning can significantly contribute to the development of skills in perspectives consciousness, the ability to recognize that people may perceive an event, issue, or idea in many different ways. Cross-cultural experiences are often the critical bench-marks in changing an individual's world view from only an ethnocentric perspective to a more global perspective.

**Sample Methods.**

- Students practice active listening by interviewing people from another culture. *Example:* students interview a Vietnamese immigrant about his perspectives on refugees and political asylum.
- Students work cooperatively with people from another culture toward common goals. *Example:* students work with employees of a local Honda plant to develop a video on cross-cultural understanding and economic cooperation.
- Either as a class or in small groups students discuss issues, topics, or questions with people from other cultures; for *Example:* through pen-pals or electronic mail hookups, students in another country share their concerns about the global environment.
- Students observe people from other cultures. *Example:* students attend a debate on the effects of NAFTA sponsored by the Mexican-American Community Center.
- Students are immersed in another culture. *Example:* students raise money and plan a study tour to visit rainforests in Costa Rica.

**Planning with These Methods.**   In order to provide students with cross-cultural experiences, the teacher needs to identify international resources within the school and community. Most schools have students, teachers, or parents who are from other cultures or who have lived in or visited other countries. Many cities have councils on world affairs, religious groups, immigrant organizations, international visitors bureaus, returned Peace Corps volunteer organizations, veterans' groups, or exchange organizations that can provide leads in finding appropriate resource people. Most large cities and state capitols have persons who are responsible for encouraging trade and cultural exchanges with other countries. Chambers of commerce are often helpful in identifying local companies or industries with global connections or international expertise. Most colleges and universities have international students who are willing to work with teachers. The federal government funds more than one hundred Title VI area studies centers (the African Studies Program at Indiana University) or international centers in universities across the United States. These programs have mandates to provide outreach services to local schools.

Usually the first step in planning a cross-cultural lesson is lining up the resource people who have the interest, knowledge, and expertise to work with students. The teacher is responsible for planning the activity with the resource person so that the overall goals as well as class procedures are clearly understood. It is critical that the students are prepared to work with a person from another culture and that the teacher help the resource person understand norms of the classroom and expectations of the students.

Cross-cultural experiences can also involve out of school activities such as a field trip to a Chinese exhibit of photographs of political protest or to a South African play dealing with human rights issues sponsored by the African Students Association of a local university. Many schools organize study tours or student exchanges to other countries.

Depending on the goals of the cross-cultural experience, the teacher may want to assess student skills in cross-cultural communication and interaction, student attitudes (such as tolerance and empathy), as well as knowledge objectives. Observations of student interaction and questioning, reflective writing assignments, and follow-up discussions or application projects that ask students to work cross-culturally over longer periods of time can identify progress in learner outcomes. One of the best ways to judge learning in the cross-cultural arena is by examining attitudinal and behavioral changes from those early experiences in the school year to those later in the year.

Resource people from other cultures can also serve as consultants to students as they study international conflict and peace and compose authentic audiences for exhibitions or performance-based assessment.

## Methods That Have Students Examine Multiple Perspectives

**Rationale.**   If we want students to understand why international conflicts arise and how they can be managed or resolved, we have to help them recognize the importance of examining multiple perspectives. Most forms of negotiation, peaceful settlement, and cooperation depend upon understanding how other parties interpret historical antecedents and perceive the issues, opportunities, constraints, and alternatives. Perspectives consciousness—skill in identifying other people's viewpoints and seeing the world through their eyes—is an important part of understanding international conflict and peace.

Although most Americans would agree that there are many viewpoints on issues of international conflict, only recently have social studies educators recognized the benefits of understanding other people's perspectives. Methods that help students practice skills in perspectives consciousness can open their minds to understanding the views of people in their local community, nation, and world. Perspectives consciousness does not mean one has to like, agree with, or accept other points of view. But it does mean that an appreciation of multiple perspectives is essential for real understanding of the multifaceted nature of managing international conflict. For instance, it is hard to understand economic conflicts among the world's peoples if one does not realize that many people in developing countries (and other parts of the world) believe the very structure of the present international economic system is such that it causes benefits to pile up in corporate headquarters in the industrialized countries, thus making it necessary for developing countries to seek aid and dooming them to perpetual dependency and poverty.

**Sample Methods.**

- Students read literature or watch a play and conclude why people see events or issues differently. *Example:* Students analyze Nigerian and British views of colonialism in Nigeria through selections from Chinua Achebe's *Things Fall Apart* and Joyce Cary's *Mister Johnson* and then discuss different perspectives and their historical contexts.

- Students examine primary sources and synthesize commonalities or differences across cultures or nations. *Example:* Students compare the Freedom Charter of the African National Congress with the U.S. Constitution and the U.N. Declaration on Human Rights to see what all three consider to be fundamental rights.
- Students research periodicals from different countries and identify how writers interpret issues or events. *Example:* Students evaluate news clippings and cartoons from the Philippines, Germany, the United States, Kenya, and Brazil to learn about majority and minority views on the use of forests.
- Students role-play individuals or positions different from their own. The role-plays could be based on perspectives of a family, community, famous individuals, or leaders of organizations or governments. *Example:* To follow up on a discussion of current events, students role-play a family who, in the midst of the bombing and starvation of Sarejavo in 1993, are discussing whether or not they should flee. *Example:* To conclude a reading assignment on the global distribution and dumping of toxic wastes, students are assigned either roles of government leaders or spokespersons for people's organizations or environmental groups in Nigeria, South Korea, France, Poland, and the United States. These leaders and representatives are "interviewed" by "reporters" about their views on what should be the international rules for the dumping, export, or import of toxic wastes.
- Students simulate a cross-cultural event. *Example:* Students take on roles of the members of the U.N. Security Council as they meet to decide what to do about the killing of U.N. peacekeepers in Somalia.

Many methods that teach about multiple perspectives can be integrated with methods involving cross-cultural experiences and cooperative learning, since all three categories reinforce each other and themes in international conflict management.

**Planning with These Methods.**   A first step in planning is to identify perspectives that are important in understanding the management of the conflict. For example, in the study of World War I and the Treaty of Versailles, whose perspectives need to be examined? Probably most teachers would agree that there needs to be understanding of the perspectives of the governments of the United States, Germany, and probably France and Britain. What about people in these and other countries? Did all people agree with their government's position? What about the peoples in German colonies around the world who now suddenly "belonged" to Britain? How many perspectives need to be taught? How does the teacher find materials on different perspectives and the time to teach them?

In their project on "balance" in global education the Alliance for Education in Global and International Studies (AEGIS), a consortium of forty international education organizations, has suggested that three to five perspectives need to be taught in ways that allow the learner to critique and learn from each with fairness and without indoctrination. Some perspectives may be more appropriate by the nature of the curriculum or the characteristics of the students or community.

It is always dangerous to generalize a perspective to a nation of people (e.g., the German view of Hitler's actions or the American perspective on the war in Vietnam) or an ethnic, racial or religious group (e.g., a white view of apartheid or a Muslim view of Palestinian self-determination) because such homogeneity of perspective is more the exception than the rule. To avoid stereotyping when planning and teaching, use perspectives of individuals, organizations, or government leaders who hold different points of view.

Once the decision has been made as to whose perspectives should be understood, the teacher must find appropriate resources. Primary sources can be excellent because they transport us to where the action is and take into someone else's thoughts and world. They may come from the past (e.g., Chief Joseph's famous speech) or present (e.g., a television interview of a Bosnian family). Although we often think of important documents such as the Magna Carta when we think of primary sources, first-hand knowledge of events and issues are all around us. During the conflict in the Persian Gulf Merry visited a class where one student read letters from his Kuwaiti grandmother who was living under Iraqi occupation in Kuwait City, and another boy read letters from his brother stationed in Saudi Arabia. In choosing primary readings consider both length and readability.

Literature is another wonderful source for learning about multiple perspectives. Most of us can remember reading some story or book that opened our eyes to a world or perspective we had not before experienced. Films, video, music, and art can also provide authentic voices and tangible evidence of people's perspectives of protest, conflict, and peace.

Role-playing and simulations are instructional methods that place students in situations of people different from themselves. When they have to think, argue, or make decisions as a Palestinian working in the West Bank or an Israeli settler facing Lebanese attacks, students often develop understandings that go beyond the facts of a history lesson, borders on a map, or events on a time line. These methods may focus on real people and an historical event (e.g., the meeting at Yalta) or a hypothetical event (e.g., a European Community discussion of immigration policies).

Because role-plays and simulations depend upon students already knowing the subject under study, they are usually chosen as culminating activities in which students apply their knowledge to the issues at hand. When conducting more complex simulations, teachers need to make sure that the students have enough background information to understand the perspectives associated with the specific roles they are taking. Students may fall back upon stereotypical misconceptions if they don't understand why they are taking certain roles and what those roles represent.

Debriefing after role-plays and simulations is critical. Students need an opportunity to reflect upon the learning experience, analyze the actions and arguments of their peers, and discuss implications of what happened. Students should be able to explain how the role-play or simulation connects to their knowledge of the subject and contributes to their understanding. Just as with any method, students have to learn how to play a role or simulate a person's thoughts and actions. One way to introduce students to role-playing in a nonthreatening way is to seize an opportunity when there is heated discussion over a topic that involves several points of view. For example, ask Joe, who is strenuously arguing that the United States should have the bombed the Soviet Union during the Cuban Missile Crisis to take on the role of a Russian missile technician stationed in Cuba. Then call for volunteers who will take roles of other people he might encounter such as a Cuban nurse or a Russian soldier. What would they think about the situation? What would they want to say to the Americans or the Soviet leaders?

Simulations such as *BaFa BaFa, Barnga,* and *Starpower* (see the appendix) put students into roles in which they are enculturated into a new set of behaviors, language, or beliefs. Through interacting during the simulation and participating in a subsequent debriefing, students come to recognize the power of cultural assumptions and the critical nature of our perspectives and those of others in understanding conflict and peace.

## Methods That Teach Students about Cooperation and Collaboration

**Rationale.** Cooperative learning in heterogeneous groups can maximize academic learning for all students as it helps them to develop tolerance, deal with conflicts, and study such key subjects as diplomacy, balance of power, or negotiation. Most of the methods for cooperative learning are characterized by rules or structures that create positive interdependence among students within small groups so that they must work together and depend on each other's accomplishments in order to succeed. Cooperative learning can promote individual accountability, motivation, and the ability to process large amounts of information. Learning in heterogeneous groups also contributes to student understanding of how people with different backgrounds and expertise can negotiate, reach consensus, and benefit from working together.

**Sample Methods.**

- In small groups each student completes a specific assignment, then all members share their work in order to synthesize what they have learned and complete the group's assignment. *Example:* The class explores the question Do nations usually compromise in order to manage conflict? Each group examines data on a different conflict such as the India's push for independence, the Korean War, terrorism in Europe in the 1980s, the Iraqi takeover of Kuwait, and so forth. Within each group one person analyzes a time line of actors and events related to the conflict, another looks at historical antecedents that led to the conflict, the third identifies what actually did happen to resolve or manage the conflict, and the fourth person generates alternatives that could have been responses to the conflict. Within the groups students share what they have learned, and then they present to the class their reasoned answer to the question.

- Everyone in the group masters the same content, group members quiz each other on that material to make sure all can present on it, and then each member goes out to teach another group what their group has learned. *Example:* Each group gets a case study of a human rights violation in a different country. Each group reviews its case (print and visuals, letters, other documents) and outlines the main points of the experience of the person whose right were violated as well as the different perspectives available on the case. Then the groups switch places, so that one person from each of the original groups is in every new group. Taking turns, each group member tells the story of what happened to the person in his/her case.

- Each group of students becomes the "experts" on a particular aspect of a subject under study. After practicing using their expert knowledge within the group, one representative from each group is called to a fishbowl (a group of desks in the middle of the room where the "experts" talk freely among themselves while the rest of the class listens), where experts from all groups discuss questions or make decisions. After a few minutes, the experts return to their home groups, and another set of group members enters the fishbowl. When a group representative is having trouble in the fishbowl, another person from his or her group may join the fishbowl and "advise" the group representative. *Example:* A class is studying the development of the European Community. Groups (France, Belgium, etc.) are given profiles of their country's economy, their concerns about trade and labor, and an overview of issues that have arisen historically between that country and other countries in Europe. In their country groups they come up with their views on possible steps in more economic cooperation or integration. Then the group members take turns at being their country's representative to a European Community meeting to make decisions on the future of European economic integration.

**Planning with These Methods.**   Unlike the typical group work of the past, methods in cooperative learning are structured so that all students must cooperate and work together in order for the group to succeed in the assignment. Students are rewarded for working collaboratively and helping each other learn. Cooperative learning is more appropriate when the assignment is complex and involves higher-level thinking and performance-based assessment. In order to encourage students take their cooperative learning groups seriously, some teachers bring in local professionals, businessmen, or labor leaders to discuss how they and their employees work as teams, make decisions, and solve problems together. If students perceive that cooperative work is an authentic part of their future careers, they will be more interested in learning skills in collaboration.

In general, key characteristics of cooperative learning are heterogeneous grouping, a positive interdependence among group members, individual accountability, clear and well-defined goals for the group and each individual, and group rewards. Each person in the group should have an equal opportunity for success. By the nature of sharing and working together groups need sufficient time to carry out assignments, process information and reflect upon what they are learning.

There are many ways to structure cooperative learning. For example, in the popular jigsaw method students share distinct parts of a common problem or challenge. Each member is given a "piece of the puzzle" so that no single group member has enough information to work successfully alone. Jigsaw methods can be used to complement multiple perspectives when each individual student becomes responsible for a particular perspective that must be shared with group members in order for them to solve a problem or answer a question. See the resources at the end of this chapter and in chapter 11 for many more methods. Integrating cooperative learning with content on international conflict is an obvious exemplar of how methods of instruction can support knowledge, skill and attitudinal goals.

*Methods That Teach Students How to Find, Evaluate and Use Conflicting Sources of Information*

**Rationale.**    It would be difficult to understand international conflict without finding and examining a variety of sources and types of information. Whether the source is CNN, the *Kenya Times,* a social studies text, a scholarly publication, or interviews with relevant people, it springs from subjective human experiences and should be critically assessed. Interpretations of "facts" or opinions differ depending on the author's education, sociocultural background, and expertise. One author's freedom fighter may be another author's terrorist. Governments, political parties, community groups, advocacy organizations, and experts often have agendas that frame their statements or publications in order to convince people of their "truth."

Finding information (student research) and dealing with multiple or conflicting sources (higher-level thinking) are social studies skills that are essential in understanding and making thoughtful judgments about issues in international conflict and peace. Imagine the differences in Ms. Smith's social studies classes, where students are taught only lower-level thinking skills (recall and comprehension) without practice in finding information, and Mr. Wright's classes, where students are taught to combine research and higher-level (analysis, synthesis, application, and evaluation) and critical thinking skills (such as detecting bias, identifying unstated assumptions, and distinguishing fact from opinion). In the former the class uses the information the teacher gives them and "learns" the literal meaning of treaty and the "facts" of the Treaty of Versailles. In the latter the students learn to find relevant information from different sources, identify the main ideas, hypothesize about unstated agendas related to power politics and perspectives of the parties who wrote the treaty, and then evaluate the treaty's effectiveness in keeping the peace.

In order to understand the complexities of managing international conflicts in the modern world, students need to know how to find relevant information and assess it critically. Ironically, this task has become especially important in our information-rich age in which vast amounts of data are continuously generated, yet much of it is biased or quickly outdated. Research projects are invaluable because they can contribute to the development of in-depth substantive knowledge and higher-level thinking skills.

**Sample Methods.**

- Students find and evaluate different sources of information on a topic under study. *Example:* In a study of peace making in world history, students research people they have identified as having contributed to world peace. Requirements for the projects include the use of different sources of data (by country of publication, author's point of view, and type of publication) and an analysis of perspectives on the person's contributions from different parts of the world and through different time periods.

- Students identify unstated assumptions, authors' biases, or opinions stated as fact (or other critical thinking skills). *Example:* As part of their research on issues related to cutting old growth forests, students evaluate selected materials in their school and local libraries for unstated assumptions (e.g., do they assume cutting forests is always bad?), possible biases (e.g., the author is a logger or a president of the Sierra Club), or opinions stated as fact (e.g., "too many trees have been cut down").

- Students analyze a topic under study. *Example:* Working with the research question, What was the role of the military in the United States and Soviet Union during the cold war? students find and analyze generalizations made by historians, political scientists, and economists from the 1950s to the 1990s.

- The teacher questions students to help them synthesize information. *Example:* After students have studied the development and effects of six regional trading agreements during the Twentieth Century, the teacher asks them questions such as, What can you hypothesize about the relationships between economic integration and international conflict? and, What evidence is there that trade agreements reduce conflict?

**Planning with These Methods.**    Either cooperative learning or individualized assignments can direct students toward finding and evaluating information. When possible, allow students some choice in the topic or problem to be researched, as student interests and ownership usually increase their motivation and effort. Research projects can be relatively simple or very complex, depending upon student abilities, experience, and educational goals. Teachers usually sequence the learning of skills so that students master easier steps before moving on to more complex ones. For example, the first unit in the course might focus on students finding five sources of information and learning to paraphrase the authors' main ideas and use those ideas to demonstrate different perspectives on an issue. In the units that follow, the assignments gradually involve more sophisticated sources of information and more complex skills in interpreting and using information.

Teachers' questioning strategies (what is the strength of that argument?), explicit use of discrete skills (students use their study of economic cooperation in American foreign policy to work with skills in classifying information), and student practice in asking and answering questions (students question a panel of international visitors about their interpretation of the International Monetary Fund's role in promoting economic development) can be used in almost any lesson in combination with other methods of instruction.

## Methods That Have Students Identify and Analyze Values and Attitudes

**Rationale.**    Students often ask, Why is there so much conflict in the world? Why do we have wars? Why can't people (or nations) agree? The answer lies in part in the fact that people, average citizens and political leaders alike, often hold very different values with respect to any given issue or problem. The importance of adhering to strict environmental standards is one example. While some people want laws to outlaw the dumping of toxic wastes, others may solicit importation and storing of toxic wastes in their community because they value the perceived economic benefits to the community more than they value protecting the environment.

Values are imbedded in the study of international conflict as they are in all topics in social studies education. Themes of diplomacy, negotiation, peaceful settlement, military power, economic cooperation, human rights, self-determination, and the global commons can be taught from many value positions. Value conflicts are often the reason that international issues and conflicts arise.

**Sample Methods.**

- Students analyze values of people, their actions or policies. *Example:* Students examine the values underlying economic agreements, trade barriers, and tariffs as part of working toward understanding the management of international conflict over trade.
- Students assess value conflicts. *Example at a personal level:* Students examine the moral dilemma of a Chinese university student who wants to work in the pro-democracy movement of the late 1980s yet knows she may disgrace her family and end up in

prison if the movement fails. *Example at a national level:* Students examine the value conflict between the United States wanting to punish China for that government's repression of the pro-democracy movement in the late 1980s and the desire to support Chinese economic reforms and trade liberalization through most-favored-nation status.

- Students analyze the role or effects of values in conflicts and peace. *Example:* Students examine a variety of types of international conflicts in the twentieth century, such as disputes over borders, fishing rights, punishment of war criminals, immigration restrictions, and the development of nuclear weapons. They identify the underlying values that led to and resolved each conflict, and then they develop hypotheses on what values are essential for negotiated settlements.

**Planning with These Methods.**    The first step in planning lessons that address values is to ask the questions, Are there values implicit in the content that students need to understand? Can the students evaluate the issues and contexts without recognizing peoples' underlying values? For example, in a study of the history of the United Nations, many teachers would want students to understand the shared values that brought nations together in the post–World War II world. To address that objective a teacher might have students examine U.N. documents, identify underlying values, and then assess to what degree those values continue to hold nations together today. This type of values analysis is relatively easy to plan, as the focus is having students assess values of key players as found in print or audiovisuals.

In studying value conflicts, students look at why people and nations have conflicting values, an important topic in the study of international conflict management. The values conflict can be as personal as a mother felt when she was called up for military service during Desert Storm—she wanted to do her job in the Army but didn't want to leave her baby. It can be as significant as the values conflict John Kennedy felt when he took the United States to the brink of an unthinkable war with the Soviet Union rather than allow nuclear warheads to stay in Cuba. Lessons on values conflict can be organized to look at real decisions (e.g., sending troops to Vietnam) or hypothetical ones (e.g., what we should do to help the Muslims in Bosnia). Students can generate alternatives and consequences of different actions as they identify the values of each. Such methods help students recognize the importance of values in the decisions that people and nations make about international conflicts and peace.

These teaching methods are easily combined with methods for experiencing cultural differences, examining multiple perspectives, practicing cooperative learning, researching conflicting sources, and developing skills in higher-level thinking. Values inquiry is an essential part of decision making and problem solving.

### Methods That Have Students Use Knowledge and Skills through Authentic Applications

**Rationale.**    The ultimate steps in teaching about international conflict management involve instructional methods that ask students to use the knowledge and skills they have gained to reflect, make decisions, and in some way address real-life problems. Students are not learning about international conflict and peace to pass a test or play Trivial Pursuit. We expect them to use what they have learned as citizens of the United States in a global age. Through the authentic application of content on international conflict management social studies teachers can help students begin to connect their academic work with issues, events, and people in their local community. Such methods can also serve to assess student learning and the ability to use new skills and information.

**Sample Methods.**

- Students apply what they have learned to new topics under study. *Example:* Having learned about self-determination in Africa and Asia, students consider the meaning of self-determination for peoples in the former Soviet Union and Yugoslavia who want autonomy.
- Students use a decision tree to identify decisions, issues, alternatives and their consequences. *Example:* As part of their study of Desert Storm, students work in groups with decision trees to apply what they have learned about international conflict to the foreign policy decision that faced the Bush administration when Iraq invaded Kuwait.
- Students collect information and apply it to complex questions as an exhibition of their learning. *Example:* In exploring the

role of the military in world history, a group of students choose to prepare an exhibition on the role of the military as peacemakers. They plan an exhibition that includes research on historical examples in which military might was used to keep the peace in places where fighting would otherwise have taken place. As part of the students' research they develop case studies of the role of the military in the Pax Romana, the Mogul Empire, the British colonialization of Uganda and Kenya, and Communist rule in Yugoslavia. Applying knowledge and skills from developing the cases, the students then present their assessment of the possibilities of using military power to bring about peace in the former Yugoslavia. Their authentic audiences include members of a local Slovenian Friendship Society and a local branch of Veterans of Foreign Wars. The audience listens to the presentation, asks the group salient questions, and contributes to the teacher's assessment of the group's work.

• Through action learning students undertake projects that lead to authentic citizen action within their own community. *Example:* Having studied the North American Free Trade Agreement, students make presentations to their local chamber of commerce or write letters to their congressional representative about alternative courses of action they support.

**Planning with These Methods.**    Methods of application can take the form of discrete steps as well as complex and structured long-term projects. Decision-trees provide a structure for student use of information. For example, in beginning the study of the Vietnam War, students use their background knowledge of colonialism and military intervention to generate alternatives (and their possible consequences) for an American response to the French withdrawal from Indochina in the 1950s.

Action learning projects are usually organized around a natural connection between content under study and an opportunity for the students to do something relevant in the local community. For an example, let us say students have been learning about the global commons and the harm that certain agricultural products cause to the earth's water when they wash out of soils into rivers and oceans. The teacher divides the class into groups to research conditions in local rivers and streams and talk with local agricultural extension workers and farmers, environmentalists, fishermen, and water quality engineers at the treatment plant. They then present their analyses of how the local community relates to the global issue of water quality at an Earth Day celebration in their city.

Action projects take considerable planning, management, and flexibility. However, such authentic tasks are usually landmarks in the students' social studies education and can be structured to maximize content, skill, and attitudinal objectives. Exhibitions require considerable knowledge, analyses that go beyond recounting factual information, autonomous creative work, and "realistic decisions and the defense of those decisions" in the real world.[2] They require the use of knowledge, skills, and thoughtful reflection we expect of citizens.

Although there are many other methods that can be used in teaching about international conflict management, those categories of teaching methods outlined above are particularly useful because they support the content and goals of student understanding and application. These methods are often integrated or combined with each other as teachers plan and sequence learning activities from day to day or unit to unit.

How do teachers integrate methods and content in actual classroom practice? Here are some examples.

## EXAMPLES OF CLASSROOM PRACTICE

As you read the vignettes of teacher planning below, think about how these outstanding teachers use methods to support content and educational goals. How do the teachers integrate methods, content, and instructional goals? How do they bring together different topics and issues related to international conflict and peace? What are the guiding principles behind the planning and teaching of these three social studies educators?

*Shirley Hoover, Upper Arlington High School,
Upper Arlington, Ohio*

At the end of Global History, a year-long course, Shirley Hoover developed a unit in which her ninth and tenth graders would apply what they had learned about themes and lessons in world history

---

[2]Theodore R. Sizer, *Horace's School: Redesigning the American High School* (New York: Houghton Mifflin, 1992), 98–101.

to their understanding of international conflict and peace in the contemporary world. She wanted them to use their knowledge of the historical development of international conflicts to evaluate implications for the state of today's world.

Shirley began with an explanation of the unit's goals and then organized the students in small groups for research on the state of the world today. Working in regional groups of "Africans," "Asians," "Europeans," and others, the students identified a number of resources that contain current data on major social, economic, and political indicators for the nations of the world. The World Bank's annual *World Development Report,* the *State of the World Atlas,* other data books, and computerized databases provided information on availability of health care, levels of education, availability of transportation, the status of agriculture and hunger, human rights violations and government repression, civil wars and wars that crossed national boundaries, participation in international weapons trade, loans and trade statistics, tariffs and non-tariff barriers, religion, linguistic diversity, access to technology and information, and many other indicators of standards of living and quality of life. The students sought out multiple perspectives and interpretations of different sources of data. Shirley also relied upon her students who had immigrated from Asian countries to share their perspectives on the data collection.

The regional groups analyzed these data to decide, based on their study of history, which were the most significant factors that related to the development of international conflict for their region. Each group developed its own indices of "conflict indicators" and created large maps keyed to their indicators to share with the class.

Then as a class the students reported on their regional findings and discussed what they had learned about the state of the world through the research. Shirley asked open-ended questions (e.g., why do you think . . . ? How do you know . . . ?) to encourage them to reflect upon their historical knowledge and antecedents to today's circumstances and global issues. For example, there was an extended discussion of the role of past empires and colonialization in global conflict today.

The students then transferred their most valued indicators to a blank world map that they had traced (using an opaque projector) on paper that covered the back wall of their classroom. As they constructed the map they discussed gaps in their knowledge and ambiguities in the available data. Questions also arose as to the effects of most data coming from American sources. Alternative sources were pursued.

The class map became a focal point for discussion and for development of hypotheses about development, conflict, and history. First through small group and then through whole class discussions the students developed detailed hypotheses to explain how historical conflicts and peaceful settlements were related to today's world. They considered what roles religion, race, or ethnicity have played in international conflict. They reconsidered some generalizations about imperialism, nationalism, democracy, and peace. Again and again they came back to how people in other parts of the world would view the data and their implications.

At times they took on the roles of their region and simulated discussions of the data and issues among Africans, Europeans, Asians, or specific countries of Russia, China, or Egypt. When students had conflicting data, they entered into debates to compare and test arguments. Critical thinking skills were addressed as students challenged the credibility of sources or biases in reporting.

Finally the students worked toward consensus and compared their hypotheses with the generalizations offered in a video, *Seeds of Conflict,* and in a current map of global conflict produced by *Newsweek.* In their final project the students wrote individual culminating essays on the development and management of international conflict and answered the question, Has mankind made progress?

*Connie White, Linden McKinley High School, Columbus, Ohio*

The Gulf War broke out as Connie White was finishing up the Crusades in her Global History class. Although she had planned to teach a unit on African civilizations next, she decided to continue with the Arabs and focus on their achievements and their connections to the world today. She began with a discussion in which her students began to make connections between their previous work on Arab civilizations and the current conflict in the Persian Gulf. The students then worked in cooperative groups to develop timelines of historical antecedents and the role of the area in global conflicts. They used their information from the timelines to make transparencies of the changing borders in the Middle East so that as a class they could examine shifts in power over hundreds of years and the role of conflict in the region.

In order to provide different viewpoints on historical as well as current events, Connie invited her own international students to join Palestinian and Israeli guest speakers in sharing their perspectives on the relationship between the history of the region and possible solutions to conflicts in the Middle East. The discussion led to a reexamination of previous work on Arab culture and more attention to themes in Arab and Middle Eastern literature.

Next Connie had her students simulate a peace conference. The students first debated which countries should be included in the peace process. Then they broke into small groups and prepared to interact as representatives of Iraq, Jordan, Syria, Israel, the United States, Britain, Egypt, and Saudi Arabia. The students decided to include the Palestinians with the assumption the Americans would use their economic clout to convince Israel to agree to sit down with them. The simulation allowed them to use their historical knowledge and understanding of multiple perspectives to examine the possibilities for resolution or management of conflict.

As a culminating activity Connie's students shared their questions and concerns about many global conflicts with high school students in Geneva, Switzerland, through the CompuServe system, which uses electronic networks and computers. As the Swiss students typed in their questions about recent news stories of violence in the United States, Connie's students raised questions about the reporting of conflicts and role of the media in conflict management.

*Steve Shapiro, Reynoldsburg High School, Reynoldsburg, Ohio*

Steve Shapiro teaches Global Studies in an interdisciplinary (science, math, language arts, art, and social studies) tenth-grade program called "World Connections." In the spring of 1993 Steve and his student teacher, Matt Shafer, developed a unit on racial conflcit in South Africa as part of their interdisciplinary team's larger unit on international conflict resolution. In planning backward the interdisciplinary team began by identifying five essential questions such as What are the ramifications of global conflict? and, Why is conflict resolution difficult to schieve? They began the unit with the viewing of *Cry Freedom*, a film that captured student interest and generated questions that led to student research on the history and development of today's conflicts.

Working with their students' questions and concerns, Steve and Matt used a combination of lecture and readings to fill gaps in their knowledge base as they pursued questions and issues that intrigued them. Part of the students' exploration of the contexts of the conflict and its international dimensions involved meeting several South Africans with different perspectives and backgrounds.

Then the instructors led a class discussion to identify and examine alternatives for resolution of the conflict. After conducting considerable research, the students chose four possible alternatives (negotiation, international pressure, violence, and mediation) for more research and in-depth examination. They worked in groups to develop proposals for resolution of the conflict; the proposals specified step-by-step plans, identified possible obstacles, and hypothesize outcomes. As part of the refinement and assessment of their plans, they presented them to their "consultants," South Africans of diverse viewpoints and experiences who worked with them in groups, reacted to their ideas, and helped them improve their work. Their final products were graded on feasibility, immediate and long-range consequences, and global ramifications.

Steve and Matt ended their work on South Africa with the simulation *Starpower* so that the students would have an opportunity to deal with the same issues of power and security in another case study of international conflict. The debriefing of the simulation focused on applying what they learned about South Africa to other conflicts around the world. The study of South Africa then served as a model for the students' own development of authentic exhibitions of other case studies of international conflict management. In chapter 2 Steve describes his and Matt's development of this social studies unit within the contexts of his interdisciplinary teaming and other school reforms.

## CONCLUSIONS

Although these teachers teach different social studies courses in different school districts, there are a number of commonalities in how they approach instruction on international conflict. They use methods that provide simulated or real cross-cultural experiences and address multiple perspectives in order to promote cross-cultural understanding and build perspective consciousness. They choose active learning strategies that call for students to practice cooperative learning and decision-making skills. These teachers integrate student research with tasks that develop higher-level thinking skills, provide depth of knowledge, and emphasize application of new learning to other content. Although their course objectives and content differ, they share a commitment to helping their students learn how to think globally about the past, present, and future. They expect their students to apply such knowledge and skills to their lives in the local community and their connections to others around the world.

Teachers can maximize student learning about international conflict management by using a variety of instructional methods that are especially congruent with their course content and goals and meet the needs of their students. Such methods help students experience other cultures, examine multiple perspectives, practice cooperative learning, research and evaluate conflicting sources, practice skills in higher level thinking, identify and analyze values, and use knowledge through meaningful applications. These methods can be integrated in lessons and units to reinforce student learning and help students connect their classroom experiences with real-life decisions in their community and world.

# CHAPTER 2

# A Case Study of Unit Planning in the Context of School Reform

## Steve Shapiro and Merry M. Merryfield

In chapter 1 we discussed integrating elements of international conflict and peace into secondary social studies and outlined categories of methods that are especially appropriate for teaching such content. In this chapter we examine how teachers bring together content, methods, and educational goals as they plan instruction for a unit in a specific course. This chapter is a case study of the development of a social studies unit that addresses resolving racial conflict in South Africa and occurs within an interdisciplinary unit on international conflict resolution. It documents the actual planning and instruction of Steve Shapiro, a social studies teacher at Reynoldsburg High School in Reynoldsburg, Ohio, and Matt Shafer, a student at the Ohio State University who worked as a preservice teacher with Steve and Reynoldsburg tenth graders from September 1992 to June 1993.

One of the goals of Ohio State University's Professional Development School (PDS) Network in Social Studies and Global Education is developing reflective practitioners. Working with ideas from the literature on case methods, teacher thinking and decision making, reflective practice and inquiry-oriented teacher education (see references at the end of part 1), we have found that case studies build and strengthen reflective practitioners in four ways. Through reading, writing, analyzing, and discussing cases, our preservice teachers (1) become better able to appreciate the complexity of teaching and synthesize their field and seminar experiences in new and profound ways, (2) learn to focus more on the processes and factors affecting how their students learn, (3) become more critical of their own planning and current practice, and importantly for long-term collaboration and growth, (4) get in the habit of seeking out multiple perspectives on their planning, teaching, and assessment.

We have our preservice teachers construct their own cases and share them with other teachers, administrators, and professors. We find the collaborative process of developing and analyzing cases to be an effective component in building our PDS learning community. Cases contribute to the professional development of us all as we delve deeper into critical, real-life issues of students, schools, and the social studies.

The purpose of this case is to illustrate how teachers develop instruction related to international conflict and peace that links content, methods, and educational goals in the context of ongoing school reform and restructuring. This is not a case of an average social studies teacher in a typical American school. It is a case study of actual social studies instruction in the real-life context of educational change. As you read through the case, think about how decisions are made. What are the factors that affect the conceptualization of the unit? How are goals, content, and methods linked? Perhaps you might reflect on a unit that you are thinking about developing related to international conflict and peace. You can sketch out and develop your ideas as we take you through our process of conceptualization and development. The purpose of this case is to illustrate the real-life process of unit development, not to provide a model unit or ready-to-use lessons.

## SETTING THE STAGE: CONSIDERATIONS AND CONTEXTS

Although teachers may approach unit planning in many different ways, they usually share several considerations and decisions. In planning units teachers must select the unifying topic, theme, or issue; delineate expectations for student learning of knowledge and skills; plan ongoing evaluation and final assessments; find pertinent resources and instructional materials; and finally develop and sequence daily lessons. Within this process most teachers consider many factors and make hundreds of instructional decisions. Let us look at some of these factors in table 2.1. First there are the people who influence the unit. As we plan we think about our students as individuals and as groups with their special needs, learning styles,

TABLE 2.1
Factors in Instructional Decision Making

**CURRICULUM AND TESTING**
state and local mandates,
frameworks, competencies,
outcomes, proficiency tests
college tests, skill or
achievement tests

**RESOURCES**
availability and quality of
instructional resources and materials,
texts, technologies, media center,
local libraries, museums,
organizations, universities

**PEOPLE**
students (individuals and groups;
their interests, experiences,
abilities), other teachers, team
members, parents, people in the
community, resource people

**SCHOOL CLIMATE**
scheduling, mandates, rules,
priorities, attitudes towards change,
stresses, traditions, problems

**EVENTS**
local, national, international events,
global issues

**THE TEACHER'S CONTEXTS**
values and beliefs, assumptions about teaching and learning,
education and background, knowledge of students and subjects, travel
and cross-cultural experiences, creativity and style, work ethic,
personal life, ambitions, time, professionalism
↓

**CREATION OF THE UNIT**

interests, backgrounds, and abilities. The ideas or expectations of other teachers or team members, administrators, parents, or other people in the community or profession may influence our thinking. Then there are all the official or informal curriculum mandates, frameworks, or courses of study from the state or district that specify course goals and content. Pressures from local, state or national tests of achievement, proficiency, or preparation for college frequently influence teachers' instructional decisions. School climate or other factors in the school may affect planning in obvious or subtle ways. Planning can be influenced by a scheduling change from fifty-minute classes to hundred-minute "double-blocking," by policies restricting guest speakers or field trips, by ongoing school reforms such as interdisciplinary teaming and a move toward performance-based assessment, or by a school climate of cynicism that constrains innovation and creativity.

Unit planning is also affected by the amount and quality of available instructional materials and other resources. Beginning teachers will find their units influenced by the "official" text, the district's audiovisual collection, the social studies department's (or other teachers') supplementary materials, and the availability of maps, VCRs, and overhead projectors. The quality of the research collection in the media center and the presence of technologies for computer simulations, electronic data bases, or electronic mail hookups such as those offered by CompuServe also affect choices.

Current local, national, or world events often influence planning in the social studies by creating student interest and new opportunities for making tangible connections to the subject under study. In recent years the pro-democracy movement in China, the war in the Persian Gulf, the unification of Germany, the breakup of the Soviet Union and demise of the cold war, and the end to apartheid in South Africa have provided dramatic history in the making for social studies teachers and students.

Finally there is the teacher (or teachers) planning the unit. The teacher's assumptions about teaching and learning, knowledge of students and the subject matter, values and beliefs, educational and life experiences, work ethic, and knowledge or interest in innovation all contribute to shaping a critical lens for instructional decision-making. The teacher ultimately decides how the other factors—the students, resources, curriculum and testing mandates, current events, and school climate—actually shape what is taught and learned.

We ask our preservice teachers to reflect upon the topic under study in the context in which they will teach it. You might want to web out your contextual factors as you think about categories of factors in table 2.1 and read about our considerations in the case below. Reflection on contextual factors provides necessary background for cases, as each case is unique. As you will learn in this case, some of the most significant factors affecting the development of the unit were the nature of ongoing school reforms, our interdisciplinary team, student characteristics, available resources, and our priorities as teachers.

## An Overview of Community and Parental Factors

Reynoldsburg, Ohio, is a small, middle-class community with an average family income in 1991 of $30,600, slightly below the average Ohio income of $30,800. Though it has rural, agricultural roots as the home of the hybrid tomato, Reynoldsburg has become one of many suburban bedroom communities surrounding greater Columbus. Its population has mushroomed from 724 in 1950 to 26,000 today as Columbus's sprawl has brought new industry, subdivisions, apartments, and strip mall shopping. The small-town atmosphere has been influenced by changing demographics, urbanization, and development, yet residents are still very proud of their community as a good place to live. Reynoldsburg has the reputation of being a politically and socially conservative community where Republicans dominate local politics.

Although the community is generally positive about education, in the last decade many efforts to raise money for the schools have been defeated by the voters. A relatively low level of funding has led school administrators and staff to seek outside grants in order to implement school reforms and restructuring. Reynoldsburg City School District's 1992 per pupil expenditures of $4,359 were among the lowest of all suburban school districts in Ohio and well below the state average of $4,741. Relatively few parents of high school students attend parent-teacher conferences or "Meet the Teacher Night." It is unclear whether the lack of parental involvement in the face of major educational reforms comes from parental trust in teachers and administrators or if it is more a reflection of apathy. Parents appear to be more interested and involved in school athletics (the Athletic Boosters are very successful in raising money) than in issues related to academic programs.

## An Overview of Our Students

All public school students in the community complete their secondary education at Reynoldsburg High School (RHS). In the last few years the school has changed considerably through growth and changing demographics. As we[1] write this case in the spring of 1994, the student population at the high school is approximately eleven hundred students in grades ten through twelve. In the fall of 1994 the district ninth graders will move from the junior high to the high school and occupy a new addition currently under construction. The school population is changing as more minorities move into the community each year. In the 1993–94 school year minorities (primarily African American) make up approximately 8 percent of the high school student body. The increasing diversity of the school population has begun to influence hiring practices, staff development, curricular reform, and the development of new approaches to prejudice reduction.

Reynoldsburg students generally perform slightly above state and national averages in most measures of academic performance. The dropout rate is less than 5 percent. Approximately 15 percent of the students choose vocational training through attendance at Eastland or Fairfield Career Center during their junior and senior years. Approximately 55 percent to 60 percent of Reynoldsburg High School graduates go on to college or technical schools. Composite scores on SAT, ACT, and state proficiency tests are generally slightly above state and national averages.

Many Reynoldsburg students work part time while attending school. Most students spend their earnings on clothes, entertainment, and cars. Many juniors and seniors own cars, and there is great competition for spaces in the student section of the school parking lot. Student values and attitudes about current events re-

[1]Authors' note: The case was written by Steve Shapiro and Merry Merryfield from Steve's point of view as the primary developer of the unit described in the case. Throughout the chapter "we" is used by Steve telling the reader about his school, program, and work. In the description of the actual unit planning, "we" at times also includes the members of Steve's interdisciplinary team and Matt Shafer, Steve's student teacher who developed and taught the global studies unit with Steve.

flect predominately conservative thought particularly related to race and social change. Affirmative action, welfare, capital punishment, and abortion are controversial issues for many students. Although all students work fairly well together in classes, there are some tensions and some self-selected separation by different ethnic and racial groups that can be observed during free time and extracurricular events.

World Connections, the interdisciplinary program described in this case study, serves the academic "middle" group of students. In restructuring the school the staff recognized that the high school needed to improve programs for middle-ability/middle-achieving students. These students are not a part of the school's programs for the academically advanced (advanced placement courses, gifted and talented programming) or programs for the least successful students (learning disabled programs and remediation courses). With a few exceptions, the students in World Connections are neither headed for advanced placement courses nor involved in learning disabled or remedial programs.

## A Climate of Ongoing School Reform and Restructuring

The Reynoldsburg City School District is engaged in an effort to rethink the process and practice of educating young people. Much of the reform effort has been spearheaded by the high school, where administrators and teachers have worked together to study and implement whole-school change. In 1990 the high school faculty selected a broad base of research from which to restructure the school and chose to become a member in the Coalition of Essential Schools (a school reform movement based at Brown University). The overall goal was to develop a new high school learning community. Since then the faculty has redesigned scheduling, programming, and delivery of education and adopted such innovations as interdisciplinary teaming, backwards building curriculum, authentic assessment, personalization of teaching, teacher as coach and student as worker, and other coalition reforms. Several of these reforms directly affect the development of the unit described in this case.

**Interdisciplinary Teaming.**    A problem inherent in the structure of the American high school is fragmentation of the curriculum. For example, students rarely have the opportunity to connect their study of Thoreau's "Civil Disobedience" in English class in November to their study of the passive resistance tactics of the civil rights movement in U.S. History in March. In most American high schools students are not taught to appreciate important relationships across different academic disciplines or to examine issues holistically. Through the development of interdisciplinary teams such relationships and connections become a part of course planning, unit construction, and student thinking.

The unit described in this case was developed at the end of the second year of our interdisciplinary teaming in World Connections, a program for sophomores that includes geometry, English 10 (college prep or general, but not advanced), biology, and global studies. During fifty minutes of team-planning every morning (and snatches of time for logistical coordination throughout the day) our World Connections team develops and teaches interdisciplinary units that make connections across our four disciplines. The global studies unit on resolving racial conflict in South Africa described below is the social studies component of the larger interdisciplinary unit on international conflict resolution.

**Personalization of Instruction.**   When students move every forty-five to fifty minutes from one crowded class to another they rarely receive any individual attention, support, or personal feedback. Most American high school students have contact with guidance counselors only for scheduling or with administrators only for disciplinary reasons. When teachers face 150 to 180 students a day it is difficult if not impossible for them to individualize instruction and assessment to meet each student's special needs. Given the amount of time it takes to grade essays or reports, teachers are also constrained by the demands of their own assignments and frequently forego those assignments that require extensive time to grade. When faced with trying to teach large numbers of students in short periods of time, teachers make compromises (as Sizer describes in *Horace's Compromise*) that diminish teaching and learning.

Personalization (knowledge of, interest in, interaction with, and care for each student as a person) decreases students' academic and social problems, alienation, and rate of drop out or failure. In the spring of 1993 when this unit was developed and taught, our World Connections team of four teachers shared ninety-five tenth graders and a daily block of two hundred minutes that we could structure in many ways to meet the needs of our students. We have found that this team structure helps to create a family environment and provide individual attention for every student. In our first period team meetings each morning, we can discuss students who are having problems and develop ways to address them immediately. Sharing students also enriches our understanding of their abilities and learning styles. Teaming improves our communication with parents. The team generates several newsletters every year to inform parents about the work of their students. Teaming also improves parent teacher conferences as parents learn about all aspects of their students' academic coursework at one time.

**Backwards Building Curriculum and Authentic Assessment.** We use the backwards building approach to unit planning. That is, we begin by identifying the critical knowledge and skills we expect students to learn. We then develop the final "performance" through which students' mastery of content and skills will be demonstrated and assessed. Only then do we begin to develop and sequence daily lessons. The final assessment drives the organization and content of lessons so that the students are prepared to succeed in the task. The word *performance* does not necessarily imply that the assessment is done through skits and reenactments. By "performance" we mean the acts through which students demonstrate their learning. Such performances require students to apply their learning to meaningful and authentic tasks, tasks similar to those that they will undertake in adult life. In order to identify an authentic assessment as we think about a prospective unit, we ask ourselves, *How do people use this material in the real world?* This question helps us begin to conceptualize possible authentic tasks. Writing is a performance, but it depends on how it is used as to whether or not it is authentic. We expect adults in our society to write reports or letters or to prepare notes for an oral presentation; therefore those tasks are authentic. But writing short recall answers, marking a multiple choice test, or filling in a blank map from memory are not real adult tasks. These types of assessments are not authentic (real) in our society. We do use such paper and pencil tests as intermediate steps within a unit to evaluate student knowledge and skills before moving on to the application of such content in an authentic assessment. As you see in figure 2.1, acquisition of knowledge and

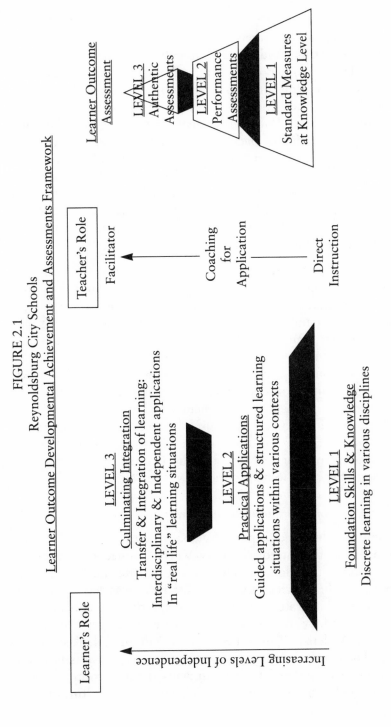

FIGURE 2.1
Reynoldsburg City Schools
Learner Outcome Developmental Achievement and Assessments Framework

Learner Outcome Assessment

LEVEL 3
Authentic Assessments

LEVEL 2
Performance Assessments

LEVEL 1
Standard Measures at Knowledge Level

Teacher's Role

Facilitator

Coaching for Application

Direct Instruction

LEVEL 3
Culminating Integration
Transfer & Integration of learning:
Interdisciplinary & Independent applications
In "real life" learning situations

LEVEL 2
Practical Applications
Guided applications & structured learning
situations within various contexts

LEVEL 1
Foundation Skills & Knowledge
Discrete learning in various disciplines

© Reynoldsburg City Schools, 1994.

Learner's Role

Increasing Levels of Independence

skills is a prerequisite for the application of student learning that leads to authentic assessment.

Our backwards building and authentic assessment approaches to unit planning differ considerably from the more traditional practice of identifying unit goals and objectives, planning lesson after lesson and then constructing a paper and pencil test at the end of the unit to see how well students learned the material. One of the major benefits of backwards building is that we begin by determining what the end target is. The teacher and students understand what is needed to achieve the final goal and succeed in the assessment, and they all work together to achieve it. Each lesson is designed to move the students toward the successful completion of the final performance. This clarity of purpose results in units that are cohesive and carefully crafted.

**Teacher as Coach, Student as Worker.** A methodological approach that supports the goals of personalization and authentic assessment is that of having teachers take on the role of "coaching" student learning and accomplishment. This metaphor suggests that students, rather than solely absorbing information given out by the teacher in front of the class, become active in processing and applying information. As students take responsibility for their own learning in terms of in-depth research, analysis, and synthesis of new information, teachers coach them by asking stimulating questions and providing a variety of useful resources and support. As you will see in the preparation for the exhibition described below, the coaching role for teachers and the worker role for students necessitate the development of new skills for all concerned.

*An Overview of Curriculum Considerations*

The unit was designed as part of global studies, the social studies component of the interdisciplinary World Connections Program. We developed the global studies course for Reynoldsburg High School as the first such course in the district. It was developed from the goals and literature on global perspectives in education as conceptualized by Robert Hanvey, Chadwick Alger and James Harf, Lee Anderson, James Becker and Willard Kniep (see references). The course is a study of world cultures, global issues, and global history intended to help students develop competence in and knowledge of perspective consciousness, cross-cultural understanding, global dynamics, local-global interconnectedness, and an awareness of the dimensions and effects of human choices. A conscious decision was made to organize the course by major themes such as conflict, culture, interdependence, and others that students would examine in depth and apply to global issues.

## The Teachers' Considerations

Reflecting on my own experiences and values, I realize what a high priority I place on cross-cultural, experiential learning. After graduating from college I spent nine months traveling around the world through twenty countries on four continents. It was on this journey that I decided to become a teacher. I made that decision because I wanted to enable others to have profound cross-cultural experiences and enjoy the world's diversity as I have. As a teacher I know that rather than simply retelling my experiences to my students, I need to design activities through which they will create their own experiences and develop cross-cultural understanding and a global perspective. As a result I use experiential methods such as simulations and interaction with resource people from the local and global community.

I also want my class to be a place where students learn memorable lessons that are relevant to their lives. Although I was always a successful student, I often felt that what I was learning in high school was unimportant. I viewed school as a series of hoops that I needed to jump through in order to reach my future goals; it was a "game" to be played in order to get to college. This recollection has led me to work at creating a learning environment where students have ownership and make decisions as active participants in learning that is authentic in their own lives.

As we discuss the steps in our development of the unit, it is important to remember that the global studies unit was designed within the contexts of the larger interdisciplinary plan that included related and overlapping biology, English, and geometry units. However, with easy modifications this unit on resolving conflict in South Africa could be taught in a self-contained global studies or global/world history class. For the purposes of this case we have sequenced the backwards building process of unit development into five steps, and we will discuss each in turn. The discrete nature of the five steps is not intended to imply that the steps occur in isolation from each other. While they are somewhat sequential, they are very interactive in nature. That is, as we worked on step two, we were looking back to our work in step one and frequently revising it. Each of the steps relates to the others, and it is important that we continually rethink each step. Unit planning is difficult and messy work that grows more complex with interdisciplinary teaming.

## STEP 1: SELECTING THE ESSENTIAL CONTENT

Units may be organized by topics, themes, issues, or even skills. In the topical approach, units focus on discrete events (e.g., the Great Depression or World War II), historical eras (e.g., the rise of Islam), peoples (e.g., the Arabs), places (e.g., East Asia), or others topics (e.g., the Constitution, the Legislative Branch). This approach can provide depth but usually treats the topic in isolation rather than placing it in broader historical, political, economic, or geographic contexts.

Through a thematic or issues-oriented approach, teachers plan units that integrate content across geographic regions, academic disciplines, and time periods. For example, the Great Depression in the United States could be studied in depth by itself (topically) or as part of a larger thematic unit, such as "Domestic Policies and International Trade in the Twentieth Century" or "Government Involvement in Economic Affairs in U.S. History." In the former the thematic approach places the Great Depression within the larger scope of the global economy, and in the latter students view the Great Depression within the context connections to governmental decisions and events that preceded and followed it.

Units may also relate to a particular competency or skill such as research skills, higher-level skills (analysis, synthesis, application, evaluation) or critical-thinking skills (detecting bias, identifying unstated assumptions, etc.). This approach is particularly useful for interdisciplinary teams in which the different courses overlap in skills more than in content. For example, our World Connections team has designed and implemented a unit entitled "Can You Prove It?" based on the skills of proving and drawing conclusions. The unit ties together the process of proof in each of our four disciplines by linking the scientific method (biology), two column proofs (geometry), expository writing and thesis statements (English) and social science methods of testing cultural theories (global studies). Units may integrate several topics in a course through a theme that is highly motivating to the students. The American Connections team at Reynoldsburg High School has developed a unit entitled "Unsolved Mysteries in American History" that enables students to pursue a variety of topics, each of which relates to the broad theme of unanswered questions in our nation's history.

## Our Interdisciplinary Theme of International Conflict Resolution

Our World Connections team identifies themes for the year by using the curriculum mapping strategy developed by Heidi Hayes-Jacobs at Columbia University (see references for interdisciplinary curriculum). Curriculum mapping is a strategy that provides analysis of how different bodies of content (in our case biology, English, geometry, and global studies) relate and connect to each other through knowledge and skills. Because of their length and complexity, we generally teach two or three major (five to seven week) interdisciplinary thematic units each school year. We attempt to plan units that bring together the content of each of the four subjects. However, we occasionally find that one of the subjects does not naturally fit the unit theme. In such cases we develop the unit within the three classes rather than attempting to force the fourth class to fit. In addition to the interdisciplinary units, we also teach units designed to meet the needs of only our individual courses. The unit discussed here was developed after our team's curriculum mapping identified that *the existence of international conflict and the desire to resolve it* is a part of the curricula of our biology, English, and global studies courses.

The global nature of our program goals shaped our approach in choosing content within each subject. We wanted the conflicts studied to have global implications and be characterized by global dynamics that have an impact across national borders and involve different types of world actors. For example, the biology teacher suggested that he could have students focus on genetic engineering as part of the unit. Genetic engineering and its moral/ethical issues potentially affect people all around the world. The biology teacher on our team used the Interact simulation *Clone* and the students studied related historical events and issues, such as the Mengele experiments on twins in Nazi concentration camps. In English the content was religious conflict, and students read *Night* by Eli Weisel, accounts of Nazi medical experiments from *Children of the Flame* by Lucette Matalon Lagnado, and poetry written by children in concentration camps. They examined alternative resolutions to a variety of conflicts related to the Holocaust. Although some connections were made through inquiry processes, geometry had minimal integration in the unit because of its limited applications to this theme.

*Selecting Global Studies Content for the Interdisciplinary Theme*

With the unit theme identified as international conflict resolution (the management or resolution of conflicts that affect people in more than one part of the world), we began making decisions on the specific content (knowledge and skills) for global studies.[2] We looked for possible connections with the curriculum guide for global studies by creating a list of topics in the course that would lend themselves to the study of conflict resolution. The list contained several historical and well as contemporary conflicts. We decided that a current conflict would be more intriguing for our students because it would enable them to consider alternative outcomes without the knowledge of how actual resolution (or lack thereof) occurred in history.

Eventually we narrowed our choice of content focus to the racial conflict in South Africa or the Arab-Israeli conflict in the Middle East. Both topics met the interdisciplinary criteria of involving global dynamics, many types of world actors, and local-global connections. Both topics were found in the news almost daily, and we had extensive instructional materials and resources in the school and community about each conflict. The Arab-Israeli theme could easily tie in historically to the English course readings.

However, in the end we chose racial conflict in South Africa because of considerations about our students. Racial prejudice, "differences" between white and black Americans and related discrimination are significant issues in our students' daily lives. They hear about and deal with racial conflicts in the school, the commu-

[2]All of what follows reflects a collaborative effort between Steve Shapiro as a field professor and Matt Shafer as a preservice teacher in the Ohio State PDS Network in Social Studies and Global Education. Collaboration between teachers is a major element in our PDS preparation of preservice teachers in social studies and global education.

nity, our nation, and the world. As social studies teachers we believe that we must prepare our students to overcome racism, particularly the black/white issues that are so much a part of history and contemporary life here and in many other countries. We also recognized that our students, like most Americans, know little about Africa and African peoples and nations beyond the stereotypes of films or the war and starvation stories that characterize most print and television coverage of the continent. We also knew that the larger interdisciplinary unit would give students the opportunity to make connections with other international conflicts, such as those in the Middle East and elsewhere, as part of their final assessment.

Racial conflict in South Africa also demonstrates how conflicts within a country spill out to affect economic choices (foreign investment and marketing, roles of multinational corporations, etc.), political relationships (e.g., bilateral decisions to boycott, ban imports or restrict movement of people; "pariah" status in the world community) and cultural matters (e.g., ban on entertainers going to South Africa, ban on participation in the Olympics) around the world. Since racial conflict is a global issue, the study of South Africa can provide insights into the management of racial conflict in other parts of the world.

## Selecting Essential Knowledge and Skills

Essential content is the body of knowledge and skills essential to a working understanding and application of the topic or theme. In identifying essential content, we ask ourselves, *If we were to see one of these students in a couple of years and strike up a conversation about South Africa, what would we expect that they would still know about the topic?* We use this question because we have found it is important not to get so bogged down in the details of the topic that students fail to understand the vital concepts or generalizations. It is important to remember that when we give a traditional test, a student who does not know 15 percent of the information *on test day* receives a very respectable grade. The same student, a week later, will certainly remember less about the topic than he or she did the day of the test. It is a sobering experience to consider how that student would do on the exact same test if it were taken a year or a decade later. It is our opinion that in an effort to "cover" everything, we have buried students under a blanket of trivia and denied them an internalized, meaningful understanding of important generalizations or the "big picture."

Our list of essential knowledge emerged from brainstorming, debate, and careful consideration of what the students needed to know in order to apply what they learn about the South Africa conflict to other international conflicts and peacemaking. During the important process of reflecting and prioritizing we developed a six-item list of points we designated as composing the *essential knowledge* for this unit:

1. major historical and contemporary steps in the South African evolution of racial conflict (including reasons for European settlement and the nature of early cross-cultural interaction) and efforts to resolve it;

2. the relative size, geography, and economic and political power of different racial and ethnic groups in South Africa;

3. multiple perspectives (of South Africans and others) on the reasons for and effects of racial conflict and apartheid on human/ civil rights and the quality of life of diverse South Africans and their families;

4. the role of economics in the racial conflict and the alternative uses of economic forces (disinvestment, boycotts, strikes, etc.) in the conflict;

5. the role of political forces struggling for power and self-determination, their leaders, their basic positions, and their relationships with nations, organizations, and individuals outside of South Africa;

6. the ways in which the military, terrorism, violence, and negotiation and other nonviolent approaches have been used by people in South Africa and other parts of the world in their efforts to maintain or overcome apartheid or racial conflict.

We also began to think about which skills would be most appropriate for the unit. We outlined the following *essential skills* during the early planning process and revised and updated them as we planned the assessment and developed the lessons.

1. abilities to conceptualize, write, present, and defend a proposal to resolve an international conflict;

2. abilities to analyze, evaluate, and predict the effects (dynamics) of a current action in both the short run and the long run using the process of dynamics webbing;

3. ability to work collaboratively with peers toward completion of a common product.

## A NOTE ON ATTITUDES AND VALUES

When developing a unit, some teachers identify essential attitudes or values. As with the essential knowledge and skills, these attitudes would be among the most important outcomes of the unit. However, the explicit identification of values and attitudes can be quite controversial as some teachers, parents, and communities feel that the school's role is not one of teaching or assessing student attitudes and values.

Our team has chosen not to list essential values along with our essential knowledge and skills for a different reason. In the process of developing a unit through backwards building, the essential content provides the basis for the creation of the unit's final assessment. The intent is that the assessment involves a performance demonstrating mastery of the essentials. It is because we do not support such an assessment of attitudes and values that we have chosen not to identify them as part of the essential content.

We do recognize that attitudes and values permeate our practice as an important, intrinsic part of education. We convey values through our policies and procedures (for example, valuing punctuality), classroom practice (respect for others during discussions), and in materials and topics (concern over human rights championed in the movie Cry Freedom). As you can infer from our essential knowledge and skills listed above, this unit focuses on valuing people's ability to cooperate and work together, valuing the management or resolution of conflicts whether international or local, and valuing the human rights of all peoples.

## STEP 2: DEVELOPING THE ESSENTIAL QUESTIONS

Just as Socrates was able to teach important lessons to his students by asking them thoughtful, fundamental questions, we as teachers use questioning to develop reflection and higher level thought processes. It is extremely valuable for teachers to think about and identify fundamental questions that get to the core of the complex issues related to a unit. The Coalition of Essential School researchers and practitioners refer to these as *essential questions*. Our entire team works together to develop essential questions for our interdisciplinary units.

There are several characteristics of essential questions. They are questions that are *open-ended* and effect serious discussion, debate, and *critical thought*. Essential questions *do not have a "correct" answer*. Rather they have many possible answers, each of which can be defended with ideas and evidence. Essential questions *go to the heart of content*. Through their study and debate of essential questions, students take apart, examine and apply the unit's most important knowledge and skills.

## Generating Possibilities

Although our team generates a single set of essential questions for an interdisciplinary unit, an individual teacher can do the same for a self-contained classroom. While there is no magic formula, our team tends to use four to six questions for a given unit. We also attempt to sequence the questions from most basic to most complex.

Our team began the process of developing essential questions on international conflict resolution by considering the nature of these questions, the content of the unit, and the characteristics of our students. As we brainstormed ideas, we wrote them on a blackboard for consideration. Questions were rejected if they did not meet the criteria of essential questions (see above), fit the demands of interdisciplinary connections to biology, English, and global studies, or meet the needs of our students. Our initial list read as follows:

1. What causes international conflict?
2. What makes a conflict "global?"
3. In what ways can international conflict be resolved?
4. Is it necessary that international conflict be resolved?
5. What causes conflict resolution to be long-lasting?
6. What are hurdles to conflict resolution?

7. What are the ramifications of conflict?
8. Why do we need to think globally?
9. How can we determine the most effective resolution to a conflict?
10. How do global conflicts affect you?
11. Why is conflict resolution so difficult to achieve?
12. How does a global perspective affect the way you understand conflict?

In looking back over the suggestions, we quickly eliminated question 8 as unnecessary (the students had been studying global perspectives all year) and too broad for the theme. Question 3 was eliminated because it does not require sufficient critical thought but can be answered by listing approaches to conflict resolution. Question 5 was eliminated because we felt that it required study that would not be included in sufficient depth in this unit. Instead, we could include this issue by revising question 7 to read, "What are the ramifications of global conflict *and its management or resolution?*" We felt that question 12 was redundant and could be eliminated because it would be answered through the revised number 7. Although question 4 was closed ended, it struck us as provocative. However, we decided it would emerge anyway when students pondered alternative approaches to conflict resolution.

After much debate and a few days to reflect on connections with our subject units, we chose these *essential questions for our interdisciplinary unit:*

1. When is a conflict global? How do such conflicts affect you?
2. What causes global conflict?
3. What are the ramifications of global conflict and its management or resolution?
4. Why is conflict resolution difficult to achieve?
5. How can we determine the most effective resolution to conflict?

*Using Essential Questions*

Essential questions are not simply reproduced on a worksheet. Rather, these are questions that students deal with in day to day activities throughout the unit. We prominently display the questions on posterboard in our classrooms and refer students to them as related issues emerge. We often begin an activity by directing students' attention to a question or questions that the day's activity will address. It is critical that the essential questions relate closely to the essential knowledge and skills and the final assessment for the unit. Sometimes as we are planning a lesson we find that it does not directly relate to an essential question. We stop and rethink our planning and revise either the essential questions (perhaps we really had not thought through some element or necessary connection) or we rework the lesson. The essential questions help us focus our lesson planning on the major goals of the unit and its final assessment. In our team's interdisciplinary units, we design performance-based assessments that require students to demonstrate their understanding of these questions through the completion of a complex, contextual, meaningful task (step 3, below).

When we plan social studies units centered on a topic rather than a theme, we design questions that are more content specific. For example, if we were teaching the South Africa unit in a self-contained classroom, our essential questions would have captured the essence of resolving racial conflict in South Africa with such questions as, *What would have to happen in South Africa for the people there to manage or resolve their racial conflicts?* Essential questions go to the heart of instruction and assessment.

## STEP 3: DESIGNING THE FINAL UNIT ASSESSMENT

The final assessment is the glue that holds the structure of the backwards building unit together. Most social studies teachers have been trained to identify the unit goals and objectives (which are similar to essential knowledge and skills) and then plan daily lessons. The underlying rationale is that we design lessons to teach the content identified in the goals and objectives. While this sequence of planning seems to make sense, it overlooks the difference between what we teach and what students learn. That is, we all know that just because we *teach* something, doesn't mean that our students will have *learned* it. In the traditional approach to planning, designing the assessment(s) frequently follows the development or even the actual teaching of lessons. It says, "Well, I have taught X, Y, and Z. Now let's see what the students have learned about these things."

### Bringing Together Backwards Building Curriculum and Authentic Assessment

We planned this unit "backwards" from the traditional approach so that we could focus on the assessment. Our reasoning is that if we want students to know X, then we need to design a task that will enable students to show us that they *understand* and *can use* X. Ideally, the task will be meaningful and authentic, something that people actually do with this particular knowledge and these skills in the real world. It should provide students the opportunity to demonstrate not only competence but also excellence in ways that "objective" tests, with their 100 percent limits, cannot.

Perhaps we can demonstrate the concept more clearly by applying it to the topic of this chapter—unit planning. Consider the options of a professor in a teacher education program who wishes to teach preservice teachers how to design an instructional unit. The professor could present information about unit planning and then give a test about the most effective ways to design a unit. However, the assessment would be more meaningful if the preservice teachers had to demonstrate mastery of the concepts by actually designing a unit (a performance-based assessment). Taking it a step further, an authentic assessment for the study of unit planning would be to give each preservice teacher a chance actually to teach the unit he or she developed to middle or high school students (an authentic audience). With this final assessment in place, the professor could then focus on what lessons needed to be planned (building backwards from the assessment) in order to prepare students to be successful in their unit planning and teaching. The authentic application makes the process of learning more meaningful, as the preservice teachers have a compelling reason to learn the lessons about unit planning.

The backwards building approach is especially valuable to beginning teachers. When working with student teachers we often sense a deep frustration or pale of impending doom as they try to figure out what they should teach. They wander through library stacks or browse through the school's resources hoping to come across something "neat." Other times they design lessons to keep students busy or to "cover" a body of factual knowledge without thinking about overall goals or teaching the students how such knowledge is used by adults in our society. For students, learning social studies may become an esoteric exercise useful only in getting a grade. Designing the assessment first makes determining what to teach much easier, as we consider what knowledge and skills students will need to learn in order to be prepared to complete the assessment performance. It is vital to remember that the final assessment must be designed in such a way that students cannot successfully complete the assignment without the mastery of the essential knowledge and skills.

*Planning the Final Assessment*

We designed the interdisciplinary unit so that the final assessment for the study of racial conflict in South Africa would provide the students with experience and knowledge that they would use in completing the final assessment for the interdisciplinary unit. *We asked the students to conceptualize and develop a plan for reducing racial conflict in South Africa.* Working in groups, students chose a method for conflict resolution and designed a step by step plan for resolving or managing conflict in South Africa. They explored a number of approaches from which they could choose for their proposal:

1. Violence
   a. Use of physical force or the threat of physical force
   b. Often a last resort after other approaches have failed
   c. May take different forms including: military force, police action, guerrilla warfare (unconventional warfare), terrorism (targeted or random), threat of force
2. Negotiation, diplomacy
   a. Conversations between representatives of groups seeking to resolve a conflict; may include outside parties to facilitate negotiation
   b. Involves compromise by both sides
   c. May be bilateral (two sides) or multilateral (more than two sides)
3. Nonviolent Action
   a. Strategic nonviolent actions aimed at forcing the end of a conflict
   b. Common tools include hunger strikes, work strikes, boycotts, sit-ins, marches, write-in campaigns, published or unpublished writings, and non-lethal sabotage

    c. Relies on political, economic, social or religious pressure to bring about change

4. Peacekeeping
    a. Use of United Nations' or another country's troops as a buffer between disputing groups
    b. Troops are lightly armed and come from a variety of different countries
    c. Troops are stationed in area between disputing groups with their permission
    d. The goal is to prevent escalation of violence between disputing groups.

As we designed this final assessment, we wanted to make sure that to complete it successfully students would have to master the essential content and skills. It is important to recognize that it is unrealistic to expect that a single performance-based assessment will encapsulate every element of each item on the list of essential skills and knowledge. Every unit should involve smaller assessments throughout the unit (quizzes, writing assignments, graded class seminars) to insure that all essentials have been mastered by all students. However, in looking back at the essential content and skills, we felt that students would definitely need to have mastered most items in both categories in order to be successful on this assignment. In fact, it seemed that this assignment required students to actually synthesize and integrate much of the knowledge to create an original product.

Perhaps more importantly, we looked to the essential questions. We designed the final assessment so that it would correspond with the essential questions. We tried to design it so that in completing the assessment the students would address the essential questions. We developed a form for their proposals to guide students through the process of designing their resolution (table 2.2).

This form was carefully designed to guide students through a new and complex process. Students first articulated their approach to conflict resolution and then described their *projected outcome*. Examples of outcomes identified by students ranged from division of South Africa into two independent nations to the creation of a single democratic nation open to participation by members of all racial and ethnic groups. We wanted the students to identify the end goal before they created the plan. We based this decision on the

TABLE 2.2
Resolution Proposal Form

---

Group:
APPROACHES TO CONFLICT RESOLUTION:

1.) PROJECTED OUTCOME (What will be the specific results of the proposed resolution?)

2.) SIGNIFICANT PARTIES (Who must be involved for your resolution to be implemented?)

3.) EXISTING CHALLENGES OR PROBLEMS (What are the hurdles that *have* to be considered?)

4.) RESOLUTION PLAN
What specific steps must be taken?
In what order should steps be implemented?
What do the significant parties need to do?
Your plan must address all challenges and problems listed in part #3.
Your plan should lead to the projected outcome named in part #1 of this proposal.

---

© Steve Shapiro, 1994

same rationale that guides our backwards building units—if you know the end target, you can then work toward it. The second item, *significant parties,* deals with essential question 4 (Why is conflict resolution difficult to achieve?). Without this section, students would propose resolutions that would be unrealistic and oversimplified. By asking students to consider all parties involved, we forced students to deal with multiple perspectives and the diverse experiences of concerned parties. The third item is *existing challenges or problems.* This question also correlates with essential question number 4. Finally, the fourth section asked students to design the plan itself. We asked students to attempt to reach the outcome identified in section 1 and to deal with the parties (in section 2) and the obstacles (in section 3).

Effective completion of this assignment would demonstrate a student's profound understanding of many of the essentials of the unit. But what if it were not done well? We knew that the products that students produced on this assessment would be only a first draft of a proposal. As a result, we arranged for four South Africans from different racial and ethnic groups, socioeconomic backgrounds, and political philosophies to come into class. We asked the groups to go through their proposed resolutions with each of the four South Africans who would serve as *consultants* to the students. Knowing that they were going to share their plans with this authentic audience, students put much thought and effort into the creation of their proposals. The opportunity to receive insightful feedback and hear multiple perspectives led to rethinking, more research, and improvement of the proposals.

Finally, in an effort to close this assessment and to deal with essential question 5 (How can we determine the most effective resolution to conflict?) and question 3 (What are the ramifications of global conflict and its management or resolution?), we had students assess their own proposed resolution. Our experience is that engaging students in a meaningful process of self-evaluation results in students who are more reflective and honest about their academic performance. It also helps students break their dependence on the teacher by empowering them to evaluate their own work. Students were provided with criteria for evaluating their proposals (table 2.3).

The first two criteria, feasibility and equity, force students to consider essential question 5 (How can we determine the most effective resolution to conflict?). The final two items require students to consider both the short-term and the long-term ramifications of their proposed resolution. While dealing directly with essential question 3, these items also help students consider the effectiveness of their proposed resolution (essential question 5).

As you can see, the final assessment process was complex and time consuming. It was a week filled with higher-level thinking and intellectual challenge. In addition to testing the students' knowledge of essential content, this assessment offered a meaningful learning experience to students.

### Connections between the Final Assessment for the Global Studies Unit and the Exhibition for the Interdisciplinary Unit

The process of proposing a resolution to racial conflict in South Africa served as a model for the final assessment for the interdisciplinary unit. We refer to this final assessment as an "exhibi-

TABLE 2.3
Criteria for Evaluating Resolution Proposals

---

**DIRECTIONS**   Describe the strengths and weaknesses of the proposed resolution in each of these areas.

**FEASIBILITY:**
Is the plan workable?

What might prevent the plan from achieving the proposed outcome?

Which significant parties might oppose parts of the plans, and for what reasons?


Rank feasibility on a scale of 0–10 (10 being most feasible).
       0     1     2     3     4     5     6     7     8     9     10

**EQUITY:**
List each significant party and predict how they would view the fairness of this plan from *their* perspective.

**IMMEDIATE GLOBAL RAMIFICATIONS:**

—What effect will implementing this plan have on the South African people?

—How will implementation of this plan affect other nations?

—How will people, governments, and businesses around the world respond to this resolution?

**FUTURE (NEXT GENERATION) GLOBAL RAMIFICATIONS:**
—What will be the political, social, and economic ramifications for South Africans?

—What will be the political, social, and economic ramifications for other nations?

---

© Steve Shapiro, 1994.

tion" because it gives students the opportunity to demonstrate or exhibit their understanding of global conflict and its resolution or management. The purpose of the exhibition was synthesis and application of the students' knowledge and understanding of the complex issues raised by the essential questions to another international conflict. Because the exhibition dealt with the concept of global conflict resolution rather than the specific content of any of the four courses, it was designed to give groups of students the opportunity to choose a conflict that interested them. The major criterion that suggested topics had to meet was that they be global in nature. Topics could be drawn from many academic fields, thus enabling students to choose from many alternatives. The process of having students identifying topics and presenting them for the team's approval was in itself an exercise in answering essential question 1. After identifying and researching that conflict, each group had to develop a plan for resolving or managing the conflict.

We developed an overview of the exhibition to introduce its process to the students (table 2.4). A detailed account of the implementation of the exhibition appears at the end of this chapter. (see pages 101-117).

TABLE 2.4
Introduction of the Conflict Resolution Exhibition

| | |
|---|---|
| PART I. | RESEARCH PAPER |
| | Identify a conflict of global importance. |
| | Analyze the conflict. (The topic needs to be divided in such a way that multiple perspectives are researched.) |
| PART II. | PRESENTATION |
| | Explain the ramifications of the conflict. |
| | Propose possible resolutions. |
| | Select the "best" resolution; project its ramifications and give the rationale for your selection. |
| AUDIENCE. | Experts in your field of study with whom you have made arrangements to evaluate your exhibition. With permission slips and sign-out by an adult driver and chaperone, you may leave campus during the exhibition period. |
| FORMAT. | How this exhibition is presented is up to your group. Specific evaluation criteria will be given to you after your research paper is completed. |

© Steve Shapiro, 1994.

With the final assessments for the global studies unit and the interdisciplinary unit in draft, we were ready to turn to the task of developing lessons for the global studies unit. Our lesson planning began with our sketching out an overview of the entire unit on racial conflict in South Africa. The process of developing a unit overview is especially useful for beginning teachers who are learning the relationships between content and methods.

## STEP 4: DEVELOPING OVERVIEWS OF DAILY LESSONS

We had determined what we wanted students to know (essential knowledge) and be able to do (essential skills) to answer the essential questions and successfully complete the final assessment for the racial conflict in South Africa unit. Next we had to consider how to choose methods that support these content and assessment goals. We also needed to identify instructional materials and resources in the school and community. But first we thought about our students' prior knowledge on racial conflict in South Africa.

### Building on Student Knowledge

Before teachers begin to plan a unit, it is important to understand what the students already know so that we can build on their prior knowledge. While we knew about the students' interests and abilities, we did not know about their background on history and contemporary life in South Africa. In order to understand what students already knew about the subject, we conducted an informal diagnostic inquiry several weeks before we began to plan the unit. We gave students a short questionnaire to determine what they knew about racial conflict in South Africa that included items such as: What comes to mind when you think of South Africa? What is apartheid and why is it significant to South Africans? Who is Nelson Mandela and why is he in the news?

We also spoke to several students informally about the subject. It was evident that most of the students had heard the word *apartheid* but that almost none of them had even the most elementary knowledge of racial conflict in South Africa. It was clear that we should assume that students had little background knowledge as we began to plan the unit.

*Webbing the Essentials and Assessment with Methods and Resources*

With our essential knowledge, skills, questions, and the unit assessment tacked up on the wall in front of us in summary form, we first checked to see if they were all congruent. Were the essential knowledge and skills needed to complete the assessment? Did the completion of the final assessment require attention to the essential questions? As we found problems, we revised the essentials, the questions, or the final assessment.

Our next step in planning was to think about how we could prepare the students for the final assessment. In order to build backwards, we began brainstorming alternative methods and resources that we could use to teach the knowledge and skills needed in the final assessment. As we thought of possibilities, we sketched them out and connected them to the appropriate content (see figure 2.2). We knew that we must decide how the students would get the information, how we would help them process it, and how we would help them prepare to use it in the final unit assessment. As you examine figure 2.2, you see that we identified

- different types of readings (the text, supplementary materials, literature, and primary sources, including documents such as the ANC Freedom Charter)
- work with maps and statistical tables and charts to learn about demographics, social and economic indicators
- several simulations and some role-playing to understand multiple perspectives and power relationships
- interaction with resource people to obtain personal stories and insights into the complexities of the conflicts
- films and video to provide visual contexts and background information
- decision-trees and debates on controversial issues to spur thinking skills and evaluation of data
- discussion, synthesis, seminars, and writing assignments to help students integrate ideas and skills

We found it useful to identify instructional materials and resources in the school and community in webbing out ideas for lessons.

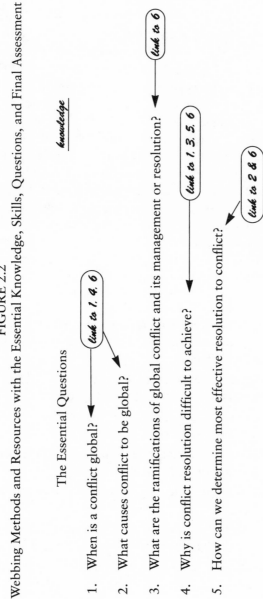

FIGURE 2.2

Webbing Methods and Resources with the Essential Knowledge, Skills, Questions, and Final Assessment

*knowledge*

The Essential Questions

1. When is a conflict global? *link to 1, 4, 6*

2. What causes conflict to be global?

3. What are the ramifications of global conflict and its management or resolution? *link to 6*

4. Why is conflict resolution difficult to achieve? *link to 1, 3, 5, 6*

5. How can we determine most effective resolution to conflict? *link to 2 & 6*

Final Assessment:
CONCEPTUALIZE AND DEVELOP A PLAN FOR
REDUCING RACIAL CONFLICT IN SOUTH AFRICA

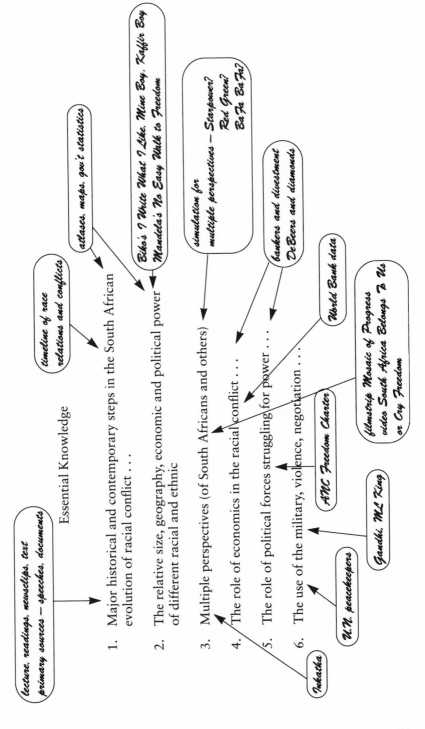

lecture, readings, newsclips, text
primary sources — speeches, documents

timeline of race
relations and conflicts

atlases, maps, gov't statistics

Biko's I Write What I Like, Mine Boy, Kaffir Boy
Mandela's No Easy Walk to Freedom

simulation for
multiple perspectives — Starpower?
Red Green?
Ba Fa Ba Fa?

bankers and divestment
DeBeers and diamonds

World Bank data

filmstrip Mosaic of Progress
video South Africa Belongs To Us
or Cry Freedom

ANC Freedom Charter

Gandhi, ML King

U.N. peacekeepers

Inkatha

Essential Knowledge

1. Major historical and contemporary steps in the South African
   evolution of racial conflict . . . .

2. The relative size, geography, economic and political power
   of different racial and ethnic

3. Multiple perspectives (of South Africans and others)

4. The role of economics in the racial conflict . . . .

5. The role of political forces struggling for power . . . .

6. The use of the military, violence, negotiation . . . .

Essential Skills

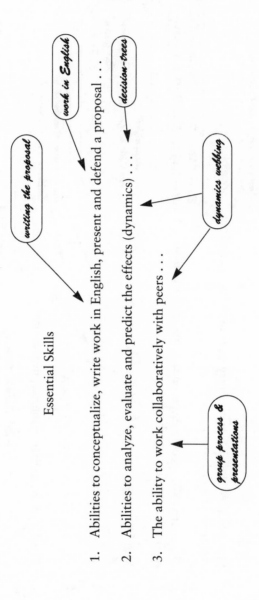

1. Abilities to conceptualize, write work in English, present and defend a proposal . . .

2. Abilities to analyze, evaluate and predict the effects (dynamics) . . .

3. The ability to work collaboratively with peers . . .

As we ran low on ideas we sat back to decide which of the alternatives that we had identified were truly needed to address the essentials and assessments that we have planned. We circled these on the web and looked for gaps between the new emerging activities and our essentials and assessment. We asked ourselves: Are all the essentials addressed? We went through them one by one, looking for ways to connect content and instructional methods. Much of our discussion at this point was similar to the discussion of alternatives found in the methods section in chapter 1. We discussed the best ways for students to understand the historical changes in the demographics of South Africa, the development of racial conflicts, and apartheid and its insidious effect on the quality of life for most South Africans. How could we help our students feel the injustice? How could we bring them into an understanding of the ethnic and racial groups, the political parties, and the effects of outsiders and other governments on the resolution of racial conflict? How could we make sure they would develop the background of knowledge they would need to evaluate approaches to conflict resolution?

*Planning and Sequencing Lessons: Making Decisions on Linking Content, Methods, and Goals*

Finally we put all the lesson ideas down on paper in a calendar format (see Figure 2.3) so that we could see the flow of activities. In the process we asked ourselves more questions: How can we interest students in South Africa? What do they need to know first in order to build a knowledge base? With some definite ideas of which methods, content, and resources we wanted to include, we sketched out a working draft of the lesson ideas and sequenced them. We started with a basic idea or conceptualization of the lesson and developed summaries that provided a brief capsule of each lesson's purpose, content, and method in a second draft. We also wrote in the interdisciplinary activities and their tentative dates so that the knowledge and skills of the global studies unit would be developed and assessed within the larger interdisciplinary unit. As you read the narrative description of our decision making as we developed and sequenced the unit's lessons below, you may want to refer to the tables entitled "Draft Lesson Summaries" (our final planning document of all the unit's lesson summaries) and the sample lesson plans that follow later in this chapter.

Figure 2.3
Unit Overview

| M | T | W | Th | F |
|---|---|---|---|---|
| | | | 1 | 2 |
| 5678 5<br>Unit Introduction | 5566 6<br>CRY FREEDOM | 7788 7<br>CRY FREEDOM | 5566 8<br>CRY FREEDOM (continued)<br>& developing questions | 7788 9 |
| 5678 12<br>Distribute QS—<br>Lecture & Research | Adv.grp/5678 13<br>Research (cont.) | Adv.grp/5678 14<br>Research (cont.) | 5678 15<br>Students present/<br>discuss answers<br>to QS | 5678 16<br>5 pres/disc.<br>cont. |
| 5678 19<br>Newsclips | 5678 20<br>Review newsclips<br>& test material | 5678 21<br>TEST | 5678 22<br>OPEN | 5678 23<br>OPEN |
| 5678 26<br>Intro to Dynamics<br>Webbing | 5566 27<br>RED-GREEN SIMULATION<br>& dynamics webbing | 7788 28 | 29<br>Divestment Issues | 30<br>Divestment Debate |

| 5678 (3) | 5678 (4) | 5566 (5) | 7788 (6) | 5678 (7) |
|---|---|---|---|---|
| OPEN | Lecture-Change Agents | Developing Resolution Proposals | Developing Resolution Proposals | Revising Resolution Proposals |
| 5678 (10) | 5678 (11) | 5678 (12) | Adv.grp/5678 (13) | (14) |
| Revising Resolution Proposals | Presenting Resolutions to Authentic Audiences | Presenting Resolutions to Authentic Audiences | Discuss Authentic Audiences | Self-assessment |
| 5566 (17) | 7788 (18) | 5678 (19) | Adv.grp. (20) | Adv.grp. (21) |
| *STARPOWER* | *STARPOWER* | Student Seminar | Prepare for First Rehearsal | First Rehearsal |
| 5678 (24) | Adv.grp. (25) | (26) | (27) | (28) |
| OPEN | Dress Rehearsal | Exhibition Day | | |

**Motivating Lessons.** It is always advantageous to begin a unit in a way that captures students' interest and involves them in the subject under study. Once they are caught up in the content, they are motivated to learn. We believed that the film *Cry Freedom* and the *Starpower* simulation would be equally interesting and intriguing to our students. The benefit of *Cry Freedom* is that it takes students into daily life in South Africa and paints powerful, bold images of the conflicts and racism. We also know that Hollywood movies grab our students' attention. *Starpower* does not deal with South Africa directly, although it focuses on the larger themes of social, political, and economic inequities that led to the creation and maintenance of apartheid. By using the simulation at the beginning of the unit, we could ensure that all of the learning about racial conflict would have had a personal meaning to the students. However, we chose to use the movie. We decided that working with *Starpower* would be better as a culminating activity at the end of the unit, at which point we could engage the students in a post-simulation seminar dealing with the factors that create and diminish racial conflict. At the end of the unit, we asked the students whether they thought the simulation would have been more effective at the beginning of the unit (it was fascinating to hear them analyze this issue!), and they were evenly divided on the timing but in consensus on the simulation's value as a learning experience. Using double-blocking classes (scheduling hundred-minute classes that meet every other day) we would be able to show *Cry Freedom*, discuss it with students and begin a follow-up activity during the first week of the unit (see Figure 2.4 week one).

**Lessons on Historical, Geographic, Political, and Economic Factors and Multiple Perspectives on the Racial Conflict.** While the film provides a look at the life of a few South Africans and alludes to their history, it leaves students with an incomplete story. We expected that students would have many questions about South Africa after viewing the movie. Wishing to build on their questions and interests, we decided to have students make lists of questions that they would like to have answered. We would compile all of their questions and let those questions (with a few of ours if some critical issues were not raised) become the basis for our initial inquiry into racial conflict in South Africa.

Generating and answering these basic questions would become

FIGURE 2.4
Draft Lesson Summaries

---

Note: All lessons related to the interdisciplinary unit and exhibition are in italics and lessons focusing on the social studies unit are in regular tupe.

Week One (April 5–9)
Monday
- *Purpose: Introducing interdisciplinary unit and global studies unit*
- *Content: Essential content, essential questions, the unit assessments*
- *Methods: Examination of essential content and questions (on posters), brainstorming of relationships between international conflict management and resolution of racial conflict in South Africa (SA), and explanation of sign-up sheet for the group exhibitions*

Tuesday through Friday
- Double blocking of social studies over four days (e.g., fifth- and sixth-period classes meet one hundred minutes on Tuesday and Thursday, seventh and eighth period classes meet one hundred minutes on Wednesday and Friday)
- Purpose: Motivating student interest, developing student questions about SA in general (includes political, human rights and economic issues) and its people and racial conflicts, and so forth
- Content: High-interest overview of SA background, perspectives on racial conflict in SA
- Methods: Show film *Cry Freedom* and ask students to work together to develop questions on SA and the racial conflict there

Week Two (April 12–16) *Monitor individual research projects through study halls.*
Monday
- Purpose: Beginning to answer student questions about SA, fill in historical and contemporary background
- Content: Historical development and geography of SA apartheid and the anti-apartheid movement, demographics of SA population and "homelands."
- Methods: Lecture; student work with handouts, maps, statistical tables

Tuesday and Wednesday    One hundred minutes each day for First Advisory Groups Meeting (Tuesday) with students developing questions for their exhibitions and Second Advisory Group Meeting (Wednesday) with students dividing up the research topics **into individual research papers.** Remaining hundred minutes divided among the four subjects
- Purpose: Answer other student questions on SA
- Content: SA socio-economic, legal and political issues related to apartheid and the anti-apartheid movement, expenditures and public

FIGURE 2.4 (Continued)

services (education, health care, etc. of different racial and ethnic groups)
- Methods: Lecture and student inquiry with statistics, primary sources from leaders, political parties, and anti-apartheid organizations

Thursday and Friday
- Purpose: Presenting and discussing questions related to essential knowledge about racial conflict in SA
- Content: Events in SA history; economics, and politics of racial conflict and apartheid; people and organizations struggling for power in SA
- Methods: Student presentation of answers to questions, discussion of student questions, teacher questioning of unstated assumptions, evidence, and biased information

Week Three (April 19–23) *Each advisor examines his/her groups work on individual research papers.*

Monday
- Purpose: Developing chronological overview and evaluating major factors influencing racial conflict
- Content: Major events, benchmarks in racial conflict, multiple perspectives
- Methods: Students examine and evaluate newsclips on SA from around the world over two decades.

Tuesday
- Purpose: Reviewing for test
- Content: Essential knowledge (numbers 1–6)
- Methods: Teacher questioning, student presentations

Wednesday
- Purpose: Testing student understanding of essential knowledge
- Content: Essential knowledge (numbers 1–6)
- Methods: Written test

Thursday
- Purpose: Reteaching background as needed, according to test results
- Content: Essential knowledge
- Methods: Students teaching their knowledge, expertise; some teacher talk if needed

Friday
- Leave open to use as needed

Week Four (April 26–30) *In study halls advisors make final check of notecards by Wednesday and outlines for research papers by Friday; students should begin to write individual research papers by the first of next week. Papers are due on May 11.*

FIGURE 2.4 (Continued)

Monday
- Purpose: Develop student understanding of dynamics webbing
- Content: Process and skills in dynamics webbing
- Methods: Demonstration and discussion

Tuesday and Wednesday   (100 minute periods)
- Purpose: Examinating alternatives in conflict resolution
- Content: Negotiation
- Methods: Red-Green Simulation and dynamics webbing

Thursday
- Purpose: Understanding some economic approaches to conflict resolution or management
- Content: Divestment, economic boycotts, strikes
- Methods: Dynamics webbing

Friday
- Purpose: Understanding some economic approaches to conflict resolution or management

Content: Divestment, economic boycotts, strikes

Methods: Student debates

Week Five (May 3–7)
Monday
- Leave open to use as needed

Tuesday
- Purpose: Understanding change agents
- Content: United Nations' role in international conflict management, international peacekeeping, effects of the media, roles of outsiders (other nations, individuals, organizations, multinational corporations)
- Methods: Lecture, visuals

Wednesday and Thursday   (100 minute periods)
- Purpose: Developing resolution proposals
- Content: Approaches to managing or resolving racial conflict on SA
- Methods: Decision making and research in cooperative groups

Friday
- Purpose: Revising resolution proposals
- Content: Approaches to managing or resolving racial conflict on SA
- Methods: Rewriting in cooperative groups

Week Six (May 10–14)
Monday  *Individual student reports for interdisciplinary unit are due.*
- Purpose: Defending/reworking resolution proposals
- Content: Approaches to managing or resolving racial conflict on SA
- Methods: Presenting, defending, rewriting in cooperative groups

FIGURE 2.4 (Continued)

---

Tuesday and Wednesday   (double blocking of social studies over two days—fifth- and sixth-period classes meet one hundred minutes on Tuesday, seventh- and eighth-period classes meet one hundred minutes Wednesday)
- Purpose: Interacting with and learning from an authentic audience
- Content: Approaches to managing or resolving racial conflict on SA
- Methods: Groups present their resolution proposals to each of four South Africans of diverse backgrounds and beliefs and respond to their questions and suggestions

Thursday   (*First one hundred minutes in Third Advisory Group Meeting*; remaining hundred minutes divided among the four subjects)
- Purpose: Discussing students' work with South Africans
- Content: Approaches to managing or resolving racial conflict in SA
- Methods: Students share the four South Africans' perspectives and advice on their proposals and discuss possible changes.

Friday
- Purpose: Assessing of resolutions and student learning
- Content: Approaches to managing or resolving racial conflict in SA
- Methods: Student evaluation and critique, discussion of issues

Week Seven (May 17–21)
Monday and Tuesday   Classes are double blocked: fifth and sixth on Monday; seventh and eighth periods on Tuesday.
- Purpose: Experiencing use of power to bring about inequality
- Content: Concept of power in negotiation and settlement
- Methods: Students participate in the simulation *Starpower*

Wednesday
- Purpose: Discussing the relationship between power and conflict and conclusion of South Africa unit in global studies
- Content: Racial conflict in South Africa, experience of *Starpower*
- Methods: Student-led seminar (see sample lesson)

Thursday
- *Purpose: Fourth Advisory Group Meeting*
- *Content: Proposals on international conflict resolution*
- *Methods: Preparation for exhibition in cooperative groups with advisor's coaching*

Friday
- *Purpose: First Rehearsal*
- *Content: Each group presents their exhibition to their advisory group*
- *Methods: Group presents exhibition followed by constructive critiques*

FIGURE 2.4 (Continued)

---

Week Eight (May 24–28)
Monday
• Leave open to use as needed
Tuesday
• *Purpose: Dress Rehearsal*
• *Content: Proposals on international conflict resolution*
• *Methods: Presentations of exhibitions to advisors and students for exhibition grading*
Wednesday
• *Purpose: Exhibition*
• *Content: Proposals on international conflict resolution*
• *Methods: Presentations of exhibitions to authentic audiences in the community*

---

the focus of lessons five through ten (see lesson summaries). We planned to distribute a master list of questions to the students and let them choose ones to research using a variety of sources including the textbook, secondary sources from the media center, and primary sources such as literature, statistics on government expenditures, distribution of wealth, social indicators, and so forth. Depending on their synthesis of background factors, we could provide some brief lectures on particularly complex issues or help them pull together evidence of multiple perspectives (see figure 2.4 week two).

**Lessons Targeting Racial Conflict and Approaches to Conflict Resolution.** Building upon their new background knowledge of South Africa the next lessons (see lesson summaries in week three) would explore more closely the development of apartheid and racial conflict and people's efforts to resolve or manage those conflicts through a variety of methods. We decided to select news articles from magazines and newspapers that depict the issues from different perspectives (including some from the United States and other parts of the world) over a number of years. We were able to get articles from South African newspapers from the Ohio State university library. *World Press Today,* the *Manchester Guardian Weekly,* the *New York Times* and the *Christian Science Monitor* are other excellent sources for articles from around the world.

We planned to give the student groups packets of undated news articles and ask them to determine (1) the chronological order in which the articles occurred, (2) perspectives on the conflict represented in the articles, and (3) methods people were using or advocating to resolve or manage the conflicts. After completing this task, each group would create a timeline tracing the changes in the apartheid system and people's approaches to combatting racism. Discussion of their findings served as a major part of the review for a test on the essential knowledge (see figure 2.4, week three). Success on the test (multiple choice; short answer; true/false-explain questions, where students must explain why a given answer is false; essay) was a prerequisite for the second step, the practical applications of writing the resolutions to resolve or manage conflict in South Africa (see figure 2.1 on authentic learning and assessment). If the students' grades had not indicated that satisfactory progress had been made with the essential content, we were prepared to go back and revisit this material using different teaching methods and strategies. We tentatively left two days open to go over the test and reteach content as necessary.

**Lessons Linking Conflicts in South Africa to Global Ramifications.**    We felt that when the students had acquired a good understanding of the foundations of the racial conflict in South Africa, it was time to give them a chance to apply what they had learned as they expanded their knowledge to see South African issues more globally. We also wanted to bring together essential questions 1 and 3 (When is a conflict global? What are the ramifications of global conflict?) and our essential skill 2 (the ability to predict the dynamics of a current action). Dynamics webbing helps students make connections, recognize complexities and visualize long-term consequences and alternatives. To introduce the skill of webbing, we chose to model using the topic of aid to Russia. We selected this example because we knew that they had strong opinions on the topic (it had come up in class discussion from time to time), yet we doubted that they had seriously thought about the ramifications of those opinions. We planned to write on the board, "Should the U.S. approve $5 billion in financial aid to the newly formed Russian government?" By asking questions, we would have the students web out alternatives and possible future ramifications, both immediate and long-term effects of a single decision. As they expanded the web, students would begin to project future ramifications that could result over time. (This lesson is used as a sample lesson; see lesson for Monday of week four.)

After spending one class period teaching and practicing this process with students, we would then have them apply dynamics webbing in the Red/Green Simulation (see figure 2.4 week four). In this simulation, groups of students participate in a series of rounds of negotiations. In each round groups submit a written vote of either red or green. Each group earns or loses points based on its own vote and the votes of the other groups. The decisions the groups make in each round and the degree to which they abide by their agreements made in negotiations (the game is structured to encourage groups to agree to cooperate and then "cheat" when they actually vote) has ramifications on the future rounds of negotiations. We would have students design webs tracing the immediate and long-term ramifications of a particular action taken in the simulation and then discuss the outcomes of a single action taken by one group early in the simulation. One goal of this lesson was to help students see that in addressing current conflicts, one must consider the antecedents that led the players in the conflict to their current positions. We also wanted students to see that a proposed resolution to a conflict, if enacted, will have ramifications for years to come. Finally the game clearly demonstrates the complexity of negotiating an agreement between competing groups. (This lesson is developed as a sample lesson; see lesson for Tuesday of week four.)

Building on the skill of predicting dynamics, we wanted to give students an opportunity to apply the skill to the content of racial conflict in South Africa. We chose the question of divestment as the specific example. The dynamics began with the South African government's past refusal to dismantle the system of apartheid. Students would be placed in the position of CEO of a multinational company that did business in South Africa. After reading the viewpoints of prominent people on the topic of divestment, students would determine a course of action that they would take as CEO. Students would then web out the immediate and long-range ramifications of their decisions about divestment. After the students completed their webs, we would engage in a class debate in which students argued for or against divestment by using arguments about the future ramifications of the two options. (See lesson summaries for week four.)

As we looked over our tentative plans for weeks one through four and compared them with the essentials and the final interdisciplinary assessment, we decided one element needed to be strengthened: Students needed a better understanding of the role of different types of external forces, such as the United Nations, the World Bank, or Amnesty International, and their potential role in resolving or managing conflicts.

We addressed these concerns by adding a mini-lecture on global agents of large-scale change. The lecture would explain how the United Nations and other nongovernmental organizations could become part of the management or resolution of a global conflict. We would link these change agents to methods of nonviolent change and the pragmatism of military and political realities. This lesson fit in quite well after the dynamics webbing of divestment and economic approaches (see figure 2.4, week five).

**The Final Assessment in the South Africa Unit.**   In examining the lesson summaries again, we felt that students would have all the tools necessary to complete the final assessment. We planned to introduce the final assessment assignment (see forms discussed in Step 3 above) and then focus on the four methods of conflict resolution. Students would work in four groups, each attempting to use a different one of the four methods: violence, negotiation, peacekeeping, or nonviolent action. Each of the four groups would have between five and seven members. While groups of this size are larger than optimum, we felt that it was important that they be large enough to have many diverse opinions. While cooperative learning research suggests that these groups are too large to function efficiently, we were comfortable knowing that the size of the groups could create challenges. We felt that the complexity of the groups would to some degree mirror issues of complexity in South Africa and raise the students' consciousness of how difficult it can be to satisfy everyone in a diverse society. We saw the possibility of disagreement within the large groups as a *teachable moment*.

Before the groups went to work, we would direct their attention to four questions written on the board:

1.  Is it feasible?
2.  Is it fair to all parties?

3. What are the short term dynamics of your proposal?
4. What are the long term dynamics of your proposal?

We would advise them to be mindful of these questions as they worked through their resolution proposals. The questions come from the form "Criteria for Evaluating Resolution Proposals" (table 2.3). As groups began to develop their proposals, we would question the individual groups to help them develop more realistic proposals. We would use the questions on the board to help keep students on track and challenge their proposals in every context imaginable. Knowing that this was a complex process of rethinking and revision, we allowed three days for groups to complete their proposals before the South Africans came to hear them (see figure 2.4, Wednesday through Friday of week five and the beginning of week six).

The next two days (Tuesday and Wednesday of week six) were the days on which we invited four South Africans to visit. In order to get a wide range of perspectives, we wanted to arrange to have South Africans representing different backgrounds and experiences with racial conflict. These members of our *authentic audience,* persons who have expertise in the subject or concepts being assessed, were to give feedback to students on their work. The students do take the challenge of presenting their work to an authentic audience very seriously. Through a desire to impress (or fear of embarrassment), students put exceptional effort into work that they know they will be presenting to and defending before an authentic audience. The authentic audience also changes the relationship between the students and the classroom teacher. The teacher becomes the coach, helping students prepare for the big game rather than being the "opponent in the game of grades."

We planned to collaborate with the English teacher to create extra class time for the students to work with the authentic audience. Having just received a stack of research papers that she needed to grade for writing mechanics, she would be able to work on grading while we orchestrated student interaction with the four members of the authentic audience in both the English and global studies classrooms. We planned for two South Africans to come the first day and two to come the second. Each of the South Africans would remain in one of the two rooms (English or global studies), and students would follow their usual class schedule. The result would be that our classes could spend fifty minutes with each one of the four South Africans during the two days.

During the fifty-minute periods, we wanted each of the groups to present orally the steps of their proposed resolution. The authentic audience would give oral feedback. (In retrospect, these sessions turned out to be very exciting, as the students experienced multiple perspectives and heard successive speakers disagree on basic issues. For example, the white South African insisted that apartheid was over, while the black and Asian speakers said that it was still very much alive. Several students had the courage to challenge the speakers on points and evidence. Every group received valuable feedback from the visitors.)

For the following day we planned a class discussion about the guest speakers. We designed questions to create discussion about what students learned about multiple perspectives, racial conflict, and possible approaches to conflict resolution in South Africa. We would also ask each individual student to assess his or her group's proposed resolution on a slightly revised version of the "Student Checklist for Exhibition" (see table 2.9). We find that self-assessment offers students an opportunity to reflect on their work and their contributions to the group process. We compared their own assessments with our assessments of their resolutions and we arranged conferences with students whose self-assessment varied greatly from our assessment to discuss the disparities.

We planned to follow their presentation of their proposal on resolving racial conflict in South Africa with the simulation *Starpower*. Although the unit provides substantive knowledge about relationships between power and conflict, we were concerned with our students' lack of empathy for victims of human rights abuse and compassion for people who have little power. In general our students have problems relating to a majority who allow a minority to have authority over them. We decided the issue of understanding and empathy for the human rights of people with little power needed an experiential dimension. We decided to combine the simulation *Starpower* with a seminar on relationships between power and conflict as the final activities in the unit on South Africa.

*Starpower* is a simulation in which three groups are formed: circles, triangles, and squares. The groups play a trading game for points. The game is set up so that the group that has the most points is allowed to make the rules for future trading. As you might imagine, a power struggle ensues in which your geometric shape determines your success. The simulation is exciting and volatile. Since we knew that the simulation would take most of the class time, we planned to assign two essay questions for homework. They were (1) In what ways were today's simulation similar to the racial conflicts in South Africa? and (2) In what ways were today's simulation different from the racial conflicts in South Africa?

On the day following the simulation, students would participate in a discussion of the answers to the essay questions and would attempt to draw conclusions about the ways in which power affects global conflict. We planned the lesson as a student-run seminar in which they would be graded on the quality of their participation. (This lesson is detailed below as a sample lesson; see lesson for Wednesday of week seven.) The lessons with *Starpower* and the seminar completed the South African unit. As with all our units, we planned to ask the students to complete a unit evaluation sheet so that we would have suggestions for revision of the unit for the future.

Remember that even a "final draft" of a unit plan will likely change several times during its implementation. To plan for flexibility, we always leave two or three days marked "open" near the end of the unit. Most beginning teachers have difficulty estimating the time that an activity will take. Preservice teachers are accustomed to the rapid pace of university classes and frequently plan a one-day lesson that requires two days or more for effective teaching and learning. While teachers often overplan, it is important with backwards building not to overplan activities essential to the completion of the final assessment. It is useful to keep some additional lessons in mind in case the open days are not needed for essential activities or reteaching. In the case of this unit, we planned a lesson with South African literature, *Kaffir Boy* and *Mine Boy*, if time allowed. Since the students had seen other literature and other lessons on multiple perspectives, the lesson was optional and could be adapted to fit any open days during the unit.

As we completed the first draft of the unit plan, we recognized that the chances of everything running exactly according to schedule were minuscule. We knew that we would have to be flexible, allowing more time for some activities and probably less for others according to student progress and interruptions to the school day. One limit to our flexibility was the scheduling of the South Africans. We made contacts and discussed tentative dates with the speakers several weeks in advance. However, we did not finalize the appointments until approximately one week before their visits so that we were sure that our students would be ready to share their proposals.

Having completed our lesson summaries, we looked at the plan as a whole unit. We used a checklist looking at individual lessons as part of a cohesive whole. This checklist helps us stay focused not only on the unit, but on the students and their experiences as learners. It is a checklist used by preservice and inservice teachers in our PDS Network.

TABLE 2.5
Social Studies and Global Education PDS Network Unit Checklist

1. Am I motivating my students to learn by building off their interests, experiences, knowledge and abilities?
2. Are students actively (rather than passively) involved in learning and reflecting during *each* lesson?
3. Is there some originality, creativity, or excitement in my unit or is it boring or "tired"?
4. Do I begin the unit with easier ideas and progress to more complex or difficult ones?
5. Within the unit are the students learning to find, process (compare, analyze, synthesize), use (apply), and evaluate information? Am I asking higher level questions or just recall?
6. Does every lesson relate to my assessment of student learning (knowledge, skills, attitudes)? If not, why not?
7. Are all lessons and activities essential to my content goals or am I using some because they are handy (e.g., I have a video on the topic) or traditional (e.g., always use a case study)?
8. Am I trying to cover too much content? Is the content/time allotted realistic for my students?
9. Does each lesson have a beginning, development, and a conclusion? Is there sufficient instructional variety?
10. Will my sequence of lessons and activities make sense to my students? Do the methods support the content goals?

© Merry M. Merryfield, 1994.

With the overview of the entire unit finished, we turned our attention to planning the specifics of each individual lesson.

## STEP 5: DEVELOPING DETAILED LESSON PLANS

With the overview of the unit completed, we began to work on the lessons week by week and day by day. Some lessons, such as the ones using news articles, would require locating specific resources. Others required development of rubrics, review of simulation protocols, organization of a lecture, or preparation of handouts. We had already outlined the purpose, content, and methods for each lesson in the summaries, and we knew their relation to the unit. However, many decisions still needed to be made that required a great deal of thought, especially for a preservice teacher.

Below we have provided plans for four of the more complex lessons. Examine the plans and think about the questions that follow. The format we have used in the lesson plans is one the teachers in our PDS selected for our preservice teachers to use in preparation for classroom teaching during methods and student teaching. It is short enough to be practical, yet it provides adequate information for the cooperating teacher.

### Sample Lesson Plan: Introduction to Dynamics Webbing

Monday of week four focuses on dynamics webbing, a process that helps students think about alternatives and future ramifications as they make decisions about the application of content. When teaching skills such as these, we find it critical that the teacher give both a visual and oral step-by-step explanation, followed by class participation in working with the skill and then individual practice under the teacher's supervision. As you read through the lesson plan, consider these questions:

1. What would you do if some students appear to be confused after step 2?
2. Suppose the students only volunteer two or three responses to the original question. What would you do?
3. As the students begin to develop their own personal webs, you see that several are really excellent while others are having trouble getting started. What do you do?

4. What would be another good match between dynamics webbing and content in a unit you are planning? Why?

**Introduction.**   In this lesson students learn a technique for graph-
ically depicting the potential dynamics of an action.

**Purpose/Objectives.**   This lesson is an introduction to a process
of generating and examining dynamic effects of decisions and actions. Students will use this process in order to understand global
ramifications.

**Materials/Resources.**   None.

**Steps in Lesson.**   Before class begins, write the following question
on the board: "Should the U. S. approve $5 billion in financial aid
to the newly formed Russian government?"

Begin the lesson by having students volunteer information about
the current situation in Russia with its new government and economic reforms. Continually direct students' attention to the question on the board. Allow time for discussion of pros and cons, and
then take a class vote. (Knowing my students, I was confident that
each class would oppose aid.) After taking the vote, explain that
the purpose of today's class is to develop a strategy for tracing the
dynamics of actions. Review the concept of 'global dynamics' (how
many historical, social, economic, political, environmental, or
technological factors around the world are mutually shaping each
other over time). Explain the concept of *dynamics webbing* (a
process for generating and examining potential consequences or
ramifications of decisions or actions).

In the middle of the chalkboard, write "U.S. votes down $5
billion in financial aid to newly formed Russian government."
Place a rectangle around these words and explain that the rectangle
symbolizes the initial action in the dynamics web. Then ask students, "Who or what will this decision affect?" Compile a list on
the far edge of the chalkboard (figure 2.5).

Choose one of these groups and ask students how they will be
affected *immediately.* For answers that project long-range effects,
ask students to think more about the immediate future. Take an
immediate ramification and place it in a circle near the rectangle.
Draw an arrow from the rectangle to the circle. Explain that the
arrow to the circle symbolizes a ramification of the event in the
rectangle.

# FIGURE 2.5
## Dynamics Web

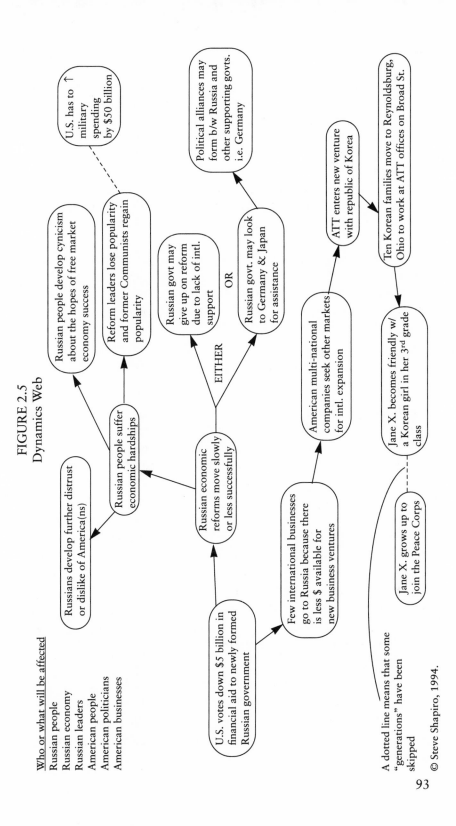

Who or what will be affected
Russian people
Russian economy
Russian leaders
American people
American politicians
American businesses

U.S. has to ↑ military spending by $50 billion

Russian people develop cynicism about the hopes of free market economy success

Reform leaders lose popularity and former Communists regain popularity

Political alliances may form b/w Russia and other supporting govts. i.e. Germany

Russians develop further distrust or dislike of America(ns)

Russian people suffer economic hardships

Russian govt may give up on reform due to lack of intl. support

ATT enters new venture with republic of Korea

Ten Korean families move to Reynoldsburg, Ohio to work at ATT offices on Broad St.

OR

Russian govt. may look to Germany & Japan for assistance

EITHER

Russian economic reforms move slowly or less successfully

American multi-national companies seek other markets for intl. expansion

Jane X. becomes friendly w/ a Korean girl in her 3rd grade class

Few international businesses go to Russia because there is less $ available for new business ventures

U.S. votes down $5 billion in financial aid to newly formed Russian government

Jane X. grows up to join the Peace Corps

A dotted line means that some "generations" have been skipped

© Steve Shapiro, 1994.

93

Then move to the first ramification and have students project ramifications that could result from it. As a class, build the web out several "generations." Ask students to identify new places on the web where other alternatives could emerge. As the web grows, students will begin to see some negative ramifications of the original decision.

When the web is well developed, ask students if this web would cause them to reconsider their earlier vote. Why or why not?

Ask students about why dynamics webbing is a valuable exercise.

For practice, have students choose an important decision they have made in the past. Have student create a web based on the ramifications of that decision. Walk around the class to observe their webbing and answer questions from students who are struggling with the concept.

**Closure.**    If time permits, have a volunteer share his or her web with the class. Answer any questions that remain. Then collect the webs to examine their skills.

**Application.**    After receiving written feedback on their personal dynamics web, students will use this skill to project the ramifications of the Red-Green simulation, the divestment decision, their proposal for resolving racial conflict in South Africa, and their interdisciplinary conflict resolution exhibition.

© Steve Shapiro, 1994.

*Sample Lesson Plan: The plan "Red-Green Simulation"*

The plan for Tuesday and Wednesday of week four includes a simulation and discussion through dynamics webbing. Simulations can be powerful learning experiences if orchestrated well by the teacher. They can also fall flat or turn into chaos if they are not structured with specific students' abilities and behavior in mind. As you examine this lesson plan, think about these questions:

1. Will you run the simulation according to the rules provided or will you modify to meet content or student needs? How do you make that decision?

2. What will you do if your students don't react as planned to the simulation?

3. How can you make sure that the students relate the process of the simulation to content on South Africa?

**Introduction.** In a hundred-minute period, students simulate negotiations and then use dynamics webbing to examine the impact of specific decisions they made in the negotiations.

**Purpose/Objectives.** The purpose of the simulation is to have students experience negotiation as one way to resolve conflict. The lesson also enables them to see negotiations and conflicts in a larger context of global ramifications through dynamics webbing.

**Materials/Resources.** Red-Green Simulation instructions (available through *Managing Conflict,* a book of lesson ideas; see reference in the appendix), large sheets of paper, markers.

**Steps in the Lesson.** Before class begins, divide each class into four groups, two composed of males and two of females. When class begins, have students join their respective groups. Each group gathers in one corner of the classroom. Place four desks in the middle of the room to serve as the conference center.

Read the instructions to the students. Their goal is to score as many positive points as possible. In each round, each group can vote red or green. Lead students through the ten rounds of the game. Points are given according how many groups vote red or green (e.g., if all vote green, each group gets fifty, but if three groups vote green and one votes red, the greens lose one hundred points each, and the group that voted red gets three hundred points).

Keep scores from each round, along with total scores on the board. Follow the rules, and don't answer student questions during the rounds.

After the simulation is over, have students move into a large circle to discuss their experience. Focus the discussion on the process of negotiation and the impact that decisions in early rounds had on the events in later rounds.

After the discussion have students identify one event in the simulation that they viewed as important. Have them place this event in a rectangle in the center of a large sheets of paper and then create a dynamics web from that event.

**Closure.** Have volunteers tape their webs in front of the room. Ask the groups to explain their webs to the class and encourage other students to ask questions or critique webbing. Collect webs to check for student mastery of dynamics webbing.

**Application.**   Students will apply their understanding of negotiation, recognition of the contexts of conflict, and dynamics webbing skills in completing their proposal for resolving racial conflict in South Africa and in their interdisciplinary conflict resolution exhibition.

© Steve Shapiro, 1994.

*Sample Lesson Plan: Developing a Resolution Proposal*

The class for Wednesday of week five engages students in the process of creating a plan to reduce racial conflict in South Africa. We chose to identify four possible strategies (from which students could chose one) for their proposal to help them focus on one approach. We had students work in groups because of the complexity of the proposal and the need for multiple perspectives. It is very important to put the assessment questions on the board or overhead and to continually refer to them as the groups draft their proposals. We always try to keep the criteria for success well defined. *If we make the target clear, students have a much better chance of hitting it.* As you read the lesson, consider the following questions:

1. What value is there in opening up the lesson with brainstorming methods of conflict management and resolution? How will you decide whether or not to use this approach?
2. What are different ways of putting students into groups? What is the rationale behind each? Which will you use for this lesson? Why?
3. What will you do if there are disagreements or disputes among members of a group? What if someone wants to change groups in the middle of the lesson?
4. How will you respond to groups that hand in unrealistic or oversimplified proposals? What are your alternatives?

**Introduction.**   In this lesson students consider several methods of resolving international conflict, choose one, and design a proposal for resolving racial conflict in South Africa. This lesson takes place in a double-blocked class (one hundred minutes).

**Purpose/Objectives.** By completing this lesson, students will begin to understand the complexity of resolving global conflicts. They will demonstrate the ability to apply knowledge about South Africa to developing their proposed resolution. They will also develop a working understanding of a model for resolving conflict.

**Materials/Resources.** Handout entitled "Approaches to Conflict Resolution." Handout explains four major approaches commonly used to resolve conflict.

**Steps in the Lesson.** Begin the lesson by having students brainstorm possible methods of resolving international conflicts. Write student responses on the board. Ask students to look for natural groupings or categories of approaches to conflict resolution.

Hand out "Approaches to Conflict Resolution." Ask students to compare what's on the board with the list. Then have students think about examples or illustrations in history or the contemporary world of the different ways to manage or resolve international conflicts. You might start off with an example of the use of violence in Vietnam in the 1960s. If students have problems in thinking of examples for each approach, give them hints or help.

Explain that the students may choose from one of these four approaches to develop proposals to resolve racial conflicts in South Africa. Pass out the resolution proposal form (table 2.2) and explain each of the items. Make sure they understand each of the steps in the process and in their presentations to a racially diverse group of South Africans. After answering questions, write the following questions on the board:

Is it feasible?

Is it fair to all parties?

What are the short-term dynamics of your proposal?

What are the long-term dynamics of your proposal?

Explain that these will be the questions by which groups' proposals will be assessed.

Allow students to choose the alternative of their choice and move into groups to work on their resolution proposal. Move from group to group and ask questions to help the groups develop thoughtful proposals.

**Closure.** With five minutes left in the period, answer any questions that students have and share observations about the overall work of the class, offering suggestions or praise as appropriate. Collect proposals in progress and write comments, suggestions, and concerns as feedback for the next work session.

**Application.** After receiving the teacher's written feedback and having time to revise and improve proposals, groups will present their proposals in four sessions with South Africans in order to receive feedback and ideas. Finally, each student will assess the strengths and weaknesses of his/her group's proposed resolution.
© Steve Shapiro, 1994.

*Sample Lesson Plan: Seminar on Power and Racial Conflict in South Africa*

The class for Wednesday of week seven engages students in drawing conclusions and making generalizations about power and conflict. By reflecting on *Starpower* and comparing that simulated experience to the situation in South Africa, the students use the seminar as a forum to draw conclusions and come to closure. We chose to use a scored discussions because they encourage students to participate and reward students for their individual contributions. We give the rubric to the students before the seminar so that they can become familiar with our expectations and be prepared to meet them. We designed the seminar to be an open conversation between students with the teacher acting as a facilitator. Students use the rubric to self-assess their performance in the seminar. As you read the lesson, consider the following questions:

1. What effect does *using a rubric or not using a rubric* have on student participation or the quality of discussion? Why?

2. How does a teacher prepare for the seminar? With what question would you start the student discussion off?

3. How can a teacher help students prepare for such a seminar? Would you help some students differently than you would help others? Why or why not?

4. Should the teacher acknowledge the quality of student comments? What are the pros and cons of giving positive feedback to insightful contributions of students?

**Introduction.**   This lesson brings together the study of racial conflict in South Africa and participation in the simulation *Starpower.*

**Purpose/Objectives.**   Students will make connections between the simulation and their study of conflict resolution in South Africa. They will be able to hypothesize about the relationships among power, conflict, and conflict management or resolution.

**Materials/Resources.**   A rubric for grading student participation (see table 2.6).

**Steps in Lesson.**   Move desks in single circle before class begins and write on the board: Criteria for assessment includes (1) number of contributions; (2) quality of contributions; and (3) listening skills, respect, and attention shown to classmates.

Explain that the purpose of the seminar is to discuss the relationships between the simulation and what they have learned about conflict in South Africa. They are expected to generate hypotheses about power and conflict.

Explain the procedures for the seminar: every student is expected to participate in the seminar at least twice: making a contribution of a new idea or evidence, questioning or challenging the contribution of a classmate, or bringing ideas or evidence together. Students should speak to each other rather than to the teacher, and students need not raise their hands to speak. Students must be courteous to each other as speakers and listeners. Students will be graded on the quality of their contributions and participation in the seminar. Quality contributions show profound thought and analysis. Making two meaningless comments to meet the requirement will not be acceptable. Pass out scoring rubric (table 2.6) and give students time to read it and ask questions.

Begin the seminar by asking the question, "In what ways was yesterday's simulation similar to the racial conflicts in South Africa?" Allow the students time to think and begin the discussion on their own. Join in to ask questions to keep students on the topic or pursue important themes that are not being considered. Assess students' performance by writing comments about their contributions (presenting new ideas or evidence, questioning or challenging others, synthesizing ideas, handing differences with respect, etc.). Use rubric.

With about ten minutes left in the class, begin to look for an appropriate place to end the seminar, perhaps a natural pause or concluding argument.

TABLE 2.6
Rubric for Grading Seminar Participation

| Grading Criteria: | 1. quantity of contributions |
| | 2. quality of contributions |
| | 3. listening skills |

| Points Earned | Combinations Made and Skills Displayed |
| --- | --- |
| 10 | 1. Made at least two contributions to the seminar<br>2. Made contributions that were of high quality<br>—introduced profound ideas<br>—synthesized comments made by other students<br>—challenged the ideas being discussed<br>—made contributions that were intellectual, not personal in nature<br>—related personal experiences to the issues being discussed<br>—made analogies using *Starpower* and the unit on South Africa<br>3. Listened to *all* contributors<br>—made eye contact |
| 7–9 | Displayed a combination of qualities from 10- and 6-point entries |
| 6 | 1. Made at least one contribution to the seminar<br>2. Contribution was of high quality (see items in ten point category.<br>3. Listened during nearly all of the seminar<br>—occasionally failed to stay focused on speakers' ideas |
| 1–5 | Displayed a combination of qualities from 0- and 6-point entries |
| 0 | 1. Did not contribute to the seminar or made contributions of low quality *or* dominated the seminar by interrupting others or preventing others from having a chance to contribute.<br>2. Made personal attacks on others by teasing or belittling others for their ideas<br>3. Was disruptive while others spoke<br>—focused on things other than the conversation (eg., a magazine, a side conversation, or homework for another class) |

© Steve Shapiro, 1994.

**Closure.** When the seminar reaches a natural breaking point, ask students to score their own performance in the seminar using the scoring rubric.

**Application.** This seminar concludes the unit on racial conflict in South Africa. Students should use their working hypotheses about conflict and power in their interdisciplinary exhibition on international conflict resolution.

© Steve Shapiro, 1994.

The process of writing out complete lesson plans may lead to revisions in the overall plan as it becomes obvious that too much or too little has been developed for a class period. We find that it helps beginning teachers to have alternatives prepared if a lesson runs longer or shorter than they had originally planned. Even experienced teachers frequently find that they need to change plans because of student abilities, interests, or learning styles.

In working with preservice teachers we find the unit checklist (see table 2.5) is effective in helping students evaluate individual lessons and the fit and rhythm of each week's lessons as well as the entire unit. We have also learned through our PDS experiences that the best way to teach preservice teachers to plan is to provide authentic experiences where they are planning for and then actually teaching real students in a supportive, nurturing environment. A few years ago in methods classes at Ohio State we had our preservice teachers develop lessons to hand in to a college professor for a grade. Through collaborative inquiry we have learned that our preservice teachers only begin to understand the connection between teacher planning and student learning when they are preparing a lesson for an actual group of students that they will be responsible for teaching and assessing.

## IMPLEMENTING THE INTERDISCIPLINARY EXHIBITION

Implementing an exhibition is a very complex process requiring a multitude of teacher decisions. The following is a detailed account of the process of implementing the interdisciplinary exhibition that we introduced on page 67. We have chosen to include this section because the exhibition process is much different than the process of traditional testing and is a process that many teachers have never experienced.

The process began with the formation of student groups for this collaborative exhibition. For this exhibition we allowed the students to select their own groups because of the amount of cooperation and work outside of school that the exhibitions required. We put groups together in many different ways (e.g., by randomly counting off or by purposefully selecting heterogeneous groups) during the school year. However, it is our experience that exhibitions benefit from self-selected groups by building on peer pressure among friends, since most students will not let their friends down. We asked that groups contain a maximum of four students, because both the research on cooperative learning and our experience tells us that groups larger than four run into problems with communication and equitable distribution of the workload. We did not want students to work individually because one of our objectives was to help students develop interpersonal skills through working with others. Specific steps were taken by students and staff to complete the exhibition (table 2.7).

It is absolutely crucial that teams attempting to create an exhibition of this magnitude realize that it is an evolving process that demands flexibility. It is imperative that the teacher monitor and help students as necessary so that some are not left behind, struggling to complete a complex task, while the teacher, focusing on a predetermined schedule, forges ahead insensitive to their needs.

*Advisor Groups*

Students were free to work with anyone of the ninety-five students in the World Connections program. As a result, the time devoted to group preparation for the exhibition required a unique schedule. To address this need we first had groups sign up and identify possible topics. The team of four teachers and two student teachers who were working with the program during the spring of 1993 organized the small groups into new larger "advisor" groups (of about four or five small groups or fifteen to sixteen students) so that each teacher could take responsibility for several groups. We made decisions about group placement based on several critical issues. We considered the teachers' knowledge and interest in the topics chosen by the groups. We sought to select groups of students with whom we had particularly effective working relationships. We tried to avoid putting with a single teacher all the students known for creating the most challenging classroom management prob-

TABLE 2.7
Steps in Completing Exhibition

| Activities | Time Used |
| --- | --- |
| Students sign up for group and possible topic | Sign up sheets posted in classrooms, students sign up between classes |
| Teachers divide up advisor groups | Done after school |
| 1st advisor period—narrowing topic to a single global conflict and state it as a question | One hour adviser schedule needed |
| Advisor approves of suggests revisions | Done outside of school |
| 2nd advisor period—students break down conflict into research topics & grade breakdown sheet explained | One and one half hours adviser schedule needed |
| Students do research | Conducted through English class |
| Advisors check working bibliography, research notecards, and paper outline | Outside of school |
| Students turn in research papers | English teachers grades for mechanics. Advisors grade for content. |
| 3rd advisor period—students share research and begin to draw conclusions | 2 hours—advisor schedule needed |
| Teachers explain assessment criteria for exhibition and audience requirements | |
| 4th advisor period—groups plan exhibition presentation | 2 hours—advisor schedule needed |
| 5th advisor period—To be scheduled as needed | |
| 1st rehearsal | Full 200 minutes used |
| Dress rehearsal | Full 200 minutes used |
| Exhibition day—students perform exhibition and complete self and peer evaluations | Full 200 minutes used |

© Steve Shapiro, 1994.

lems. We also looked at individual student needs, and each teacher chose to work with a group including particular individuals who would require extensive time and attention. During the preparation for the exhibitions teachers were called "advisors" because they were working as coaches of independent student work. The teacher and all of the groups he or she was advising were known collectively as an "advisor group."

On days when we wanted to give groups time to work, we scheduled "advisor periods" during portions of our two hundred minutes of class time. Instead of attending regular classes, students reported to the room of their advisor. In the unit overview you will see advisor days scheduled (figure 2.3) These represent days that global studies and the other subjects were either shortened or canceled so that groups could work with their advisor on the interdisciplinary exhibition. Because the exhibition was interdisciplinary, it required the use of the concepts related to conflict resolution from all of the classes. Shortening our traditional class meetings did not result in students getting less time for "our" subject. Rather, it meant that they were getting support from a team of teachers so that students could apply the knowledge and skills from our individual classes.

## The Exhibition Process

While the global studies class was contributing to the exhibition by using racial conflict in South Africa as a model for resolving global conflict, English class was meeting its curricular goal of having students write a research paper by relating that research paper to students' group exhibitions. Students identified research topics corresponding to the subject of their group's exhibition. Through the research process they developed the expertise necessary to successfully complete this complex assessment. The English teacher taught the research process and graded all research papers for writing mechanics. However, the advisors helped students determine the topic of their papers and graded them for content.

The ongoing process of preparing for the exhibitions began with the first advisor session. Groups worked with their advisor to narrow and develop their exhibition topics. For example, one group was interested in terrorism. Since the topic was far too broad to look at as an individual conflict, students began to explore how to break it down into a manageable topic. They considered airport security issues, terrorism in Northern Ireland, and use of the HIV virus as an instrument of terrorism.

Once a group narrowed down its topic, the students then developed it in the form of a question in order to focus on the specific conflict they were analyzing. In the case of our sample group, these questions came from the narrower topics the students discussed:

1. Should international security standards be set and enforced at all airports serving international flights?

2. Are the Irish Republican Army's tactics an effective approach in managing or resolving conflict in Northern Ireland?

3. Should antiterrorism experts prepare to defend the world against a future wave of HIV-related terrorism?

Each group submitted to its advisor a proposed question for the exhibition. Advisors looked over each group's question to make sure that it met several criteria. First the question had to have *global ramifications*. For example, one group wanted to work on a conflict related to abortion rights. They began with the question "should girls under eighteen years old be able to get abortions without parent permission?" Their advisor did not see significant global ramifications. After conferencing, the students revised their question to "should the FDA approve the French abortion pill for use in the United States?" This issue has much broader global implications.

A second criterion that advisors considered was whether the question was *realistic*. A question such as, *Should the United States stop all military spending?* fell outside realistic boundaries. A third criterion was whether the question was *appropriate in scope*. A group of students was interested in our judicial system in the wake of the Rodney King verdict and curious about judicial reform in the newly independent republics of the former Soviet Union. They posed the following question: "Should Russia model a newly formed judicial system on the American system of justice?" While this question is fascinating and impressively complex, it is far too broad in scope for a project of this nature. As their advisor, I "coached" the group by providing feedback, asking questions and providing ideas for how to narrow focus of the question, but I left the rethinking and rewriting to the students.

The second advisor session gave groups the opportunity to develop topics for each individual member's research paper. The goal was to divide the research so that each student would have his or her own unique inquiry and yet contribute to the group's exhibition. For example, if there were four people in a group asking the Northern Ireland question listed above, they might devise the following research topics:

1. Northern Ireland: a history of conflict
2. The Irish Republican Army: objectives and tactics
3. British responses to IRA terrorism
4. Alternatives to violent action: political change according to Gandhi and King

The purpose of the first three papers is obvious. The purpose of the fourth paper is to explore alternatives to terrorism in resolving the conflict in Northern Ireland. Similarly, in a group pursuing the question, "Should Nazi war criminals have been punished for crimes against humanity?" one student examined experiments on obedience to authority in order to consider arguments for answering their question in the negative.

At the end of the second advisor group session, advisors went over the Conflict Resolution Exhibition: Grade Breakdown Sheet with the students (table 2.8). We explained that the completion of the exhibition was a long process and that students' grades would be based on performance throughout the process of preparing for the exhibition. Since the exhibition was assessing the skills developed in more than one academic discipline, the 175-point score would be recorded in English, global studies, and biology. The grade combines individual grades (accounting for 67 percent of the total) with group grades (33 percent). We believe that the emphasis on individual grades ensures accountability in the exhibition and the ultimate success of the group's final product.

Each group divided up its research topic according to student interest and began the data collection process in English class. Our team of teachers, while depending upon the English teacher to assist individual students with research methods, realized that we could not expect her to also make sure that each student's research was actually helping them answer his or her group's exhibition question. Therefore, each advisor took the responsibility for supervising and coaching the students in each of his or her groups. Advisors regularly checked the bibliography cards and notecards of their advisees to see that they were using a variety of sources and

TABLE 2.8
Conflict Resolution Exhibition: Grade Breakdown Sheet

INDIVIDUAL GRADES:

| TASK | POINTS | DUE DATE |
|---|---|---|
| Working Bibliography | 5 | April 19 |
| Notecards | 5 | April 23 |
| Notecards | 5 | April 28 |
| Outline | 10 | April 30 |
| Research Paper (content) | 25 | May 10 |
| Work in Advisor Groups | 5 | _____ |
| Work in Advisor Groups | 5 | _____ |
| Work in Advisor Groups | 5 | May 21 |
| Dress Rehearsal | 30 | May 25 |
| Self Evaluation | 10 | May 26 |
| Peer Evaluation | 10 | May 26 |
| GROUP GRADES: | | |
| First Rehearsal | 10 | May 21 |
| Dress Rehearsal | 30 | May 25 |
| EXHIBITION | 20 | May 26 |
| | 175 points | |

© Steve Shapiro, 1994.

that their notes were relevant and complete. This process enabled advisors to evaluate both individual and group progress.

The third advisor group session focused on having students share their research with their group so that each student could begin to examine the whole picture, not just the segment of the issue that he or she had been researching. The advisors asked each group to begin to develop an answer to the group's question and coached each group as it attempted to apply the evidence that group members had collected. At the end of this two-hour session, advisors gave each student a Student Checklist for Exhibition (table 2.9) and the Rubric for Assessing the Exhibition (table 2.10). The checklist helped students literally check off steps in their preparation, and the rubric (assessment tool for the assignment) explained the qualitative differences in the four criteria of meeting the assignment, indicating depth of knowledge, organization, and engaging the audience. Advisors explained the expectations and answered questions about the assessment of the final exhibitions.

TABLE 2.9
Student Checklist for Exhibition

---

The following list of questions and criteria indicate the areas in which you will be assessed during your exhibitions. Keep this list in mind as you plan your presentation so you can be sure to "cover all the bases."

DOES THE EXHIBITION MEET THE ASSIGNMENT?
—Does it include multiple perspectives?
—Does it discuss global ramifications to the conflict?
—Does it present a rationale for the resolution?

DOES THE EXHIBITION INDICATE DEPTH OF KNOWLEDGE?
—Is it "profound?"
—Does it cover a sufficient amount of information?
—Can questions from the audience be answered well?

DOES THE EXHIBITION INDICATE GOOD ORGANIZATION?
—Is the group well-prepared for the presentation? (Did all group members participate?)
—Does the presentation have a logical beginning, middle and end?
—Does the presentation flow smoothly with good transitions and lack of repetition?

DOES THE EXHIBITION ENGAGE THE AUDIENCE?
—Is the presentation creative?
—Does it use audio/visual aids wisely? (Or do the aids control the presentation?)
—Does the group use proper speech techniques?
(clearness, loudness, memorization, etc.)

---

© Steve Shapiro, 1994.

At this point we advisors also explained the process of arranging an audience for the exhibition. Each group would present their exhibition directly to an authentic audience, not just in front of a class of peers. We reviewed the concept of authentic audience as people who have real world expertise, interest, and involvement in the topic. We also explained that each group must identify experts in their field of study and make arrangements for them to serve as the audience and assessors of their exhibition. Advisors would help them identify appropriate audiences, but it would be each group's responsibility to contact the people and to arrange the meeting for the exhibition. We required not only that the members of the audi-

TABLE 2.10
Rubric for Assessing the Exhibition

| * Most Important | Meeting the Assignment* | Depth of Knowledge* | Organization | Engaging the Audience |
|---|---|---|---|---|
| Outstanding | Presentation fairly represents the complex perspectives of all parties in the conflict<br><br>Presentation identifies both the obvious and the *subtle* global ramifications that the proposed resolution would create<br><br>Group presents a thoughtful rationale for its resolution, and offers a thoughtfully reasoned explanation for choosing their resolution over other options | Analysis of issue and conclusions demonstrate profound thought/insight<br><br>Presentation demonstrates extensive knowledge of topic, including detail and critical analysis of sources<br><br>Group appears to have anticipated potential questions, and can answer them with detail and authority | Presentation has an even balance in the contributions of group members<br><br>Presentation has a very clear and logical beginning, middle and end<br><br>Presentation has smooth transitions shows evidence of thoughtful planning | Presentation is highly creative/original<br><br>Audio and visual aids are meaningfully integrated into the presentation<br><br>All group members consistently utilize effective speech techniques |

TABLE 2.10
(*Continued*)

| *Most Important* | *Meeting the Assignment** | *Depth of Knowledge** | *Organization* | *Engaging the Audience* |
|---|---|---|---|---|
| Satisfactory | Presentation represents the perspectives of all parties, but seems to favor one perspective over others | Analysis of issue and conclusions demonstrate basic competence of knowledge | All group members participate, with relatively even balance | Presentation is somewhat creative/original |
| | Presentation identifies the most obvious ramifications that the proposed resolution would create | Presentation demonstrates knowledge of the essential information needed to understand the topic | Presentation has a clear beginning middle and end, but the parts may not be logically sequenced | Audio and visual aids support presentation, but are not effectively integrated into the presentation |
| | Group presents a thoughtful rationale for its resolution, and offers simplified reasons for selecting this resolution rather than other options | Group can answer most questions with thoughtful responses | Transitions are used between speakers, but segments of the presentation are repetitive or leave gaps of omission | Group members utilize effective speech techniques through most of the presentation |

| Substandard | Presentation fails to consider the perspective of all parties involved in the conflict<br><br>Presentation fails to consider obvious ramifications that the proposed resolution would create<br><br>The resolution proposed appears to have been chosen randomly—the group fails to offer a clear rationale for choosing their proposed resolution | Analysis of issues and conclusions are based on inaccurate information or faulty logic<br><br>Presentation fails to consider vitally important information<br><br>Group is stumped by most audience questions—knowledge of the topic seems limited to the information in the presentation | One or two members dominate the presentation<br><br>The presentation appears to be a sequence of unrelated parts, ending when the last person is finished<br><br>There are no transitions made between discreet segments of the presentation | Presentation lacks creativity<br><br>Audio & visual aids are inaccurate, distracting or overshadow the rest of the presentation<br><br>Poor speech techniques are distracting and detract from the content of the presentation |
| --- | --- | --- | --- | --- |

© Steve Shapiro, 1994.

ence be experts in the field but also that each group made an effort to have representatives from different sides of the conflict in question. We allowed for audience members to come to school, or for group members to arrange to present their exhibition in the community. For example, the group on airport security went to the FBI building in Columbus to present their exhibition.

The final advisor sessions provided time for groups to prepare their exhibitions. Advisors coached groups as they made decisions about how to resolve their conflict and how to present their conclusions. These final advisor sessions counted toward students' exhibition grades. Advisors assigned each student a score from one to five based on his or her work in the advisor periods. The complexity of designing the exhibition was such that every group spent significant time outside of school working on its presentation. One of the most difficult challenges for the groups was developing a creative format for presenting their findings that would engage their audiences. Some of the formats that students used were courtroom reenactments, debates, simulated peace conferences, and simulated news broadcasts.

An exhibition is a major academic performance. It is the equivalent of the big game in sports, the Winter Show for the choir, or the major play presented by the Drama Club. In each of these cases, we would never expect students to face an audience without practice or rehearsal. The same holds true for the performance of an exhibition in front of an audience. In preparation for exhibitions our team generally provided two rehearsals for the groups.

A *first rehearsal* is the first time that groups have to present their work publicly. We blocked off the entire 200 minutes of the World Connections schedule for the first rehearsal, and the time went quickly as each group of students presented its exhibition and listened to the critique of the rest of the advisor groups. Former students who had completed similar exhibitions came to these sessions to give feedback to the groups. At that stage the presentations were quite far from meeting exhibition standards. (First rehearsals usually leave the advisors very nervous and the groups somewhat overwhelmed with the work left to be done.) In the absence of this session, the overall quality of the final products would have been significantly diminished. Generally, the presentations were short, but the feedback sessions after each group's presentation were long. It was very impressive to see students work with their peers to help improve the quality of other groups' exhibitions. As we sat in these collaborative sessions we thought, *This is why we went into teaching.*

During the time that remained after the rehearsals and feedback, groups began the process of improving their work. The first rehearsal accounts for a ten point group grade because the purpose of the session is diagnostic, and we do not want to leave students overly discouraged after receiving an already intimidating wave of constructive criticism. Assessors used an evaluation form (table 2.11, with slight modifications) to assess the first rehearsal as well as the dress rehearsal and final exhibition. Note how the form is parallel to the student checklist (table 2.9) and the rubric for the exhibition (table 2.10). This demonstrates the consistency and clarity of our expectations.

The final rehearsal, or *dress rehearsal,* was four busy days later. A dress rehearsal is always the day before the exhibition is presented to the authentic audience. While advisors and peers did offer final suggestions after each group presented its dress rehearsal, the primary purpose of the performance was to give the advisor an opportunity to assess the final product. The largest portion of the grade (thirty points individual and thirty points group) came from this rehearsal because we wanted the advisor who had worked with the group and understood the criteria and student abilities to hold primary responsibility for evaluating the performance. The authentic audience would be made up of "experts" (a term used by the Coalition of Essential Schools) who have some special knowledge or experience with the subject under study. However, members of an authentic audience usually are not experienced with the process of the exhibition or knowledgeable about the ability levels of the students. The authentic audience's evaluations did count twenty points, just over 10 percent of the total exhibition grade.

Exhibition days are the most emotionally charged days of the year for both students and teachers. There is an emotional shift from nervousness and tension before the exhibition begins, to stress and enthusiasm during the actual performances, to exhilaration and relief after the presentations are complete. This particular exhibition required a great deal of teacher coordination because many groups presented simultaneously. The team divided up the exhibition day responsibilities, which included signing out stu-

## TABLE 2.11
### Conflict Resolution Exhibition
### First Rehearsal Evaluation

Group Members: _____

Indiv. Grade (30) _____

Topic: _____

| | Outstanding | Satisfactory | Substandard |
|---|---|---|---|
| *MEETING THE ASSIGNMENT:* | | | |
| **multiple perspectives** | | | |
| **global ramifications** | | | |
| **rationale for resolution** | | | |
| *DEPTH OF KNOWLEDGE:* | | | |
| **profundity** | | | |
| **thorough information** | | | |
| **answering questions** | | | |

ORGANIZATION:

**well-prepared**

**beginning/middle/end**

**flow smoothly**

ENGAGING AUDIENCE:

**creativity**

**audio-visual**

**speech techniques**

Group Grade:        (of 30)
Comments:

© Steve Shapiro, 1994.

dents who had permission (and parent chaperons) to leave campus for their presentations, greeting audience members as they arrived at the school, coordinating the room assignment of presentations, and handling crises and problems as they arose.

One of the most exciting elements of this exhibition was that a small group of students and a small expert audience were together without a teacher in the room. After hearing the presentation, members of the audience asked the students questions and then completed an evaluation. However, in many cases the interaction did not end there. Several groups spent more than an hour, and in one case more than two hours, discussing their topics with their expert audiences after they had finished their presentations. The group exploring the question, *Should the United States revise its immigration policy to be more equitable to people of color?* spent more than an hour in conversation with representatives of the local NAACP. The group considering trial of Nazi war criminals presented to an attorney, a doctoral student in political science, and the assistant superintendent of schools (who lost family members in the Holocaust). The group's outstanding presentation lasted thirty minutes. However, the students and their audience spent another ninety minutes in a compelling discussion of the issues. Beyond the obvious educational implications, we were impressed that our students could captivate an attorney, a doctoral student, and an assistant superintendent for that amount of time.

Exhibitions create benchmarks of learning in the memories of all present. We witnessed a school board member (selected because he was accustomed to making difficult spending decisions) sit with two Somali women and fire tough questions at students whose question was, Should the United States commit military troops to a humanitarian mission in Somalia? As the group's advisor, I felt the same kind of adrenaline rush that the football coach must feel as he watches his team drive down the field in a league championship game. The members of the audience and the students were equally caught up in the discussion and the stimulation of "expert" debate.

After completing an exhibition, we ask students to fill out a self- and peer evaluation because we believe that it is important to engage students in a meaningful examination of their academic performance. We also want to demonstrate that we value their self-assessment by counting the scores that students give themselves and their peers as part of the final exhibition grade (see table 2.8

for the grade breakdown). Peer evaluation gives students an opportunity to reward other students who provided leadership or made important contributions. It also sends a powerful message to those who failed to make appropriate contributions.

Student exhibitions have several very positive effects on students' academic growth, cognitive development, and perspectives on the relationships between school and adult life. First, exhibitions provide students with an intensive, in-depth inquiry that traditional assessment rarely permits. They learn the power of their own research and its value in the community. Second, success in an exhibition creates an immeasurable boost to the self-esteem of students as they learn how hard work leads to accomplishment and pride in their abilities and expertise. Many students comment that they have worked harder for these performances than they have ever worked in school before. They are genuinely proud of what they accomplish, and they see their accomplishments mirrored in the questions and praise of the adult community beyond the school. Finally, exhibitions also provide excellent public relations for the school. After observing the high quality of the students' work, audience members carry away a very positive impression of the school and its programs. The use of the outside audiences also brings the schools and community closer together as a single community of learners.

## CONCLUSION

Our unit planning on international conflict and peace within the context of school reforms such as interdisciplinary teaming, personalization, backwards building curriculum and authentic assessment demonstrates that it is both possible and desirable to restructure the way we teach to meet the needs of our students in the late twentieth century. While some schools and teachers use the familiar excuses of too many students, fifty-minute periods, too much in the curriculum, or past reforms that have failed, others are moving forward, experimenting, and finding ways to rethink schools. Just as global education is a new way to look at the study of the world and its peoples, restructuring can help us bend the old paradigms and improve student learning.

Effective teaching in our global age means giving more attention to connecting students to topics in international conflict and peace. In chapter 1 we identified six ways that social studies teachers can prepare students to understand and apply global knowledge and skills as they learn about international conflict and peace. In chapter 2 we have documented such methods in the context of a preservice teacher and an inservice teacher's work together in a high school in the midst of restructuring. Think about the relationships between content and methods as you develop your next unit plan. Ask these questions:

1. What experiences can I provide to help my students experience cultural differences and similarities as they study other people, issues, and events?

2. How can I arrange for my students to understand and appreciate multiple perspectives as they learn about history and the contemporary world?

3. How will my students learn about cooperation and collaboration as they study conflict and peace?

4. In what ways will I ensure that my students can find and evaluate conflicting sources of information?

5. How will my students come to recognize and analyze the values and attitudes that shape people's choices and actions?

6. How can I plan so that my students will use their knowledge and skills in applications that are authentic in the real world?

In the essays that follow in Part Two of this book you will find substantive content about approaches and issues in international conflict and peace. Just as we infused approaches to conflict resolution into our unit on South Africa, we hope that you will improve your social studies units with scholarly content on peace tools, the use of the military, diplomacy, negotiation, economic cooperation, human rights, self-determination, and cooperation over the global environment.

## REFERENCES AND SUGGESTED READINGS FOR PART 1

*Alternative Assessment*

Coalition of Essential Schools. "Performances and Exhibitions: The Demonstration of Mastery." *Horace* 6, no.3 (March 1990): 1–12.

Newmann, Fred. "Linking Restructuring to Authentic Human Achievement." *Phi Delta Kappan*. 72, no. 6, (February 1991): 458–63.

Spady, William G., and K. J. Marshall. "Beyond Traditional Outcome-Based Education." *Educational Leadership* 49, no. 2 (October 1991): 67–72.

Wiggins, Grant. "Teaching to the (Authentic) Test." *Educational Leadership* 46, no. 7 (April 1989): 41–47.

Wooster, Judith S. "Authentic Assessment: A Strategy for Preparing Teachers to Respond to Curricular Mandates in Global Education." *Theory Into Practice* 32, no. 1 (winter 1993): 47–51.

*Backwards Building Curriculum*

McDonald, Joseph P. *Dilemmas of Planning Backwards*. Providence: Coalition of Essential Schools, Brown University, n.d.

Sizer, Theodore R. *Horace's School: Redesigning the American High School*. Boston: Houghton Mifflin Co., 1992.

*Cases*

*Journal of Teacher Education* 42, no. 4 (September-October 1991). Theme issue on case methods: six articles and book reviews.

Kleinfeld, Judith. *Cross-Cultural Teaching Tales*. Teaching Cases in Cross-Cultural Education, no. 4. Fairbanks: Center for Cross-Cultural Studies, College of Rural Alaska, University of Alaska, Fairbanks, 1989. Other cases are available from the center.

Shulman, Judith H., ed. *Case Methods in Teacher Education*. New York: Teachers College Press, 1992.

Shulman, Judith H., and Joel A. Colbert, eds. *The Intern Teacher Casebook*. San Francisco: Far West Laboratory for Educational Research and Development, 1988.

Wassermann, Selma. *Getting Down To Cases: Learning to Teach with Case Studies*. New York: Teachers College Press, 1993.

*Cooperative Learning*

Aronson, Elliot, Nancy T. Blaney, Cookie Stephan, Jev Sikes, and Matthew Snapp. *The Jigsaw Classroom*. Beverly Hills: Sage, 1978.

Cohen, Elizabeth G. *Designing Groupwork*. New York: Teachers College Press, 1986.

Johnson, David W., and Roger T. Johnson. *Learning Together and Alone: Cooperative, Competitive and Individualistic Learning*. Englewood Cliffs, NJ: PrenticeHall, 1987.

Slavin, Robert E. *Cooperative Learning: Theory, Research and Practice*. Englewood Cliffs, NJ: Prentice-Hall, 1990.

Stahl, Robert J., ed. *Cooperative Learning in the Social Studies: A Handbook for Teachers*. Menlo Park, CA: Addison-Wesley, 1992.

## Conventional Unit Planning

Banks, James A., with Ambrose A. Clegg. *Teaching Strategies For the Social Studies.* White Plains, NY: Longman, 1990.

Dobkin, William S., Joel Fischer, Bernard Ludwig, and Richard Koblinger. *A Handbook for the Teaching of Social Studies.* Boston: Allyn and Bacon, 1985.

Martorella, Peter H. *Teaching Social Studies in Middle and Secondary Schools.* New York: Macmillan, 1991.

Zevin, Jack. *Social Studies for the Twenty-First Century.* New York: Longman, 1992.

## Experiential Learning for Cross-Cultural Understanding

Gilliom, M. Eugene. "The Many Ways of Being Human." *Kappa Delta Pi Record* 29, no. 3 (spring 1993): p. 79.

———. "Social Studies Teachers and World Citizenship: Bridging the Credibility Gap." *Social Studies Teachers* 22, No 3, Fall 1971): 227–280.

Wilson, Angene H. "A Case Study of Two Teachers with Cross-Cultural Knowledge: They Know More." *Educational Research Quarterly* 8, no. 1 (1983): 78–85.

———. "Conversation Partners: Gaining a Global Perspective through Cross-Cultural Experiences." *Theory into Practice* 32, no. 1 (winter 1993): 21–26.

———. *The Meaning of International Experience for Schools.* Westport, CT: Praeger, 1993.

## Global Perspectives in Education

Alger, Chadwick. F., and James E. Harf. "Global Education: Why? For Whom? About What?" In *Promising Practices in Global Education: A Handbook With Case Studies,* edited by Robert E. Freeman, 1–13. New York: National Council on Foreign Language and International Studies, 1986.

Anderson, Lee F. "A Rationale for Global Education." In *Global Education: From Thought to Action,* edited by Kenneth A. Tye, 13–34. Alexandria, VA: Association for Supervision and Curriculum Development, 1990.

Becker, James M., ed. *Schooling for a Global Age.* New York: McGraw-Hill, 1979.

Hanvey, Robert. G. *An Attainable Global Perspective.* New York: Global Perspectives in Education, 1975.

Kniep, Willard. M. "Defining a Global Education by Its Content." *Social Education* 50, no. 6 (October 1986): 437–66.

Merryfield, Merry M. "Responding to the Gulf War: A Case Study of Instructional Decision-Making." *Social Education* 57, no. 1 (January 1993): 33–41.

Tye, Barbara B., and Kenneth A. Tye. *Global Education: A Study of School Change.* Albany: State University of New York Press, 1992.

*Interdisciplinary Curriculum*

Brady, Marion. *What's Worth Teaching? Selecting, Organizing, and Integrating Knowledge.* Albany: State University of New York Press, 1989.

Jacobs, Heidi-Hayes, ed. *Interdisciplinary Curriculum: Design and Implementation.* Alexandria, VA: Association for Supervision and Curriculum Development, 1989.

*Less Is More, Depth Over Coverage*

Brophy, Jere. "Fifth-Grade U.S. History: How One Teacher Arranged to Focus on Key Ideas in Depth." *Theory and Research in Social Education* 20, no. 2 (spring 1992): 141–55.

Dempster, Frank N. "Exposing Our Students to Less Should Help Them Learn More." *Phi Delta Kappan* 74, no. 6 (February 1993): 433–37.

Newmann, Fred M. "Can Depth Replace Coverage in the High School Curriculum?" *Phi Delta Kappan* 69, no. 5 (January 1988): 345–48.

Parker, Walter C. *Renewing the Social Studies Curriculum.* Alexandria, VA: Association for Supervision and Curriculum Development, 1991.

Woyach, Robert B., and Richard C. Remy. *Approaches to World Studies: A Handbook for Curriculum Planners.* Boston: Allyn and Bacon, 1989.

*Reflective Inquiry*

Dewey, John. *How We Think.* Boston: D.C. Heath, 1933.

Engle, Shirley H., and Anna S. Ochoa. *Education for Democratic Citizenship: Decision Making in the Social Studies.* New York: Teachers College Press, 1988.

Martorella, Peter H. *Teaching Social Studies in Middle and Secondary Schools.* New York: Macmillan, 1991.

*Social Studies Reform*

California Department of Education. *History-Social Science Framework for California Public Schools.* Sacramento: California Department of Education, 1988.

National Commission on Social Studies in the Schools. *Charting A Course: Social Studies for the 21st Century.* Washington, DC: National Commission on Social Studies in the Schools, 1989.

National Council for the Social Studies. *Social Studies Curriculum Planning Resources*. Dubuque: Kendall/Hunt Publishing, 1990.

## Teacher As Coach, Student As Worker

Wiggins, Grant. *The Metaphor of Student As Worker*. Providence: Coalition of Essential Schools, Brown University, n.d.

## Teachers as Reflective Practitioners

Calderhead, James, and Peter Gates, eds. *Conceptualizing Reflection in Teacher Development*. London: Falmer Press, 1993.

Clift, Rene T., W. Robert Houston, and Marleen C. Pugach, eds. *Encouraging Reflective Practice in Education: A Analysis of Issues and Programs*. New York: Teachers College Press, 1990.

Goodman, Jesse. "Using a Methods Course to Promote Reflection and Inquiry among Preservice Teachers." In *Issues and Practices in Inquiry-Oriented Teacher Education*, edited by B. Robert Tabachnich and Kenneth Zeichner, 56–76. London: Falmer Press, 1991.

Merryfield, Merry M. "Reflective Practice in Teacher Education in Global Perspectives: Strategies for Teacher Educators." *Theory into Practice* 32, no. 1 (winter 1993): 27–32.

"The Reflective Practitioner," *Educational Leadership* 48, no. 6 (March 1991). Special issue.

Russell, Tom, and Hugh Munby. *Teachers and Teaching: From Classroom to Reflection*. New York: Falmer Press, 1992.

Ross, E. Wayne, Jeffrey W. Cornett, and Gail McCutcheon. *Teacher Personal Theorizing: Connecting Curriculum Practice, Theory and Research*. Albany: State University of New York Press, 1992.

Schon, Donald A. *The Reflective Practitioner*. New York: Basic Books, 1983.

## Teaching Thinking Skills

Beyer, Barry K. "Teaching Critical Thinking: A Direct Approach." *Social Education* 49, no. 4 (April 1985): 297–303.

Bruer, John T. *Schools for Thought: A Science of Learning in the Classroom*. Cambridge: MIT Press, 1993.

———. "The Mind's Journey From Novice to Expert." *American Educator* 17, no. 2 (summer 1993): 6–15.

Ladwig, James G., and Bruce M. King. "Restructuring Secondary Social Studies: The Association of Organizational Features and Classroom Thoughtfulness." *American Educational Research Journal* 29, no. 4 (winter 1992): 695–714.

Parker, Walter C. "Achieving Thinking and Decision-Making Objectives in Social Studies." In *Handbook of Research on Social Studies Teach-*

*ing and Learning*, edited by James P. Shaver, 345–56. New York: Macmillan, 1991.

Remy, Richard C. "Civic Decision-Making in an Information Age." In *From Information to Decision-Making: New Challenges for Effective Citizenship* edited by Margaret Laughlin, N. M. Hartoonian, and N. Sanders. Washington, DC: National Council for the Social Studies, 1989.

Newmann, Fred M. "Classroom Thoughtfulness and Students' Higher Order Thinking: Common Indicators and Diverse Social Studies Courses." *Theory and Research in Social Education* 19, no. 4 (fall 1991): 410–33.

## Values Education

Fraenkel, Jack R. *Helping Students to Think and Value: Strategies for Teaching Social Studies*. Englewood Cliffs, NJ: Prentice-Hall, 1980.

Gilligan, Carol. *In a Different Voice: Psychological Theory and Women's Development*. Cambridge: Harvard University Press, 1982.

Hahn, Carol, and Patricia Avery. "Effect of Value Analysis Discussions on Students' Political Attitudes and Reading Comprehension." *Theory and Research in Social Education* 13, no. 2 (spring 1985): 47–60.

Shaver, James P., and William Strong. *Facing Value Decisions: Rationale-building for Teachers*. New York. Teachers College Press, 1982.

PART 2

# Essays
# in International Conflict
# Management & Peace

CHAPTER 3

# Building Peace: A Global Learning Process

## Chadwick F. Alger

The Feminist Perspective
Peace Education
Applying the Peace Tools
Conclusion

As I write these words, headlines in newspapers, television, and radio are reporting brutal violence between Serbs and Croats; between Bosnians and Serbs; and between Croats and Bosnians. At the same time, headlines are reporting intercommunal violence in Somalia, Cambodia, Zaire, India, and other countries. Some people would say that these events underline the desperate need for education about international peace and conflict resolution. But others might say: "Why bother? Human beings have always killed each other and they always will. To confirm this, you need only follow the daily headlines and study history."

On the other hand, one might reply that Bosnians, Serbs, and Croats lived in the same cities, towns, and neighborhoods for years without violence. But this was never the subject of headlines. Why not? Upon reflection we quickly realize that headline news tends to focus on wars, depressions, floods, earthquakes, and other disasters. Actually, peace is not news because most people live in peace with their neighbors most of the time, and most countries live in peace with neighboring countries most of the time. Isn't it ironic— the fact that wars are given headline status is good news! This means that they are not the normal state of affairs. This simple truth is an element of encouragement for those who hope for a more peaceful world, but it also makes teaching about peace more difficult. Educators must overcome the partial view of the human condition propagated by bad news in the headlines and by histories that emphasize battles and wars. They must help focus students' attention on the continuing quest for peace.

## THE EVOLUTION OF PEACE TOOLS

Understanding the quest for peace begins with an appreciation that the interstate system will not continue as it is today. This system is continually evolving. It was created by human decisions in response to specific historic circumstances. As conditions have changed this system has undergone dramatic transformations, as reflected in changes in the political map after World Wars I and II, the creation of the United Nations system, the breakup of overseas colonial empires, and the fragmentation of the Soviet Union. There is no doubt that the character of the interstate system will continue to undergo transformations.

One of the most important transformations in the interstate system has been the development of new approaches for resolving conflicts and for building peaceful human relationships. Most people, including our students, are aware of the phenomenal growth in the destructiveness of weapons in the twentieth century, and of their inter-continental reach. Indeed, the fear generated by these weapons has contributed to both the recently negotiated cuts in the nuclear arsenals of the United States and Russia and in the efforts of the international community to halt the spread of nuclear weapons to other states in the system, such as Iraq and North Korea. But few people are as cognizant of simultaneous progress made in this century in dealing with conflict.

*What Are Peace Tools?*

The quest for peace in the twentieth century is on the one hand a story of the development of a definition of peace that can accommodate a diversity of threats to the fulfillment of human potential—not only the quick death of bombs, but also the slow death of preventable disease; not only the diminution of physical and mental capacity by gunshot wounds, but also the curtailment of mental and physical capacity by malnutrition and pollution. On the other hand, it is also a story about the development of twenty-one identifiable approaches to managing, resolving, and avoiding international conflict; to building peace. We can refer to these twenty-one approaches as "peace tools." During this century new peace tools have emerged as a result of the fact that earlier tools were unable to cope with specific kinds of situations. Figure 3.1 shows how these peace tools have evolved in the context of the League of Nations and the United Nations.

Using the notion of "tools" gives us a handy way to provide an overview, a kind of conceptual map, of practical ways individuals and groups over time have sought to deal with conflict and violence in the world. At the same time, you must recognize that these tools are not equally accepted by either scholars or policymakers. Some people place emphasis on those tools that are significant in their professions or their discipline. Some are unwilling to accept more recent innovations, like nonviolence, preferring to place em-

FIGURE 3.1
The Emergence of Peace Tools

| | 19th Century | 1919 | 1945 | 1950– | |
|---|---|---|---|---|---|
| | | League Covenant | UN Charter | UN Practice | NGO/People's Movements |

NEGATIVE

Diplomacy (1)
Balance of Power (2)

I

Collective Security (3)

Peaceful Settlement (4)
Disarmament/Arms Control (5)

Collective Security

Peaceful Settlement
Disarmament/Arms Control

Collective Security
Peacekeeping (9)

Peaceful Settlement
Disarmament/Arms Control

Disarmament/Arms Control
Track II Diplomacy (15)
Conversion (16)

POSITIVE PEACE

Functionalism (6)
Self-Determinism (7)
Human Rights (8)

III

Functionalism
Self-Determinism
Human Rights

Economic Development (10)
Economic Equity (NIEO) (11)
Communications Equity (12)
Ecological Balance (13)
Governance for Commons (14)

IV

Non-Violence (17)
Citizen Defense (18)
Self-Determination
Human Rights

Self-Reliance (19)
Feminist (20)

Ecological Balance
Peace Education (21)

V

phasis on more traditional approaches such as diplomacy or balance of power. Others find it difficult to accept the involvement of nongovernmental organizations such as Amnesty International, believing that matters relating to peace should be left in the hands of government officials.

This chapter assumes that people must be broadly educated about all available tools and encouraged to attain knowledge that will enable them to have informed opinions as citizens about which tools should be applied in different circumstances. Indeed, their informed participation is required in any country that aspires to fulfill the expectations of democratic governance.

## Our Nineteenth-Century Heritage

As we entered the twentieth century, the state system had already acquired significant experience with two peace tools, diplomacy and the balance of power.

**Diplomacy.**　The so-called art of diplomacy is a significant human achievement that deserves much credit for the fact that most states have peaceful relations with most other states most of the time. The system of embassies that each country has in the capitals of many other countries has developed over many centuries. Formerly consisting primarily of career diplomats representing their Foreign Ministry, now many embassies include representatives of other government departments responsible for health, labor, education, trade, environment, and the like.

There remain, however, significant limitations in the capacity of the interstate diplomatic system to permit sustained contact among all states. Large states have embassies in virtually all other states—some 185. And all of the smaller states tend to have embassies in the large states. But many smaller states cannot afford to have permanent embassies in all other states, and sometimes they may not really need permanent representation in distant small states. Instead, one embassy may be accredited to a number of states in a region. Thus, it is important to understand that there are limitations in the capacity of the diplomatic system to sustain contact among all of the countries in today's world.

**Balance of Power.**　Although the interstate diplomatic system preserves the peace most of the time, disputes do arise nevertheless and create situations in which states fear aggression by others. In such cases balance of power may be used to deter aggression; this involves the attempts by a country to acquire sufficient military and related capacity to deter aggression, or attempts to deter aggression by making alliances with other states. In some cases, when balance of power is employed as a deterrent it does indeed deter aggression. On the other hand, reciprocal application of balance of power does sometimes lead to arms races. When state A fears the aggression of state B, it may not perceive that it has an accurate estimate of B's military strength, so A tends to exceed the military competence of B just to play it safe. In turn, B tends to assume that A has aggressive intentions and feels a need to have a slight advantage over A. Thus begins an arms race, which then spirals out of control as suspicion and distrust escalate. Although balance of power may sometimes preserve the peace, many believe that balance of power and accompanying arms races contributed significantly to the outbreak of World War I. Nevertheless, many policymakers, particularly in more powerful states, still tend to rely heavily on balance of power.

*The League of Nations Covenant*

In the aftermath of World War I, states created the first world organization (members from Africa, Asia, Europe, and North and South America) devoted to preserving the peace. As many as sixty-three states became members of this League of Nations, but there were never more than fifty-eight members at any one time. Although the League made only modest contributions to restraining interstate violence, as the first world "laboratory" devoted to interstate peace, it made significant contributions toward the development of the United Nations in 1945. The League of Nations Covenant, which came into force in 1920, provided members with three peace tools: collective security, peaceful settlement, and disarmament/arms control.

**Collective Security.**    This peace tool was devised as a way to overcome the weaknesses of balance of power as a deterrent to aggression. Collective Security obligated all who were members of the League to "undertake to respect and preserve against external aggression the territorial integrity and existing political independence of all Members of the League." Those who advocated collective security hoped that the pledge of *all* to resist aggression by *any* member would be such an overwhelming deterrent that none would have reasonable ground for fearing aggression. But the obvious common sense of collective security in the abstract ignores concrete situations in which *all* may not be able or willing to resist aggression by *any* other member. This may be explained by long-standing friendships and alliances and perhaps by fear of retribution by powerful neighbors. Also, when the aggressor is very powerful, the practice of collective security in the pursuit of peace may produce an even larger war than the initial aggression. For reasons such as these, collective security did not prevent aggression by Germany, Japan, and Italy that led to World War II.

**Peaceful Settlement.** This tool is intended to prevent the outbreak of violence in those instances when routine diplomacy fails to do so. In cases where a dispute could "lead to a rupture" the Covenant required states to "submit the matter either to arbitration or judicial settlement or to inquiry by the [League] Council." In other words, members involved in a dispute agreed to involve certain "third parties" when they alone could not control escalating hostility. In employing third parties, states were drawing on human experience in a variety of other contexts: labor-management disputes, disputes between buyers and sellers, marital disputes, and so forth. In giving third-party approaches a place in the Covenant, the League obviously drew on earlier provisions for employment of third parties developed in the Hague Conferences of 1899 and 1907.

Different forms of peaceful settlement assign different kinds of roles to third parties. Their responsibilities can vary from merely making suggestions, to actively participating in discussions between parties, to binding arbitration, which requires the parties to accept the judgment of the third party. Judicial proceedings, as, for example, those conducted in the Permanent Court of International Justice (League of Nations) or the International Court of Justice (United Nations), also produce binding judgments. Sometimes *peacemaking* is used as a synonym for peaceful settlement. Another term that is frequently encountered is *conflict resolution*.

Peaceful settlement continues to be an important peace tool today. Experienced practitioners and scholars have refined and added to this tool. One such refinement, called "integrative bargaining," attempts to clarify the underlying interests of each side toward the end of finding a mutually advantageous settlement. For example, a dispute over a boundary between states may not really be about possessing territory but rather be about access to markets for local products for one country and military security for the other. Integrative bargaining would seek to satisfy these different needs other than by giving the territory to one country or the other. For example, there are cases, as between Switzerland and France, where an economic zone permitting free trade extends beyond the political border. Thus, there can be one border for military security and another for economic security from which both parties jointly gain.

**Disarmament/Arms Control.** The third main peace tool in the Covenant was disarmament/arms control. Those who believed that arms races had contributed to the outbreak of World War I thought that elimination, or at least reduction, of arms would enhance chances for peace. This was an effort to codify disarmament and arms control proposals that had been advanced in earlier times. Although covenant provisions for disarmament/arms control never fulfilled the aspirations of advocates, they did provoke the negotiation of numerous arms control measures in the 1930s. These provided valuable experience, and also a great deal of skepticism, for those who would again face similar circumstances after World War II.

*The United Nations Charter*

Following World War II, the victorious states once again endeavored to create a world organization that would maintain the peace. When the United Nations Charter was drafted in San Francisco in 1945, it incorporated collective security, peaceful settlement, and disarmament/arms control. Past experience under the League of Nations Covenant led those drafting the charter to strengthen collective security by explicitly providing for procedures through which members would make armed forces available for collective security response and a Miliary Staff Committee that would plan for the use of these forces and advise and assist the Security Council in their employment. In some respects, means for pacific settlement are more fully defined in the UN Charter. Although disarmament/arms control is again made available, the Charter emphasizes it less than does the Covenant.

But the most significant differences between the Covenant and the Charter consist of the addition of three peace tools: functionalism, self-determination, and protection of human rights. As the horizontal line in figure 2.1 shows, these tools employ "positive peace" means, in contrast with the "negative peace" means of the first three tools. The term *negative peace* has come to be applied to the first three because they are employed in stopping something—that is, violence or preparation to employ violence. On the other hand, positive peace strategies are seen as doing something that will build peaceful social structures over the long term. This is often referred to as "peacebuilding." One implication of the positive peace terminology is that war is not the only violation of peace—there are also other forms of *peacelessness*.

**Functionalism.** The first of three tools added by the UN Charter is functionalism, in which states cooperate in efforts to solve common economic and social problems that might disrupt normal relationships and even lead to violence. As advocated by David Mitrany, functionalism asserts that wars are caused by economic and social dislocations, which can be averted if states work together to solve common problems. Mitrany believed that states could overcome their hostility to each other by assigning expert representatives to cope jointly with their least conflictual common problems. Mitrany then expected that successful collaboration on easier problems would lead to "spillover" making collaboration on more difficult problems possible. Thus, he foresaw that escalating cooperation might replace escalation in arms races and other forms of hostility. The problems that drafters of the Charter had in mind included worldwide depression in the 1930s and the inability of states to collaborate in coping with this disaster. The depression led to strikes, extreme social unrest, and violence in many countries, and it significantly contributed to the development of totalitarian governments and, in some cases, aggression against neighboring states.

The League of Nations provided a kind of "laboratory" for developing the knowledge that led to giving economic and social cooperation a prominent place in the UN Charter. Although the League Covenant gave relatively slight attention to economic and social activities, in practice, the League became significantly involved in a great number of economic and social issues. Indeed, as the days of the League drew to an end before World War II, proposals had already been made to create a League economic and social council.

Emphasis on economic and social cooperation in the UN Charter is signified by the creation of the Economic and Social Council (ECOSOC) alongside the Security Council (responsible for collective security), which had been the only council in the League. According to the UN Charter, ECOSOC was created "with a view to the creation of conditions of stability and well-being which are necessary for peaceful and friendly relations among nations." Its mission includes the achievement of higher standards of living; full employment; solutions to international economic, social, health, and related problems; and international cultural and educational cooperation. At the same time, ECOSOC has the responsibility of coordinating the activities of some thirty agencies in the UN system with responsibility for health, labor, education, development, environment, population, trade, atomic energy, and a number of other global problems. Some employ the term *peacebuilding* to refer to the approach to peace taken by functionalism as well as to the eight tools that follow. The word refers to the building of long-term relationships among peoples such that problems are not created that lead to inequities, seething dissatisfactions, and perhaps violence.

**Self-Determination.**    The second peace tool added by the UN Charter was self-determination. Here, again, the UN built on the League experience. In granting independence to many nations formerly in the defeated Austro-Hungarian and Ottoman Empires, the World War I peace settlements recognized self-determination as a tool for building future peace. In addition, parts of the former Ottoman Empire outside of Europe and other colonies of defeated states were placed under a Permanent Mandates Commission of the League of Nations; such areas included Iraq, Syria, and Lebanon. These mandated territories were administered by countries that were members of the victorious coalition. The mandate system established reporting procedures through which administrating countries were responsible to the members of the League. This laid the foundation for later growth in the belief that those governing colonies have some responsibilities to the rest of the world. The mandates were called "trusteeships" in the UN Charter and were placed under a third council, the Trusteeship Council. But most important for self-determination in the Charter was the inclusion of the "Declaration Regarding Non-Self-Governing Territories" which covered the many overseas colonies not under trusteeship. This declaration asserts that those administrating colonies are obligated "to develop self-government, . . . and to assist them in the progressive development of their free political institutions."

Eventually, this declaration provided the foundation for prodding the overseas colonial powers to begin relinquishing control of their colonies. This led to a strengthened declaration by the UN General Assembly in 1960: "Declaration on the Granting of Independence to Colonial Countries and Peoples." Both the Trusteeship Council and the General Assembly played a very significant role in the largely peaceful dismantlement of the overseas empires. In this respect, self-determination has proven to be a very useful peace tool. This remarkable transformation of the interstate system more than doubled the number of independent states and the number of UN members.

**Human Rights.**    The third peace tool added by the UN Charter was human rights. Although these words were never used in the League's covenant, human rights are mentioned seven times in the UN Charter, including the second sentence of the preamble, which announces determination "to reaffirm faith in fundamental human rights, in the dignity and worth of the human person, in the equal rights of men and women and of nations large and small." As in the case of economic and social cooperation, the Charter states that human rights shall be promoted in order to "create conditions and well-being which are necessary for peaceful and friendly relations among nations." Building on the Charter, the UN General Assembly produced the Universal Declaration on Human Rights in 1947. The declaration is now widely accepted as part of international common law and has even been applied by domestic courts in the United States.

In order to strengthen the legal status of the declaration, its principles were put in treaty form by the General Assembly in 1966, as the International Covenant on Civil and Political Rights and the International Covenant on Economic, Social and Cultural Rights. In addition, an array of more specialized treaties have been developed on genocide, racial discrimination, women's rights, children's rights, forced labor, cruel and inhumane punishment, rights of refugees, and other human rights problems. Many would say that all of these help to prevent the creation of conditions of human depravity that lead to social unrest that leads to violence.

*United Nations Practice*

The post—World War II context in which the United Nations emerged provided two severe challenges to those attempting to apply the six "peace tools" incorporated into the Charter. The first was the cold war; the confrontation between the United States and the Soviet Union and their military blocs, the North Atlantic Treaty Organization (NATO) and the Warsaw Pact. The Charter assumed that these two states would collaborate in the Security Council in employing peaceful settlement and collective security in order to preserve the peace. Instead, these "policemen" threatened world war with each other by becoming indirectly involved in conflicts in Africa, Asia, and the Middle East. There was particular danger that conflicts in the Middle East and the Congo, now Zaire, would escalate into a world war.

**Peacekeeping.**   As result, peacekeeping was invented. Although some variations have been employed, peacekeeping essentially involves a cease fire, followed by the creation of a demilitarized corridor on each side of a truce line. This neutral corridor is patrolled by a UN peacekeeping force.

Peacekeeping is fundamentally different from collective security in several respects. Peacekeeping forces require the permission of states on whose territory they are based. Although big powers have provided logistical support, the troops normally come from smaller states, deemed to be politically acceptable by the parties to the conflict. The troops normally carry only small arms that are used in self-defense. Their primary protection is the fact that their blue helmets and UN emblems on their jeeps are given legitimacy by the members of the United Nations, under whose authority they are acting. UN peacekeeping forces have successfully kept the peace in the Congo (Zaire), Middle East, Cyprus, and other places for many years. But there has not been equal success in resolving the conflicts that have made them necessary.

The end of the cold war has permitted rapid expansion of UN forces to Bosnia-Herzegovina, Croatia, Cambodia, and Somalia. But these forces are not traditional peacekeeping forces, which are dispatched after a cease fire between warring parties. Instead, the U.N. "laboratory" is attempting to fabricate a new peace tool that falls between the small, lightly armed forces of peacekeeping and the large military forces of collective security. This new kind of force is attempting to cope with conflict between parties within states, often between ethnic/nationality groups. These U.N. forces are at the same time attempting to stop violence, patrol areas of potential violence, and facilitate acquisition of basic needs by the population. They tend to be much larger than peacekeeping forces and are more highly armed. But, like peacekeeping forces, they use their arms only in self defense. Some are calling this emerging new kind of force "peace enforcement" (table 3.1).

The second postwar challenge to the United Nations has been the struggle for, and acquisition of, self-determination by overseas colonies of European-based empires. This not only transformed the interstate system but also brought fundamental changes in the United Nations. A rapid doubling of the UN membership took place, largely by the addition of new members from Africa, Asia, the Caribbean, and Pacific islands. Widespread poverty in most of the new states has widened the gulf between the rich and poor U.N. members. Among the terms applied to the rich and poor countries have been *Developed Countries* (DC) and *Less Developed Countries* (LDC), respectively. Also, the term *Third World* has often been used for the poor countries of Africa, Asia, and Latin America, as distinguished from the *First World* (free market

TABLE 3.1
Uses of the Term "Peace"

Scholars and policymakers make a distinction among several terms that sound the same to most people

*Peacekeeping:* stopping violence, followed by the introduction of peacekeeping forces which maintain a cease-fire, using small arms, only in self-defense.

*Peacemaking:* resolving conflicts that have, or might, lead to violence. This is synonymous with peaceful settlement, and is sometimes called conflict resolution.

*Peacebuilding:* making efforts to build, over the long-term, economic and social relationships and structures which do not lead to violence and other forms of peacelessness.

*Peace enforcement:* using larger, and more highly armed, forces than peacekeeping forces in an effort to impose peace among parties engaged in violence. Of course, this should not be confused with the large military forces employed by collective security, in order to repel or prevent aggression.

industrialized countries) and *Second World* (the former Soviet bloc).

The entry of so many Third World countries into the United Nations significantly affected how the three new peace tools added to the U.N. Charter—functionalism, selfdetermination, and human rights—would be employed. Functionalism, it was discovered, does not work very well between countries that are very rich and have significant technological advancement and those that are poor and technologically underdeveloped. In such situations, the more advantaged partner, will tend to dominate the weaker partner who will, in turn, fear domination. This does not provide good conditions for mutually beneficial collaboration.

Second, policymakers learned that political independence for Third World countries did not necessarily lead to independence from economic and cultural domination by European centers. Once the dramatic struggles for independence were over, the degree to which the new states were creations of European colonial administrators became more apparent. For example, many of the new African states were made up of African peoples divided by arbitrary political boundaries that had little relation to the centuries-old boundaries. Thus, even after the granting of independence to colonially created states, it was apparent that a new generation of self-determination problems would be confronted in the future.

Third, the entry of so many Third World countries into the interstate system, and into the United Nations, produced a challenge to the human rights priorities of western countries like the United States. Western countries have a tendency to give priority to civil and political rights—voting, free speech, privacy, freedom of movement, organizing, freedom of religion, equality before the law, and so on. On the other hand, Third World states tend to give priority to economic and social rights—right to education, equal pay for equal work, food, clothing, medical care, and so forth. Significantly, the Universal Declaration on Human Rights, approved by the UN General Assembly in 1948, tends to list civil and political rights first and economic and social rights next. The western emphasis tends to be that "freedom" has priority before all other rights. But the Third World emphasis is that unless basic economic and social needs are acquired, one has no capacity for enjoying opportunities provided by "freedom."

Thus, United Nations attempts to deal with problems caused by the growing division between the rich and the poor after World War II prompted the development of three new peace tools: economic development, international economic equity, and international communications equity. These tools were largely a product of growing insight on the relevance of economic conditions and relationships for peace.

**Economic Development.** This peace tool is based on the idea that the rich-poor gap could be diminished if the rich countries provided development aid to the poor countries, so that they could "take off" and become developed. Many assumed that development in Third World states should be patterned after that in the industrialized countries of Europe and North America. Emphasis was placed on heavy industry and economic infrastructure such as roads, railroads, airports, and dams. In the earliest efforts, food and agriculture tended to be given low priority. Aid was primarily provided by special development loan funds and technical assistance programs that emphasized the transfer of know-how, often through providing technical experts and the tools they require. Economic development programs were established not only by the UN agencies and regional international governmental organizations but also by governments in the industrialized countries.

Many people would argue that economic development programs have often contributed to peace by diminishing poverty. But, overall, they did not diminish the rich-poor gap in the world. Indeed, as economic development programs grew in the 1950s and 1960s, the rich-poor gap continued to grow. Critics of these development programs began to argue that the gap was growing because the very structure of the global economic system kept Third World countries dependent upon the industrialized countries. Seen from this perspective, the rich-poor gap would continue until this dependency relationship was overcome by a fundamental restructuring of the international economic system.

**International Economic Equity.** The rich-poor gap led to Third World demands for International Economic Equity. The Third World movement for a more equitable international economic system was centered in the Non-Aligned Movement, an organization of some 100 countries from all parts of the world that were aligned with neither the NATO states nor the Warsaw Pact states, and in the United Nations conference on Trade and Development (UNC-TAD). UNCTAD began as a United Nations Conference in 1964 and later became a permanent U.N. organization, with headquarters in Geneva. The Third World caucus in UNCTAD came to be known as the "Group of 77," although it eventually included some 120 states.

In these two organizations the Third World devised a program for a new international economic order (NIEO). Among their demands were (1) stabilization of the prices of Third World commodities (coffee, tea, cocoa, etc.) in order to build a predictable economic base for development programs, (2) a system pegging the price of these commodities to the price of manufactured products that the Third World buys from industrialized countries, (3) access of Third World products to First World markets, (4) Third World access to technology useful in development programs, and (5) international regulation of the activities of transnational corporations in Third World countries. The purpose of these demands was to create an international economy structured so that the Third World could "earn a living."

The Third World waged an extensive campaign in the UN General Assembly for NIEO principles. For the most part, the industrialized countries were very unresponsive. This generated considerable animosity in the Third World as the gap between the rich and the poor continues to grow. At the same time, there was puzzlement over the apparent inability of the Third World to reach the people of the industrialized countries with the reasonableness of their appeal. For example, there was a tendency for the press in the United States to picture Third World demands in the General Assembly as reckless demands for special privileges by an "African-Asian-Latin American horde," which was not grateful for all of the aid that it had received.

**International Communications Equity.**    Frustration over the failure to convince people in industrialized countries about the justness of their NIEO appeal contributed to demands of the Third World for International Communications Equity. Third World leaders pointed out that the headquarters of the major world news agencies like United Press International, Associated Press, and Reuters were in industrialized countries. Further, they cited examples of biased reporting on the Third World. Thus, the Third World began to ask for a New International Information and Communications Order (NIICO). The demands for a NIICO were also stimulated by technological change in communication, particularly the introduction of communications satellites, which, circling in geostationary orbit, make it possible for those having the technology to reach into every country and virtually any village in the world. This technology has been developed and is largely controlled by giant communications corporations headquartered in the industrialized countries.

The struggle for a NIICO has been largely waged in the United Nations Educational, Scientific and Cultural Organization (UNESCO), with its headquarters in Paris. This dispute illuminates how technological change may transform the context in which a peace tool is applied and thereby generates conflict in its definition and use. UNESCO's constitution, adopted in London in November 1945, asserted "that ignorance of each other's ways and lives has been a common cause . . . of that suspicion and mistrust between peoples of the world through which their differences have all too often broken into war." The constitution asserted that these conditions could be overcome through education, pursuit of objective truth, and "the free exchange of ideas and knowledge." The last would be employed "for the purposes of mutual understanding and a truer and more perfect knowledge of each other's lives." In practice, what was believed to be the essential spirit of these words was incorporated into the words of "free flow of communication."

Those emphasizing the free flow of communication as a prerequisite of peace in the aftermath of World War II were thinking of totalitarian governments as the primary threat to its fulfillment. But as newly independent peoples in the Third World became increasingly sensitive to the quality of their recently won political independence, they became aware of the one-way international flow of news, radio and television broadcasts, films, books, and magazines. Indeed, some Third World cultures have been so deeply penetrated by the media from industrialized countries that their cultural integrity is in jeopardy. Out of this dissatisfaction has come a replacement for the earlier communications slogan: "free and balanced flow of communication."

But how is "balance" to be achieved while still remaining "free?" This is a vitally important peace issue that must be resolved through international dialogue and debate. On the one hand, the western democracies fear that intrusions on the "free flow" will lead to government interference that will prevent fulfillment of the essence of the UNESCO aspiration—unfettered possibility for people to obtain a "truer and more perfect knowledge of each other's lives." On the other hand, the Third World fears that the "free flow" mediated by giant global communications corporations will be largely a one-way flow, with content dictated by these corporations. Neither outcome is in the interest of people in any part of the world. Communications is a vital aspect of peaceful global relations. Ways must be found to structure communications in such a way that they foster peace rather than produce deeply felt animosity.

**Ecological Balance.**    Another peace tool to emerge out of the UN practice is ecological balance. Although environmental issues have been seen as significant human problems at least since the Industrial Revolution in the late eighteenth century, ecological balance became a widely recognized problem in world relations as a result of the U.N. environment conference held in Stockholm in 1972. But, this time, there was a tendency for the industrialized countries to take the lead and for the Third World countries to see it as a strategy to prevent them from industrializing too—thus as a way to keep them poor. But by the time of the United Nations Conference on Environment and Development (UNCED) in Rio de Janeiro in 1992, the so-called Earth Summit, most countries agreed that ecological balance is a problem confronted by all peoples. Furthermore, whereas in 1972 very few tended to see ecological balance as a dimension of peace, this perspective is now widely shared.

Ecological balance and peace are related in at least two ways. First are disputes about who is responsible for global pollution, which ecological problems should receive priority, and who should pay "to clean up the mess." In a context of growing pollution, and increasing sensitivity to the negative effects of pollution, these questions are likely to create increasing conflict in the future. Second, by disrupting normal relationships between specific human beings and their environment, pollution directly produces peacelessness for these people. In some cases, as with the destruction with bulldozers and explosives of the habitat of people in rain forests, it is as quick and devastating as war. Although not directly resulting in loss of human life, the total and irreversible destruction of habitat, culture, and way of life can in some ways be more devastating than air bombardment of cities. In other cases, the result may be death, as in the case of poisoned air, water, earth, and food. Although this form of death may be slower than war, it also may be more painful. In many respects it shares some of the long-term characteristics of injuries sustained by those wounded in war.

**Governance for the Commons.**    Another peace tool to emerge from the UN practice is governance for the commons. The commons are areas outside the territorial boundaries of countries that are assumed to be spaces available to all; the term *commons,* once associated with the village green in the center of small towns, is also now used for city parks. In the international context, the oceans and space are generally thought of as commons, and many would add Antarctica.

The oceans, for example, are an exceedingly significant commons because they cover 70 percent of the surface of the globe. Before the days of more intrusive technology, the two main issues in the ocean commons tended to be establishing agreed upon borders of states, early set at a three-mile limit, and insuring "freedom on the seas" in the rest of the oceans. But new technologies for ocean transit, fishing, drilling for gas and oil, mining minerals on the seabed and ocean research—as well as increased use of the oceans as dumping grounds for waste produced on land—have raised a host of new problems with respect to the ocean commons. Occasionally these problems reach the headlines through stories on disputes over fishing rights and limits or oil spills from tanker collisions at sea and tankers running aground.

A historic step in building for positive peace was taken in 1982 with the completion of a comprehensive treaty for governance of the oceans, the United Nations Law of the Sea Treaty. Completed after ten years of negotiation, the treaty provides a new organization in the U.N. system, the International Sea-Bed Authority. This authority would have its own assembly, council and secretariat, as well as an International Tribunal for the Law of the Sea and a branch to oversee the mining of manganese nodules on the sea bed—the Enterprise. The treaty has already received fifty-five ratifications, with sixty required before it goes into operation.

## NEW PEACE TOOLS FROM NONGOVERNMENTAL ORGANIZATIONS AND PEOPLE'S MOVEMENTS

There is a rather strong tradition that holds that foreign-policy making, which includes peace issues, requires very special competence possessed by only a very few high officials in government. In traditional thinking, only they could divine the so-called national interest. Even in democracies such as the United States, this view is still widely held. Today, however, escalating global interdependence is causing a growing challenge to these assumptions.

In every town and city, people are increasingly involved in global networks for manufacturing, marketing, investment, employment, communications, pollution, drugs, crime, and disease. If the international dimensions of all of these issues were left to "foreign policy experts," democratic institutions would be vacuous. Thus, there are a growing number of avenues through which people outside of government are becoming involved in peace issues. Although mainstream teaching and research in international relations have tended to pay slight attention to these involvements, we shall see that they are not entirely new. Furthermore, they are highly significant for those teaching peace studies because they reach into the everyday lives of communities in which students live. Thus, they offer easily accessible possibilities for student inquiry as well as for present and future participation. Concrete examples to be found in every city, and many towns, include groups working for disarmament, human rights groups such as Amnesty International, groups advocating self-determination for specific peoples, and environmental groups such as Greenpeace and the Sierra Club.

## Nongovernmental Organizations

'Nongovernmental organization' (NGO) is a concept that has evolved out of international organization research and practice to distinguish interstate organizations such as the United Nations that have governments of states as members from organizations (both national and international) whose members are not government officials. Prominent examples are organizations such as international professional associations (e.g., of doctors or lawyers), international scholarly associations (e.g., of political scientists or sociologists), international religious organizations (virtually all faiths and denominations), and international organizations focusing on specific issues, such as Greenpeace or Amnesty International. Indeed, included in more than four thousand NGOs are international organizations that mirror virtually all those to be found within single countries. Many of these NGOs focus on peace issues, but most do not. In addition to NGO's, people's movements sometimes arise to address specific peace issues such as disarmament, poverty, human rights, and ecological balance. At times these movements are coalitions of already existing NGOs, but they may also include, and may be led by, others who become mobilized in response to a specific issue. Thus, because of a considerable overlap, we combine NGOs and people's movements in our discussion.

## People's Organizations

*People's organization* (PO) is a useful short title for the growing involvement of people outside of government in world affairs in general, and peace issues in particular. POs have mobilized people for peace action by bringing pressure on governments to employ all of the peace tools that we have enumerated. For example, during the cold war, it was often peace movements that kept disarmament and arms control on the public agenda when governments of both of the superpowers seemed disinterested. Many organizations have had a sustained involvement in movements advocating economic aid for the Third World countries and adjustment in international economic practices. Many would assert that the evolution of international human rights standards has been attained largely because of sustained PO initiatives and pressure on individual states and U.N. organizations. At the same time, many would give POs considerable credit for placing environmental issues high on the global agenda. This was reflected in the widely reported activities of the assembled POs from all over the world at the Earth Summit in Rio de Janeiro in 1992.

As organizations of the U.N. system become increasingly important in efforts to deal with an array of global problems, such as those related to human rights, the environment, unemployment, drugs, and violence, there are those who see the need for a concurrent growth in the participation and influence of POs. Such growth is viewed as a means for insuring that global institutions are responsive to the needs of the people of the world. There are even those who advocate the establishment of a second U.N., assembly composed of representatives of POs from around the world, which would operate alongside the present U.N. General Assembly, composed of representatives of states. But for the foreseeable future, POs will continue to focus their efforts on shaping the foreign policies of states and lobbying in organizations of the U.N. system. At the same time, they will also continue their direct efforts to provide food, shelter, health care, and other forms of aid to those in need around the world.

*New Peace Tools*

POs have been the inventors and advocates of at least seven new peace tools. It must be made clear that these do not replace the tools already employed, but they do illuminate weaknesses of old tools, or the fact that there is no tool for coping with a specific cause of peacelessness. These seven tools are:

1. second-track diplomacy
2. conversion
3. nonviolence
4. citizen defense
5. self-reliance
6. feminist perspectives
7. peace education

**Second-Track Diplomacy.**    This tool addresses the limitations of diplomacy and peaceful settlement by recognizing that negotiations stalled or broken off by governmental representatives may be revived by initiatives outside of government. Consisting at least in part of people outside of government, this approach offers a "second track" that may reach into alternative representatives of governments, often at a lower level. Second track diplomacy has been advocated and employed largely by scholars, often including those who have had wide governmental experience.

One form of second track diplomacy originated by John Burton, an Australian official turned scholar, is given the name of "problem solving workshop." Burton is concerned that representatives of states often do not resolve conflicts but arrange settlements that "paper over" underlying grievances, which will be the source of escalating conflict in the future. This is because representatives of states sometimes do not adequately represent the needs of all who will be affected by the settlement.

Problem solving workshops try to overcome this shortcoming by assembling both governmental and nongovernmental people who can widely represent the needs of all parties, including those not adequately represented by representatives of states. The workshops consist of meetings between these people and social scientists who help them to probe deeply into the basic roots of the conflict, stimulate dialogue between the parties in search of mutually acceptable solutions, and introduce social science insights where they are deemed to be useful. Burton is particularly reluctant to have these social scientists pose solutions, because he believes that viable solutions must come from the participants themselves. Not all practitioners of this approach share Burton's reluctance. Problem solving workshops have been widely practiced in international disputes, including those in Cyprus, the Middle East, and northern Ireland, and in the Argentine-British war over the Malvinas/Falkland Islands. Although this approach has occasionally been useful, it is difficult to assess its impact precisely.

The exceedingly slow progress in arms control negotiations has provoked the development of three approaches—conversion, nonviolence, and citizen defense—that could in some instances be viewed as supplements to negotiations and in others as substitutes. These approaches sometimes diminish the need for specific kinds of weapons and at other times attempt to offer nonviolent substitutes for weapons.

**Conversion.**   This approach targets the conversion of military production to that which satisfies civilian needs, such as those for housing, appliances, and the like. Arms production is often advocated as a way to create jobs for factory workers, engineers, and researchers. It follows that the communities in which those employed in arms development and production live come to depend on arms production to keep the local economy prosperous. But arms production as a means for providing employment may, of course, contribute to arms races by provoking other countries into responding by building more weapons. Conversion plans, drafted largely by POs in local communities, advocate ways in which more jobs can be created through investment in civilian production than through less labor-intensive military production.

**Nonviolence.**   Used by POs in the pursuit of social change, this approach can be viewed as a substitute for the use of arms. Most people have heard of the power of nonviolence as a result of the movement developed by Mahatma Gandhi in the struggle for Indian independence. Most also know that Martin Luther King applied the same technique in leading the civil rights movement in the United States. Nonviolent movements have also been successful in ousting dictatorial regimes that have seized power and in deterring seizure of state power by coup d'etat.

Nonviolence can diminish the need for police and military forces within a state to use weapons. This, in turn, may help reduce the need for armed forces in countries where the military is expected to make a significant contribution to maintaining internal order. Indeed, in much of the arms trade, purchasers are less motivated by fear of neighboring states than by fear of internal uprisings.

Presently there is growing interest in nonviolence throughout the world as an increasing number of people acquire first-hand knowledge of the failure of the use of weapons to bring peace. Training in nonviolent techniques can give those involved a deep understanding of reasons for the often thoughtless impulse to respond with violence when provoked by others and of the long-term negative consequences of responding with violence. At the same time, trainees learn reasons why nonviolent responses are more likely to receive nonviolent reactions in return. This restrains the launching of violence spirals, which escalate into ever larger violent reactions.

Some people tend to perceive nonviolent action wrongly as passive. Instead, nonviolence actively engages in conflict, but without inflicting violence on others and without violating its fundamental values. This strategy is based on the insight that social change created by violence often establishes institutions of violence that outlast the revolution and may put in power people who habitually use violence. Those who advocate nonviolence first try to reach opponents through petition, argument, and discussion. If that fails, they may employ direct action such as noncooperation with authorities, civil disobedience, and fasting.

The recognition of opponents as fellow human beings is fundamental to the use of nonviolence. As stated by Mahatma Ghandi in his campaign against British imperialism: "Whilst we may attack measures and systems, we may not, must not attack men. Imperfect ourselves, we must be tender towards others and slow to impute motives."

Those who advocate nonviolence are often confronted with the question, But would you have employed it in resisting Hitler or Stalin? No doubt some, who fervently believe that one should never violate one's own values, even under severe provocation, would answer yes. But this kind of question makes a fundamental mistake in assuming that a peace tool must be useful in all situations. The essential questions are whether it is useful in some situations and in what these situations are. Most would agree that both Stalin and Hitler represented situations that called for other responses.

**Citizen Defense.** This tool would substitute the threat of massive civilian resistance for the use of military forces as a deterrence to invasion by an external force. In other words, a country using this tool would try to convince a potential invader that there would be no payoff from invasion because civilians would "defend" their country by a massive refusal to cooperate with the invader's military government. Police would refuse to arrest local patriots, teachers would refuse to introduce the invader's propaganda, and workers would use strikes and delays to obstruct the invaders from acquiring their needs. Politicians, civil servants, and judges would ignore the invader's orders. Local plans would be made to maintain local media, schools, and other local services. This kind of resistance would have to be backed up by underground broadcasting stations and presses, storage for food, medicine, water, and fuel; and plans for dispersion of people to places where these facilities would be located.

This peace tool has never been employed as a total substitute for military defense and with comprehensive governmental planning and training that reaches into every community. However, Gene Sharp, a civilian defense advocate argues that there have been many instances of effective nonviolent defense, such as early resistance by American colonists, 1773–75; Hungarian passive resistance against Austrian rule, 1850–67; Finland's disobedience and noncooperation with the Russians, 1898–1905; and resistance in several Nazi-occupied countries, especially Norway, the Netherlands, and Denmark.

**Self-reliance.** Peace researcher Johan Galtung advocates self-reliance as an economic development strategy in which a country or group of countries in a region develops the capacity to produce the necessities of life, particularly foodstuffs, for itself. According to Galtung, the "first step is to rely on your own forces and own factors, on your own creativity, your own land, raw materials, capital—however limited they are." Self-reliance does not mean complete self-sufficiency, or the absence of trade, but it does mean "reliance on oneself to the point that your own capabilities are so well developed that if a crisis should occur, then one could be self-sufficient." (Galtung, no date, p. 12–13)

The idea of self-reliance arose in response to the belief that some efforts to create a more equitable international trading system—as called for by developing countries—could actually be harmful to those countries. For example, increasing the use of land in rural areas of the Third World for producing agricultural exports would require those tilling small farms to become employees of large plantations. This would, in turn, make the rural masses dependent on trade in an international economic system in which profits would gravitate to owners of agricultural industries, thereby increasing the gap between the rich and the poor. At the same time, rural people would become increasingly dependent on external sources for food and other necessities that had been produced at home. In making this argument, critics of calls for a new international economic order (NIEO) point to African areas formerly self-sufficient in food production that now import food from abroad.

The self-reliance critique of NIEO shifts attention to the consequences of international economic relationships for the mass of individuals. It asks: what will be the impact of economic development and international economic equity strategies, designed and implemented by decisions in national capitals, on the mass of individuals who have not participated in making these decisions? These questions can help us realize that discussions of peace often focus on relations between leaders of states and nations, even though the presence or absence of peace is most accurately measured by the degree to which the masses are experiencing peace in their daily lives.

**The Feminist Perspective.**    Another peace tool that has developed essentially from the action and thinking of people's organizations is the feminist perspective. It is particularly useful in shedding light on the degree to which values associated with militarism and military organizations permeate societies and how this came to be. At the same time the feminist perspective provides a vision of alternative kinds of societies. It is necessary to consider the feminist perspective as a separate tool, because women's perspectives and experiences have been largely omitted in most works on international relations and peace. One need not be a female in order to approach human behavior with a feminist perspective, but there is no doubt that the actual experiences of women have sharpened their perceptions and understanding of the roots of violence. This understanding is provoked by the violence experienced by women from the hands of men within societies through rape and family violence. At the same time, it is women and children who suffer most extensively from militarization and war. This includes not only the growing destruction of civilian societies by war but also the diversion of resources away from the needs of families into military weapons and organizations.

The feminist perspective takes note of male dependence on violence within societies as a means for satisfaction of needs, for solving problems, and for signaling individual significance and identity. Why are these attributes so prevalent in men and rare in women? Why are they much more prevalent in some cultures than in others? Why are they so prevalent in some men but not in others? In responding to these questions, feminists conclude that the tendency to employ violence as a tool for coping with problems in human relationships is learned through early socialization of males in certain cultures. They are taught that to be a man you must be aggressive and respond to provocative frustrations with violence. Not to reply with violence is not to be in control and to deny one's "manhood." This form of socialization is then easily transferred in response to disappointments and frustrations in relations between gangs or between labor and management, and is readily applied to questions of national and international peace and security.

Thus, the fundamental contributions of the feminist perspective as a peace tool are (1) to question the inevitability of violence as a tool in the pursuit of peace and security, (2) to illuminate its negative consequences, and (3) to provoke thought about where the roots of the "violence habit" are to be found. Very significant is the fact that the last question directs our attention beyond arenas of interstate conflict and into the daily life of individual societies— including our own.

**Peace Education.**   A peace tool of particular interest to users of this book is peace education. The successful employment of what we have learned in the twentieth century is dependent on peace education. Broadened interdependence directly involves everybody in a diversity of human enterprises that either contribute to or detract from peaceful human relations on a global scale. This is why it is now necessary that all begin to comprehend the peace potential generated in a diversity of "peace laboratories" in this century.

Over and over again in real-life "experiments" with an array of peace tools, practitioners have found the need to probe deeper and deeper into the causes of peacelessness. At the end of the quest, a diversity of nongovernmental/people's movements have been found to be necessary because the roots of peacelessness extend into domestic societies, local communities, and even families. Thus, the seeds of peace must be planted, watered, nurtured, and cultivated there. This means, of course, that all require peace education. It is not a topic only for present or future government leaders. Indeed, implementation of their peace plans requires the active support that only a citizenry with comprehensive peace education can provide. But there is another reason why wider participation is needed. It will deepen insight on peace potential, particularly with respect to certain positive peace tools, and most specifically those requiring broad participation. It is obvious that the full extent of this potential has not yet been realized. Most people have not been challenged to join the quest for peace. This should be the purpose of peace education.

At the same time, it is essential that those teaching peace studies bear in mind that the quest for peace has gradually drawn on more and more academic disciplines and professions. At the opening of the twentieth century, the quest for peace was perceived to be primarily a job for professional diplomats and the military, with diplomatic and military history and international law as the relevant academic disciplines. But as the century closes, virtually all professions and academic disciplines are contributing knowledge relevant to peace. This obviously includes all of the social sciences and humanities, but also physics, chemistry, and biology. At the same time, virtually all professional schools now contribute to the peace mission—law, agriculture, journalism, engineering, medicine, and nursing. The teacher who has an understanding of all of the tools should be able to clarify for every student in a class how her/his chosen discipline or profession can contribute to the quest for peace.

The mainstream of all of these disciplines and professions may not be highly conscious of the contributions of their field of knowledge and practice to conflict resolution and peace; nevertheless, there is an interdisciplinary community of social scientists, physical and natural scientists, doctors, nurses, lawyers, engineers, and journalists who discern a peace mission for themselves and are often involved in national and international governmental and nongovernmental institutions in which they are engaged in peace practice. At the same time, it may be observed that all of these disciplines and professions are contributing to an ever changing vision of peace. As advancing knowledge has revealed that war, violence, malnutrition, disease, poverty, pollution, slavery, and authoritarian rule are not inevitable, human visions of peace have at the same time expanded to cover ever more dimensions of life, accompanied with growing human unwillingness to accept conditions that had been thought to be unavoidable.

Peace education with a comprehensive view is also essential, because formal education will probably offer the only occasion in which young people are challenged to put into words their vision of a peaceful world. Because the media emphasize extreme conflict and violence, and because the academic study of international relations tends to emphasize the same phenomena, young people tend to assume that a world with widespread violence is inevitable. As a result, when students are asked to describe their personal vision of a peaceful world, they find it difficult to describe anything other than their perception of the present world. But peace education with a broad perspective cultivates the capacity of students to perceive both widespread peace in the world and significant achievements in efforts to diminish the scope of peacelessness. This enhancement of capacity to perceive peace potential makes it easier for students to employ their own values in envisioning their preferred peaceful world for the future.

Approaching peace education as a quest for ways through which one's personal vision of a peaceful world could be achieved is absolutely necessary if people in an interdependent world are to join the quest for peace. Students soon learn that pursuit of their vision requires two other kinds of knowledge. First, they must have an accurate picture of the present world. Second, they must have knowledge about how the present might be moved toward the preferred world. Since the achievement of significant goals always takes time, they must also think about what the first steps should be and what should follow. It should be obvious that this kind of peace education: (1) requires a very intensive study of the present state of human relations with a broad perspective, (2) requires systematic thinking about strategies for change based on knowledge about the past successes and failures of these strategies, and (3) constantly challenges students to clarify and revise their preferred future. This third requirement might prompt students to ask themselves questions such as: Did my first vision leave out the special problems of the Third World? Was my proposal for a stronger world court too simplistic? Was my view of human rights too narrow? Why did I leave out the commons? Did I adequately recognize that, for many people, peace means more than stopping the shooting? Thus, having a personal vision of a peaceful world is absolutely necessary if peace education is to be meaningful. This makes possible a challenging dialogue between the world as it is and the world as it might be, mediated by theories ("tools") about how to get there.

## APPLYING THE PEACE TOOLS

The tool analogy, which we have used throughout this chapter, is particularly helpful when practical problems in peacebuilding are confronted. Like an auto mechanic or surgeon, one must first learn the purpose of each tool as well as its strengths and weaknesses. Most peace problems require the employment of several tools. Following careful analysis of each situation, one must make a diagnosis before selecting the appropriate tools. Some people tend to apply a single preferred tool in all situations, but this strategy should be avoided. For example, it seems in retrospect that when the state of Yugoslavia began to disintegrate, self-determination (in terms of independence) was a good peace strategy for Slovenia. But it seems to have been a mistake for Croatia and Bosnia-Herzegovina. In those cases, there was also need for explicit guarantees for the human rights of minorities.

Another example includes cases in which peace tools should be applied in combination, as in advocacy that UN peacekeeping forces be combined with explicit procedures for peaceful settlement of the dispute between the conflicting parties. This prescription emerges from difficulties encountered in settling disputes once peacekeeping forces have insured cessation of violence. In Cyprus, for instance, UN peacekeeping forces have been in place since 1964 but negotiations between Greek and Turkish Cypriots have not yet succeeded.

The tool analogy is also helpful when we reflect on the standards applied by auto mechanics and surgeons in making their diagnoses. Significant to each diagnosis is a vision of a smoothly running automobile or a healthy person. Thus, a person who would effectively apply the tools of peace must have a vision of a peaceful world. I find that undergraduate students whose view of human experience is largely determined by news headlines and histories highlighting wars have great difficulty in creating visions of a peaceful world. At the same time, students whose courses in international relations have centered on big power conflicts, with little attention to the development of the UN system and other cooperative agencies, also have been deprived of the ability to create visions of a preferred world.

This incapacity is often encouraged by a view of international relations that labels the struggle for power, often measured by military means, as "realism" and collaboration in solving international problems as "idealism." Yet, using knowledge in the pursuit of one's vision of a peaceful world can be quite realistic. The same might be said of collaboration in the solving of common problems when this leads toward a preferred world. As we shall see in chapters 6 and 9, interstate cooperation offers a very realistic approach to solving a variety of economic and environmental problems.

On the other hand, it must be recognized that conflicts arise between those who have different visions of a peaceful world. These often arise from the tendency of people to give priority to that which most intrudes on their personal peace. For example, during the cold war most people in the United States were primarily concerned about the threat of nuclear bombs, or what scholars in peace studies call "direct violence." Most people in the Third World tended to fear more the shorter life span and lesser development of human capacities that accompany extreme and sustained poverty. This is often referred to by peace scholars as "indirect violence" or "structural violence." The term *indirect violence* refers to the fact that it is often possible to identify those who commit direct violence but that it is much more difficult with structural violence, because infant mortality and other causes of shortened life span, as well as mental retardation and other results of lack of medical care and nutrition, are the result of certain kinds of social structures. It would be much more difficult to blame these consequences on specific individuals.

Because people with different visions of peace live in a world of increasing interdependence, world peace can be possible only if people with different visions of peace reach some accommodation. This means that there must be a political process through which different definitions of peace are accommodated. For example, those whose material needs are satisfied must realize that deprivation of basic needs (structural violence) may lead to violence. At the same time, those whose material needs are in part met by resources from areas where basic needs are not met must recognize that violence may deprive them of needed resources. These kinds of interdependencies suggest the necessity of accommodating different peace priorities. In other words, although the wealthy may not tend to view satisfaction of basic needs as a peace issue, their interdependence with the poor may require them to do so.

In a fundamental sense the United Nations system can be viewed as a political process in which people from all parts of the world are engaged in developing a global vision of peace out of debate and struggle among partial visions. Out of this struggle has emerged a vision of peace that now includes four prime dimensions or values: eliminating violence, and achieving economic well-being, social justice, and ecological balance. The presence of violence or the deprivation of the other three dimensions can adversely affect life, health, and full development of human capabilities and potential. But people in different geographic areas, and in different social and economic strata, tend to suffer from different modes of deprivation. Indeed, as we now look back over the development of the peace tools, we can see how the growth of the United Nations system into a truly global organization made the addition of new peace tools inevitable, as people with different peace deprivations entered the political process. The important lesson here for would-be peacemakers is that, under conditions of interdependence, there must be a political process through which the peace needs of all can be responded to.

Finally, some readers have no doubt been wondering why we have not included *regional government* or *world government* in our list of peace tools. Some advocate forming regional governments as a way to approach world government gradually. A prominent example of an emerging regional government is the European Community in which a variety of economic and social issues are handled by European Community institutions that now include a European Parliament. The visions of some are that a world government may eventually emerge out of a federation consisting of regional governments from all parts of the world. On the other hand, there are reasons to be dubious about this expectation. In the present world, it is the most powerful states that tend to be least willing to enter into multilateral collaboration with other states. Generally, it is the smaller countries that tend to perceive the greatest need to collaborate with others. Thus, there are reasons to doubt that a world of big regional states would offer a route to achieving world government. It could produce a world of big power conflicts in a context in which there are no smaller states available to serve as mediating "third parties."

Perhaps one reason why various world government proposals have never been implemented is that they tend to resemble the constitution of the author's own state. Would not a world government have to draw on ideas and institutions from many cultures? Perhaps a world government for the future may emerge out of the United Nations, a system of some thirty organizations, whose functions reflect those of most national governments. This should not be surprising, because the agencies of the U.N. system were created to cope with problems that flow across the boundaries of states. Now, as the United Nations struggles to find solutions to these problems in larger territorial space, it serves as a laboratory for global governance. Thus, the UN laboratory will likely be a prime source of the most useful ideas for a future world government. At the same time, this future world government may not mimic the centralized assumptions of the territorial state but reflect the decentralized tendencies of the UN system today. In other words, a world government for the future could be an edifice constructed out of the twenty-one tools already discussed and additional ones yet to be developed.

## CONCLUSION

In the chapters that follow, six different scholars will briefly summarize experience in six dimensions of the quest for peace: diplomacy, negotiation, and peace settlement (chapter 5); the use and control of military power (chapter 4); economic cooperation (chapter 6); human rights in international perspective (chapter 7); self-determination (chapter 8); resolution of conflict over the global commons (chapter 9). The reader can readily see where these topics fit in the framework for peace studies developed in this chapter. Indeed, the topics were selected because each fills in a very significant dimension of the twentieth-century quest for peace.

On the other hand, it will be useful for readers to recognize that the volume as a whole is the product of independent scholars. Thus, each author brings to bear a different academic background, research specialization, and related assumptions. As a result, the volume offers a variety of perspectives. This chapter has attempted to offer an integrated overview. But the others offer extended discussions of their parts of the whole. In many respects, these efforts are complementary, but there are disagreements and contradictions. This is a good thing because these disagreements and contradictions reflect the actual state of peace studies today. But this should not be surprising, for the same conditions prevail in every other dynamic, and growing, field of knowledge.

## ANNOTATED BIBLIOGRAPHY*

Barash, David. *Introduction to Peace Studies*. Belmont, CA: Wadsworth, 1991.
A comprehensive university text covering all of the topics in this chapter except communications, the commons, feminism and peace education. An excellent source for additional reading on topics not covered in the six chapters that follow.

Boulding, Elise. *Building a Global Civil Culture: Education for an Interdependent World*. New York: Teachers College Press, 1988.
Part one places present transitions in the organization of humankind in a two-hundred-year perspective, from 1900/2100. Part two encourages using the mind in new ways not found in schooling, emphasizing the importance of social imagination and the craft and skills of doing peace.

Boulding, Kenneth. *The Three Faces of Power*. Newbury Park, CA: Sage, 1989.
A challenging view of the nature of power and its use in social relations, with emphasis on destructive power (weapons), economic power, and integrative power (love, reciprocity, respect). Particularly challenging is Boulding's discussion of the integrative power of communication and

---

*Not included here are basic works dealing with one of the topics of the six chapters that follow.

learning, including the integrative power of ability to create images of the future and to persuade others that they are valid.

Brock-Utne, Birgit. *Feminist Perspectives on Peace and Peace Education.* New York: Pergamon, 1989.
Illuminated by a diversity of feminist perspectives, this Norwegian author offers a broad analysis of perspectives on peace and peace education in both formal and informal sectors. Particularly useful in applying notions of positive and negative peace to the condition of women.

Burton, John. *Conflict: Resolution and Prevention.* New York: St. Martin's Press, 1990.
A comprehensive presentation of (1) the factors which induce "deep-rooted" conflicts, (2) those which contribute to conflict management and resolution, and (3) strategies for conflict "prevention" (long-term policy eliminating the sources of conflict). This successful Australian diplomat turned prolific scholar takes a broad multidisciplinary approach.

Fischer, Dietrick. *Preventing War in the Nuclear Age.* Totowa, NJ: Rowman and Allanheld, 1984.
A broad approach to war prevention by an author of Swiss origin, covering arms races, defensive arms, balance of power, nonmilitary defense, alliances, forms of power, conflict resolution, and proposals for the future.

Galtung, Johan. *The True Worlds: A Transnational Perspective.* New York: The Free Press, 1980.
A comprehensive analysis of factors inhibiting the struggle for peace and of potential for its achievement by a Norwegian sociologist who has been a leader in the development of peace research as an academic field. Emphasized are both world central authority and individual self-reliance and activation.

Hollins, Harry B., Averill L. Powers, and Mark Sommer. *The Conquest of War: Alternative Strategies for Global Security.* Boulder: Westview Press, 1989.
Presents six alternative approaches to global security: the United Nations, a world peacekeeping federation, minimum deterrence, qualitative disarmament, nonprovocative defense, civilian-based defense, and strategic defense. Concludes with issues common to all approaches and prospects for transformation.

Reardon, Betty. *Sexism and the War System.* New York: Teachers College Press, Columbia University, 1985.
A probing analysis of the societal roots of the war system and military institutions, with a focus on sexism. Particular attention is given to

patriarchy, violence against women, sexism in the social sciences and peace research, and possibilities for transcending sexism.

Sharp, Gene. *National Security through Civilian-Backed Defense.* Omaha: Association for Transarmament Studies, 1985.
A succinct statement of nonviolent alternatives for defense based on this scholar's lifelong study of efforts to resist internal usurpations and foreign invasions through nonviolent noncooperation and defiance which deters and prevents tyrants and attackers from achieving their goals.

Smoker, Paul, Ruth Davies, and Barbara Munske, eds. *A Reader in Peace Studies.* New York: Pergamon Press, 1990.
A reader of thirty-two excerpts from other works covering theoretical approaches, different forms of conflict, nuclear decision making, economic development, feminism, psychological contributions and nonviolence. Average length of chapters is ten pages. Glossary of more than hundred terms.

Vayrynen, Raimo, Dieter Senghaas, and Christian Schmidt, eds. *The Quest for Peace.* Newbury Park, CA: Sage, 1987.
Contributions from twenty-one peace researchers from around the world cover many of the topics discussed in this chapter, such as functionalism, disarmament, peace movements, and peace education. Also chapters on human consciousness and violence, cultural perspectives on war, international law, the global military order, violence in the Third World, and other topics. Writing is at a somewhat more advanced academic level than most other works listed.

Wallensteen, Pete, ed. *Peace Research: Achievements and Challenges.* Boulder: Westview Press, 1988.
With contributions from leading peace research scholars, the volume opens with a focus on the origins of peace research and concludes with challenges. The three sections in between focus on war, conflict resolution, and armament economics. Also written at a somewhat more advanced academic level.

*Journals*

Although many scholarly journals include pertinent articles, these are particularly useful:

*Alternatives*
*Journal of Peace Research*
*Peace and Change*
*Security Dialogue*

CHAPTER 4

# The Use and Control of Military Force

## Peter D. Feaver

If you want peace, prepare for war. Rightly or wrongly, this proverb accurately describes international relations for thousands of years. The problem is that preparations for war may produce peace, but they also make war that much more possible and deadly. Countries thus face a dilemma: if they are not armed, they could become victims of another's aggression; if they are armed, they must con-

163

trol that military capability lest it lead them into an even bloodier conflict. The plight of Bosnian Moslems makes it clear that being defenseless can be deadly in the modern age; the plight of Somalis makes it equally clear that being armed is not much better. If we are ever going to resolve this dilemma, we must first understand the sources of international conflict and how in the past states have tried to manage that conflict.

This chapter first analyzes these sources and how the international system drives states to acquire military forces, balance power, and threaten their neighbors. It next examines several ways states have tried or might try to manage their power relationships so as to control the use of military force and avoid war. It concludes with a brief look at whether the end of the cold war offers hope for a lasting resolution to the dilemmas that have plagued international relations for hundreds of years.

## ANARCHY: THE TAPROOT
## OF INTERNATIONAL CONFLICT

States develop military forces and go to war because they can; and because of this, states must be prepared to fight lest their enemy catch them unawares. Many scholars describe the international system as *anarchic*, meaning there is no supranational authority or government that can effectively regulate relations among countries by punishing aggression, enforcing promises, and protecting innocent parties. Without this authority, without what the philosopher Thomas Hobbes called a "sovereign," states are left to fend for themselves in a *state of nature*, which Hobbes described as a state of war of all against all. States may place their trust in others for a time, but ultimately each must look after its own interests. In a world of saints, this self-help system might not be a problem; but since the human condition is imperfect and often marred by greed, hatred, and suspicion, the absence of a sovereign puts countries at risk. For better and for worse, international relations comprises the interaction of different countries responding to this risk.

Since states must rely on themselves, all states seek to position themselves advantageously by accumulating power. Theorists debate whether countries seek power exclusively, primarily, or simply as one of many conflicting goals. Theorists also debate the ingredients of power: Is military power the only important element?

Can economic power substitute for military power? Are other factors like demographics, culture, and geography important? The dominant theory of international relations, *realism,* provides answers that have stood the test of time. States primarily seek power because power is the key to attaining every other goal; and military factors are the chief ingredients to state power, although a healthy economy is vital as well since it circumscribes a state's ability to build military forces. Given international anarchy, then, each state will seek to build up its own military power in order to protect itself against the designs of neighboring states.

## Security Dilemma

The interaction of these individual quests for power poses a **security dilemma** for international relations. One state's efforts to improve its own security tend to make another state feel more insecure. This will cause the second state to take steps that ultimately undermine the efforts of the first state to become more safe. Since military forces intended to defend against an attack can also be used to launch an attack against someone else, states know that any arsenal in a neighboring state can be a threat. Moreover, since it is especially difficult to gauge with confidence the intentions of another, countries are likely to be suspicious about what their neighbors are actually up to.

The dilemma works like a vicious circle. While state A may be busy building up its forces in order to become safe, neighboring state B must consider whether those forces are not in fact intended for aggressive purposes. State B will begin to build up *its* forces, just to guard against this eventuality. State A must now build up its power even more, however, to compensate for the larger potential threat its newly armed neighbor poses. So state A renews and intensifies its buildup of power. State B is likely to view this fresh effort with suspicion; why would state A want so much military power, if it did not have some fiendish designs in mind? So state B responds by duplicating, or surpassing if possible, state A's accumulation of power. An arms race ensues, with each state trying to match the other man for man, and tank for tank, lest the other gain a decisive advantage that could be exploited.

What started out as an innocent effort to make state A more secure—albeit by making it more powerful than any of its neighbors—ends up making it less secure overall as neighboring states are goaded into building up their forces.

*Balance of Power*

The security dilemma leads states to try to balance perceived threats. This, in turn, leads them to seek a **balance of power,** in which no side has a decisive advantage over the other. Because states cannot depend on the altruism of other states, they must meet head-on every threat to their own security. If they had perfect knowledge about what other states were planning and why, states would only have to address real and certain threats. But since states cannot be certain of others' intentions, they tend to focus on capabilities. What can the other guy do to me, if he decides to play nasty? States evaluate the power of potential threats and try to offset that power as best they can. Even if no state in fact had aggressive designs on another, the security dilemma would lead everyone to seek a balance in capabilities (or power) among the various players.

Some states are better suited than others to this competitive environment. Large, geographically favored states typically have a lot of resources for building up forces; small states are usually at a disadvantage. Thus, large states are likely to pose a greater apparent threat to their neighbors who must then seek a solution. Sometimes the smaller neighbors will try to accommodate the larger power with especially close and friendly relations, as Canada and Mexico have done with the United States. At other times, accommodation may be impossible or undesirable, and so the other countries will band together in an *alliance,* each promising assistance against an attack from their common enemy. A classic example of this kind of alliance is the North Atlantic Treaty Organization (NATO), in which the nations of Western Europe joined together with the United States and Canada to form an alliance emphasizing collective defense against any Soviet military attack against its individual members.

Of course, the security dilemma works to make an apparently defensive alliance appear threatening to others, and so it will be met by a counteralliance. As this spreads, the alliance map begins to resemble a checkerboard; each state checks its next-door neighbor by cultivating a balancing alliance with that neighbor's neighbor according to the maxim, the enemy of my enemy is my friend. An excellent example of the formation of a counteralliance is the case of the Warsaw Pact, which was formed by the Soviet Union and its Eastern European allies in response to the creation of NATO by the West.

The arms races and competing alliances generated by the security dilemma need not lead inevitably to war. A balance of power can remain relatively peaceful. The cold war between the United States and the Soviet Union from 1945 to 1990 never escalated to direct war despite forty-five years of hostility. During the nineteenth century, the great powers of Europe—Austria-Hungary, Britain, France, Prussia, and Russia—avoided the conflicts that bloodied that region during the previous and subsequent centuries.

In general, the fate of any balance of power depends upon two things: (1) whether the states successfully wield strategies of *appeasement* and *deterrence,* the basic tools of balance of power; and (2) whether the states finesse the security dilemma with any of the six power management schemes discussed later in this chapter.

**Appeasement.**    In order to avoid war, countries will try to appease or deter potential adversaries. Appeasement consists of giving a potential adversary a little of what he wants in the hopes of satisfying him, thereby avoiding further conflict. By accommodating the interests of a competitor, states can stabilize shaky balances of power. Appeasement has developed negative connotations ever since allied efforts to appease Adolf Hitler at the Munich conference in 1938 failed to prevent World War II. Neville Chamberlain, then prime minister of Britain, granted Hitler's demand for the Sudetenland, then a part of Czechoslovakia; Hitler annexed the Sudetenland and yet still pursued his aggressive aims, invading Poland scarcely a year later. In fact, however, appeasement can work if skillfully employed, and if the party to be appeased has limited aims. Britain appeased the United States in the late nineteenth century, avoiding what might otherwise have been a costly competition for power in the Americas. Britain essentially agreed to recognize North and South America as part of the U.S. sphere of influence from that point on, deferring thereafter to the United States on all security matters in this region.

**Deterrence.**    Deterrence is defined variously by international conflict theorists, but the basic meaning is quite simple: using threats to discourage another state from doing something. There are two principle variants, *deterrence by threats of denial* and *deterrence by threats of punishment.* Under deterrence by denial, the defending state threatens to defeat the attack of the aggressor state, thereby denying the aggressor of any gain. Deterrence theory postulates: if there is no chance at victory, the aggressor will decide not to attack.

Deterrence by punishment also seeks to prevent war, but by using a slightly different kind of threat: the defending state threatens to strike back against the aggressor, destroying targets the aggressor holds dear in order to persuade the aggressor the prize is not worth the pain. Deterrence by denial involves destroying the enemy army on the battlefield; deterrence by punishment involves striking targets in the enemy's homeland. Under deterrence by denial the threat is to stop an enemy advance; under deterrence by punishment the threat is to *inflict so much pain* that the enemy will choose to abandon the advance. The ultimate goal of both forms of deterrence is the same: preventing war by threatening the enemy with unacceptable consequences.

Throughout the cold war, NATO forces used a mix of deterrence by denial and deterrence by punishment in an effort to deter any possible attack by the Soviet-led Warsaw Pact. Thus, NATO deployed forces along the border tasked with stopping an enemy attack (deterrence by denial); NATO also deployed long-range bombers and missiles, both conventional and nuclear, that could strike targets deep in the homeland of Warsaw Pact countries (deterrence by punishment). While we do not know for certain whether the Soviet Union ever really wanted to attack Western Europe, it is clear that the deterrent threats made any such plan very difficult and perhaps unacceptably costly.

Deterrence can help prevent war, but it is not a sure thing; deterrence can fail. Given the anarchic nature of international relations, two paths to deterrence failure are particularly salient: (1) miscommunication and misinterpretation of threats and (2) military balances that reward going first in a war. If the deterrent threat gets garbled in diplomatic exchanges between potential adversaries, the threat loses its efficacy. Countries can miscalculate the enemy's resolve, as Japan did before World War II when it attacked the United States at Pearl Harbor. Countries can also fail to make their threats sufficiently credible; for instance, the United States made only ambiguous threats in the months leading up to Iraq's invasion of Kuwait in August 1990, possibly convincing Saddam Hussein that he could act with impunity. Military balances also affect deterrence. If defensive forces have a decisive, or perceived, advantage over offensive forces, neither side will go first since each knows the attack is likely to fail. When offense is superior, there is an incentive for one side to initiate conflict and so gain the upper hand in the conflict. If the attacker can achieve a knockout blow by going first, deterrence will likely fail; after all, if you cannot hit back no one will take your threats seriously. Deterrence is likely to fail if either side *perceives* an advantage in striking first, whether or not the advantage is real. Thus, the major participants in World War I—Austria-Hungary, Britain, France, Germany, and Russia—all believed incorrectly that offense had the advantage over defense; once war appeared likely, they made war inevitable by trying to get the jump on their adversaries with a rapid mobilization and a first strike. World War II had a similar result, only this time Hitler correctly gauged that his blitzkrieg doctrine gave offense a decisive advantage. Evolving military technology, doctrine (how the military plans to use force), and the relative balance of forces all work to change the real and perceived advantage of offense or defense over the other.

Since appeasement and deterrence can fail, violent conflict remains an everpresent hazard in international relations. Theorists and policymakers alike have variously sought ways to finesse the dilemma, either by dramatically reshaping the international system or by tinkering with the mechanisms of international relations, such as the balance of power, alliances, appeasement, and deterrence. The following five approaches, ranging from the most to the least radical, are the chief variants: (1) world government and disarmament, (2) collective security, (3) concerts and great power condominium, (4) arms control, and (5) crisis management.

## WORLD GOVERNMENT AND DISARMAMENT

One way to solve the security dilemma inherent in an anarchical international system is to get rid of the anarchy. If the world could build a supranational (above-the-nations) authority with the muscle to enforce the rule of law among states, the security dilemma would go away. Countries would not worry when their neighbor grew in strength, because they could trust the *world government* to protect their interests. Indeed, states would not feel the need to arm themselves if a global policeman kept order. Just as frontiersmen could shed their six-shooters as the sheriff gained in stature and authority, so could states forgo military build-ups if some sort of supranational authority could assure their security. World government is thus usually associated with plans for *disarmament*, the complete eradication of weapons of war or, at the very least, the transference of all such weapons to a single authority (the global sheriff).

## Difficulties with World Government

World government and disarmament are extreme, some would say utopian, visions of how to restructure the international system in order to eliminate war. The community of nations has never truly tried to implement world government, although attempts to establish a universal empire have been numerous. During the middle ages, the pope and the Holy Roman Emperor served something of this function for Christendom, but they never achieved the kind of complete control over local lords and potentates needed to make world government work. More recently, some of the founders of the League of Nations and the United Nations hoped these organizations would form the kernel of a world government, but, as explained in chapter 3, the League was and the UN is too weak to qualify. Experiments in supranational government on a regional scale have had little success as well. Only the European Community (EC) has been able to overcome the divisions of separate nation-states on certain issues; and the difficulty the EC had in 1992 moving to the next level of integration is a telling sign that establishing a supranational government, even among like peoples, is a devilishly elusive aspiration.

Countries have been reluctant to move to a world government for the simple reason that they think the benefits of anarchy— independent state sovereignty—outweigh the costs, the possibility of war. Nation-states with different cultures, clashing value systems, and diverse standards of living are unwilling to surrender control over their own affairs to a central authority that may take steps hostile to their interests. Rich states do not want their wealth taxed and distributed to less fortunate states; small countries do not want to see their rights trampled upon by the votes from more populous regions; and so on. Moreover, there is no guarantee that world government will end war. History reminds us that the bloodiest conflicts have been civil wars in which brother fights brother; indeed, since 1945 far more people have been killed in civil wars than in interstate wars. A world government might be too unwieldy and too prone to disintegration to regulate effectively the conflicting interests of its parts.

## Difficulties with Disarmament

Disarmament has been a similarly slippery goal. There have been various efforts to eliminate certain weapons (discussed below in the section on arms control), but there has been no serious global effort to disarm completely. Part of the difficulty is that disarmament is both a result and a necessary condition of world government. If world government could be achieved (a big if), disarmament might be possible; but disarmament may itself be a necessary step to take before world government is possible. The only thing more dangerous than everyone having guns in the wild west would have been if only the bad guys had had guns, especially in the transition period before the sheriff could enforce order. States will be unwilling to disarm unilaterally, without some firm assurances that their neighbors (and hence potential adversaries) will disarm at the same time. Thus, some sort of supranational authority is needed before the countries will be willing to surrender the arms on which they currently rely for their security. But world government cannot exercise control over heavily armed constituent elements; unless the individual states disarm first, they can and probably will resist the central government.

These problems have bedeviled every proposal for world government and are likely to make the quest intractable for the foreseeable future. World government may simply be impossible unless the international community first reaches the kind of consensus and harmony that would make such a radical step unnecessary in the first place. The nation-state has proven a very resilient form of political organization and is likely to remain the chief building block of any international conflict management system. Consequently, most practically minded leaders have searched for revisions to the international system that do not require the complete elimination of the nation state.

## COLLECTIVE SECURITY

*Collective security* is a somewhat less radical response to the security dilemma. Under collective security, the individual countries remain major players, but they lose much of their independence of action, because membership in collective security obligates states to behave in certain ways. This arrangement requires that all countries agree to come to the defense of any victim of aggression; an attack on one is an attack on all. The response must be virtually automatic, unhampered by other considerations: for example, is the aggressor country a friend, is the victim an enemy, does the conflict concern vital national interests? If a state is party to a collective security agreement, that state must get involved in every budding conflict; it loses the right to abstain in matters it deems less important.

Collective security seeks to eliminate the vulnerability anarchy imposes on small states. The combined weight of every other state is pledged to the defense of even the tiniest, least consequential member of the collective security system. It also attempts to avoid the security dilemma and the vicious cycle of arms races and alliance races. If a state knows the world community will defend it from an attack, it will not feel the need to build up military forces or solicit powerful allies. If properly implemented, collective security should work to eliminate war. The certain prospects of facing an overwhelming coalition will deter even a determined aggressor from launching an attack. Collective security is deterrence without uncertainty.

## The League of Nations and the United Nations

The world community has never actually tried pure collective security, although the League of Nations was and the United Nations is based in part on this vision of world affairs. Woodrow Wilson, the founder of the League, clearly intended his masterpiece to reflect the principles of collective security, but the members soon abandoned the score in favor of a repeat of the old balance-of-power song. The League was reasonably successful in reconciling minor disputes among small powers but became helpless when a great power was involved. Japan carved up Manchuria (1931) with impunity, and Italy invaded Ethiopia with barely a slap on the wrist (1936). Key countries, most notably Britain, refused to honor their collective security obligations. The United States did not even join the League; and France relied on alliances with its Eastern European friends to counter rising German power during the 1920s and 1930s.

The United Nations fared only somewhat better after World

War II. Key provisions designed to counter the weaknesses of the League—including giving each of the five great powers (Britain, China, France, the Soviet Union, and the United States) a permanent seat on the Security Council and a veto over security decisions—ended up paralyzing the United Nations when the cold war brought great power cooperation to a halt. The United Nations was able to come to the defense of South Korea after North Korea invaded (1950) only because the Soviet Union had temporarily walked out of the Security Council in protest. Moreover, the United Nations does not have the ability to raise its own army and must depend on contributions from member nations. The richer, more powerful nations are the prime contributors; if they do not approve of a military action sponsored by the United Nations, they can effectively kill it by withholding support. The United Nations is less a pure collective security arrangement than it is a glorified concert of great powers (see discussion below).

*The Persian Gulf War*

Perhaps the closest we have come to witnessing collective security in action was the world's response to Iraq's invasion of Kuwait (1990). The response was relatively quick, virtually unanimous, and undeniably effective, as the United States led a coalition of United Nations members in restoring Kuwait's sovereignty. But the Gulf War is notable chiefly as an exception. The United Nations has been slow to act in other areas of fighting, conspicuously so in the civil war in former Yugoslavia, and it intervened in Somalia only after the situation there reached truly cataclysmic proportions. Kuwait, though tiny, happened to sit astride one of the world's greatest proven reserves of oil. Arguably, the coalition acted not so much for the sake of the ideal of collective security as for the sake of continued access to cheap oil. In other words, national interest may have been the necessary precondition for UN action to counter Iraq. This does not make the action illegitimate, but it does make it attributable less to collective security than to more traditional balance of power politics.

## CONCERTS AND GREAT POWER CONDOMINIUM

Great powers tend to be unwilling to surrender their independence of action to some collective security deliberative body. Rather, they are more likely to try to thwart the security dilemma by joining in special agreements with other great powers. Two such arrangements, *concerts* and great power *condominiums,* have had some mixed success in preventing specific types of war for certain periods of time.

## A Concert of Nations

A *concert* is similar to a collective security arrangement but considerably less sweeping and usually involves only the great powers in a region. Concert participants agree to maintain a balance of power among the principal members, promising to come to the aid of any individual great power if under attack from another great power. Medium-sized and smaller powers are more vulnerable in a concert. Their security is not assured; great powers can invade them, provided that doing so does not disrupt the balance among the primary members. A successful concert will prevent major wars between the great powers (and will preserve the relative strengths of the great powers) but will tolerate smaller conflicts, even if these lesser struggles result in the conquest of an independent country.

The most famous concert was the Concert of Europe, which flourished during what is known as the "Classical Balance of Power" period. This arrangement lasted for some one hundred years, from 1815 to 1914, more or less keeping the great power peace. There were, however, many small wars in Europe during this time—some, like the Crimean War (1854, France and Britain against Russia), involving the great powers—and the concert collapsed catastrophically into the bloodiest war up to that time, World War I. Some have suggested the possibility of reviving the Concert as a way to keep peace in a post–cold war Europe.

## Condominiums of Great Power

Great power *condominium* is a concert variant in which the key countries agree not to fight each other in order to free their hands to dominate the other states in the international system. At various points throughout the cold war, experts discussed (often in worried tones) the possibility that the two superpowers, the United States and the Soviet Union, might suspend their rivalry and cooperate to rule the world. It is rumored Leonid Brezhnev, when he was General Secretary of the Communist Party, made precisely this offer to Richard Nixon, then President of the United States, in one of their summit meetings. The outlines of a condominium emerged toward the end of the cold war as Mikhail Gorbachev and George Bush began to cooperate on resolving various regional conflicts. The collapse of the Soviet Union, however, changed the dynamic completely.

Concerts and condominiums have some attractive qualities, especially for large countries. They do not require the members to sacrifice a great deal of autonomy and so are more easily achieved. They also hold out some realistic hope of preventing major wars. All League and United Nations successes could be recast as instances of great power concert rather than as cases of universal collective security. Pragmatic proposals for the future, therefore, usually incorporate healthy doses of concert and/or condominium features. But since concerts and condominiums are not very kind to small powers, the features are usually masked in collective security rhetoric.

## ARMS CONTROL

If the gaps separating the great powers are unbridgeable, a concert (or condominium) may be impossible. Under these circumstances, the security dilemma kicks in, triggering the arms races that can break out into war. A qualified form of cooperation is still possible, however, if the rivals pursue carefully circumscribed goals. The enterprise of this sort with the longest pedigree is *arms control*, defined as specific limitations on certain aspects of the military competition, whether of weapons or behavior.

Arms control is not disarmament. Disarmament means eliminating all weapons; arms control means containing and channelling, but still permitting, military competition. Arms control tries to cope with the problems of international anarchy rather than solving them once and for all. The goal of arms control is reducing the insecurity and uncertainty that makes the security dilemma so dangerous. Oftentimes, arms control succeeds only in codifying the status quo, reassuring countries that the known evils will remain for a while and will not be replaced by unknown, potentially worse, ones. Successful arms control, then, addresses specific maladies that can produce spiralling arms races or deterrence failures with equally specific, if short-term, treatments. There are three basic variants of arms control: quantitative, qualitative, and operational.

## Quantitative Arms Control

Quantitative arms control involves limiting the numbers of certain types of weapon systems either through restrictions on growth or cutbacks in the arsenal. The Washington Naval Conference (1921–22) is an early example; the major naval powers agreed to limit the number of battleships each navy could possess, forcing Britain and the United States to decommission many operational ships. In the nuclear age, quantitative arms control has received the most popular attention, although it has by no means represented the most important strand of nuclear arms control. The Strategic Arms Limitation Talks (SALT) begun in 1968, produced the Strategic Arms Limitation Treaty in 1972. It limited the number of launchers the United States and the Soviet Union could deploy. SALT is best known for what it did not do, however: it did not require cutbacks in the arsenal since the number was set higher than either side had at the time; it did not limit the number of warheads on each launcher, so the offensive power of the arsenal could grow significantly under the terms of the treaty; and it did not cover strategic nuclear weapons deployed aboard submarines and bombers.

Despite its limitations, SALT did mark a turning point in the cold war. The superpowers agreed to restrictions on their arsenal and, more importantly, committed themselves to ongoing arms control. Several important qualitative and operational arms control measures discussed below emerged out of the SALT process, even while quantitative arms control remained at center stage. SALT I begot SALT II, a more restrictive treaty that set overall limits on delivery vehicles and put restrictions on certain subcategories, including the number of missiles with multiple warheads and the number of warheads each missile could carry. Although signed by President Carter, the treaty was never ratified because of objections from conservative senators who viewed the treaty as conceding too many advantages in land-based missiles to the Soviets and who feared the Soviets might cheat in any case. The arms control process temporarily foundered when the Soviet Union invaded Afghanistan in 1979, and prospects looked bleaker still when the Reagan administration came into office in 1981 after a campaign heavily seasoned with anti–arms control rhetoric.

Ironically, President Reagan and his successor President Bush achieved the most striking quantitative arms control success with the Strategic Arms Reduction Talks (and then treaty). President Reagan criticized SALT for merely limiting the expansion of the nuclear arsenal, for managing rather than lessening the arms race. He proposed START as a mechanism for reducing the arsenal with meaningful cuts. After years of negotiations, this approach produced results in the START I agreement signed in 1991 and START II signed in 1993. Both treaties require deep cuts in each side's strategic arsenal; if fully implemented, the START agreements would leave the arsenals at approximately 30 percent of their previous levels, or roughly three thousand to thirty-five hundred warheads apiece. Unfortunately, the collapse of the Soviet Union and the desire of newly independent states, such as the Ukraine, to preserve some of their nuclear capabilities as a hedge against any renewed Russian threat to their sovereignty has delayed the final achievement of the START cuts.

## Qualitative Arms Control

*Qualitative arms control*—eliminating certain categories of weapons —has achieved some important successes as well. This brand of arms control traces its roots to the Hague conventions of 1899 and 1907, which produced restrictions on chemical weapons and dum-dum bullets (bullets that break up when they hit a person, producing far more lethal wounds). In the nuclear era, there have been three important qualitative arms control agreements: the Nonproliferation (NPT) Treaty, the Antiballistic Missile (ABM) Treaty, and the Intermediate Nuclear Forces (INF) Treaty.

**Nonproliferation Treaty.** The NPT (1968) sought to limit the spread of nuclear weapons to new countries. Although many key countries have not signed it (including France, China, India, and Pakistan), the NPT has made it very difficult for other countries to develop nuclear weapons by restricting access to the requisite fissionable materials and technical know-how. However, as the recent efforts of Iraq and North Korea, both signatories to the NPT, to covertly develop nuclear weapons illustrates, the NPT has been unsuccessful in completely halting states from pursuing nuclear capability.

**Antiballistic Missile Treaty.** The ABM treaty (1972) was signed as part of the SALT I agreement and severely restricted the ability of the superpowers to deploy defenses against ballistic missiles. The Reagan administration challenged the ABM treaty with the Strategic Defense Initiative in the 1980s, but the prohibition on effective defenses has remained intact to date.

**Intermediate Nuclear Forces Treaty.** The INF treaty is perhaps the most successful qualitative arms control treaty ever. Signed in 1987, it requires that the United States and the Soviet Union dismantle all intermediate range, land-based nuclear missiles deployed in the European theater. If fully implemented, START II will also have a qualitative arms control component, eliminating all land-based intercontinental missiles that carry multiple warheads.

*Operational Arms Control*

*Operational arms control* is a less-heralded, but nonetheless significant, variant of the overall effort to regulate military competition. Whereas quantitative and qualitative arms control seeks to limit, reduce, or eliminate *weapon systems,* operational arms control addresses *dangerous behaviors.* Throughout the cold war, the rivalry often brought the militaries of the superpowers into close and sometimes direct contact. Without "rules of the road," these situations could potentially escalate to a crisis or even war. The Incidents at Sea Agreement (1972) restricted risky naval maneuvers— like playing "chicken" with ships or "buzzing" enemy ships with aircraft—in order to prevent occasions for military operations to go awry. The famous hotline established in 1963 after the Cuban Missile Crisis is another example of operational arms control; it provides a direct telephonic link between the White House and the Kremlin so the leaders can communicate directly in case of a crisis. Operational arms control can also limit the arms race, and its ecological consequences, through restrictions on key activities like nuclear testing. One of the earliest successes in cold war arms control was the Limited Test Ban Treaty (1963), which prohibited above-ground test explosions of nuclear weapons.

Arms control enthusiasts have even suggested developing operational arms control arrangements to govern the kinds of military doctrines countries may pursue. The goal here is to develop non-offensive military postures, ones capable of mounting a robust defense but not equipped to mount an attack in the first place. If achieved, this approach would eliminate one of the problems that has plagued deterrence in the past, that of eliminating any perceived advantage to the offense. Although popular with nontraditional security theorists, nonoffensive defense has yet to develop any serious momentum, in part because it is almost impossible to provide for a capable defense without simultaneously developing the capability, at least potentially, to launch a credible offense.

*Limitations and Possibilities of Arms Control*

Arms control, whether nuclear or conventional, seeks to minimize the uncertainty and mistrust that plague international relations under conditions of anarchy. By making competition more stable, and therefore more predictable, successful arms control can thwart the security dilemma, dampening conflict before it spirals out of control.

Arms control is not a panacea for international conflict, however. Just as with world government, arms control tends to be more possible when it is less needed, and vice versa. When tensions are great and mistrust is high, arms control could have the biggest impact in reducing conflict and reassuring adversaries about the intentions of their opponents; but in such times, arms control is especially difficult if not impossible to achieve. States are reluctant to accept restrictions on their own arsenals unless they can be sure their adversaries will not cheat and thereby gain a decisive advantage. In times of acute tensions, each side will have ample reason to doubt the trustworthiness of the other making meaningful limitations untenable. Adequate **verification**—making sure the other side honors its obligations-is thus a crucial requirement for successful arms control. But verification procedures, like on-site inspections themselves, require a fair amount of cooperation in the first place. Since the end of the Gulf War in 1991, the ongoing difficulty of enforcing the restrictions placed on Iraq's military offers eloquent testimony to the challenge of making arms control effective in the face of a stubborn and dishonest opponent. Similarly, efforts to get North Korea to open its nuclear sites to international inspection to verify that it is not developing nuclear weapons has also run into these problems.

In contrast, the United States and the former Soviet Union were able to agree to the biggest cuts in their arsenals only after the cold war ended, that is, after the risks of nuclear war had already been reduced substantially through a reduction in tensions. Indeed, some of the most impressive arms control successes by the two superpowers were attained when they engaged in a series of sequential unilateral cuts in 1991 and 1992. By that point, the United States and the Soviet Union were already cooperating substantially on a variety of issues, and so it was relatively easy to introduce cutbacks in strategic programs without raising fears that the other side would take advantage of those cuts.

Arms control is thus of limited value in resolving the basic dilemmas that drive international conflict. It is not worthless, however. Merely by bringing adversaries together at a negotiating table, arms control can dampen tensions. More importantly, as with the SALT process, arms control can provide a mechanism whereby adversaries who *want* to improve relations can do so. It focuses their attention on areas of mutual concern and can improve each side's understanding of the other, thus addressing the distrust that lies at the heart of the security dilemma.

## CRISIS MANAGEMENT

*Crisis management,* the last broad category of approaches to restraining the use of military force and resolving international conflicts is the least ambitious, but perhaps the most important. Far from attempting to eliminate conflict, the crisis management method assumes conflict is at some level inevitable and seeks only to maneuver that conflict to a peaceful conclusion. It is a bit of an oxymoron: *crisis* implies circumstances spiralling out of control while *management* connotes the careful supervision of mundane matters. But crisis management recognizes that miscalculation, misperception, and uncertainty can turn a small confrontation into a big one. This approach involves a variety of tactics, from formal legal treaties to informal, even tacit, rules of the game.

The hot-line agreement mentioned above is an example of a formal treaty designed to improve crisis management. During a crisis, leaders often must guess at what their counterparts actually mean in the ambiguous language of diplomacy. The hot line allows direct communication at the highest levels. Confusion, deliberate or unintentional, is still possible even with such a frank and personal link, but the likelihood is reduced. Toward the end the cold war, the superpowers developed "risk-reduction centers," neutral hubs where senior military and diplomatic officials from both sides could meet and possibly nip an emerging disagreement before it blossomed into direct confrontation.

Informal and tacit understandings can also contribute to crisis management. For instance, refusing to back your opponent into a corner and giving him time to review the situation can help defuse a potential showdown. Maintaining open communication throughout the crisis also helps minimize the misperceptions that plague diplomacy.

Clear signals of restraint and resolve encourage an adversary to seek accommodation and simultaneously warn of the dangers of not doing so.

In the first fifteen years of the cold war, the world endured several superpower crises: Berlin (1948 and 1959–61), Hungary (1956), and Quemoy-Matsu (1954; small islands in the straits between Taiwan and mainland China). John Foster Dulles, the American secretary of state throughout much of this period, even claimed to seek crises deliberately as a way of forcing the hand of the Soviets, calling the policy *brinksmanship*. The worst crisis, the Cuban Missile Crisis (1962), however, underscored the dangers of brinksmanship and dampened any enthusiasm there might have been among policymakers for this risky approach to diplomacy.

The crisis began when the United States discovered that the Soviet Union was deploying medium-range nuclear-tipped missiles in Cuba, barely ninety miles from the Florida coast. President Kennedy demanded that Premier Khrushchev remove the missiles; Khrushchev refused just as adamantly. For two tense weeks, the world waited in suspense as the superpowers pushed each other to the brink of global nuclear war. The crisis ended peacefully when the Soviets agreed to dismantle the missiles in exchange for an American promise not to invade Cuba. Recently, scholars have learned that President Kennedy also promised to remove U.S. missiles from Turkey, although he explicitly denied making any such quid pro quo arrangement at the time.

Despite its outcome, the Cuban Missile Crisis confirmed many of the worst fears of the dangers of uncontrolled competition between the superpowers. Consequently, the arms control movement gained momentum after the crisis, and policymakers turned their attention to refining mechanisms for reducing, if not preventing, future crises. Scholars pointed to the way President Kennedy conducted his end of the affair as being exemplary of good crisis management techniques. Kennedy quickly established a special deliberative body, the Executive Committee, which reviewed various options, taking care to consider as many points of view as possible given time constraints. He also moved decisively to assert civilian control over military operations; indeed, just prior to the crisis, Kennedy had read *The Guns of August,* Barbara Tuchman's gripping account of the 1914 crisis that escalated into World War I, and he was determined not to let military exigencies drag the world into World War III.

Skillful manipulation of these techniques can resolve crises without bloodshed. International conflict need not breed international war. But crisis management can fail, as can deterrence and appeasement, and so it is not a final solution to the security dilemma. Crisis management is best viewed as a temporary coping mechanism, capable of dampening conflict until such time as the international community develops a more lasting solution to the puzzle of cooperating under conditions of anarchy.

## WHERE TO FROM HERE?

The end of the cold war has helped reduce a sense of urgency, at least among Americans, about international conflict. In some ways, the nuclear shadow has lifted a bit and the specter of a global conflagration has receded. Absent a major turnabout in Russia, we can expect a period of relative peace among the great powers in the foreseeable future.

Military conflict remains a major international problem, however; and in some ways the coming years may be even more disagreeable than those of the cold war. The likelihood for smaller wars has increased in direct proportion to the declining probability of a superpower clash. The paralyzing threat of global nuclear war stifled many of the conflicts now bubbling to the surface. For better or for worse, the superpower contest suppressed nationalist ambitions in central Europe and the former Soviet republics. Among the new freedoms unleashed by the collapse of the Soviet Union is the freedom of national and subnational groups to seek redress for past injustices, by the sword if necessary. The civil wars in Yugoslavia, the former Soviet republic of Georgia, and Somalia may well be harbingers of the kind of conflicts the world will face in the next several decades: groups wielding modern weapons to exact revenge for centuries-old grievances. The perversity of the security dilemma, the growing interdependence among states, and the continued global diffusion of weapons dictate that even peaceful countries will feel the effects of this new strife.

To counter this, many have called on the world community to refine and employ new variants of the power management techniques discussed above. Some have seen in the coalition fighting Iraq the outlines of a new great power concert, one more dedicated to protecting small countries than advancing the interests of the large. Any new concert would probably use the newly reinvigorated United Nations as a base of operation. The United Nations' role has increased dramatically in the last five years. The United Nations has peacekeeping missions in well over a dozen countries, including many of the hot spots that flared up during the cold war: Indochina, the Horn of Africa, the Middle East, and the Balkans. These efforts fall somewhat short of ideal collective security, and well short of a utopian world government. But they speak to the possibility for greater community involvement in preventing the spread of international conflict in the future.

Countries seeking peace continue to prepare for war. Unless the world community finds a way to move beyond the nation-state, the logic of international relations dictates that military force, and the control thereof, will remain crucial factors for the foreseeable future. Yet, the remarkable events attending the end of the cold war offer some encouragement for those who seek to manage and perhaps reduce conflict among nations. At the very least, the world community seems less fatalistic about the inevitability of military confrontations. And with the renewed hopefulness comes a fresh determination to find a workable and lasting peace.

## ANNOTATED BIBLIOGRAPHY

Art, Robert J., and Kenneth N. Waltz, eds. *The Use of Force: International Politics and Foreign Policy.* 3rd ed. Lanham, MD: University Press of America, 1988.
A useful collection of essays on the relationship between force and national objectives.

Blainey, Geoffrey. *The Causes of War.* 3rd ed. New York: Free Press, 1988.
An analytical treatment of the question, somewhat impressionistic in organization but useful nonetheless.

Bull, Hedley. *The Anarchical Society: The Study of Order in World Politics.* New York: Columbia University Press, 1977.
A thoughtful review of the challenge of order in an anarchical international system.

Claude, Inis L. *Power and International Relations.* New York: Random House, 1962.
The classic treatment of balance of power and collective security as mechanisms for managing power in the international system.

Craig, Gordon A., and Alexander L. George. *Force and Statecraft: Diplomatic Problems of Our Time.* 2nd ed. New York: Oxford University Press, 1990.
A thoughtful treatment of the theory and history of great power conflict in the modern era.

Brodie, Bernard. *War and Politics.* New York: Macmillan, 1973.
A classic overview by one of the deans of U.S. strategic studies.

Gaddis, John Lewis. *Strategies of Containment: A Critical Assessment of Postwar American National Security Policy.* New York: Oxford University Press, 1982.
A scholarly treatment of the first three-plus decades of the cold war by the most prominent historian of contemporary American foreign policy.

George, Alexander L., and Richard Smoke. *Deterrence in American Foreign Policy: Theory and Practice.* New York: Columbia University Press, 1974.
A scholarly overview of the conditions under which deterrence succeeds and fails.

Lynn-Jones, Sean M. *The Cold War and After—Prospects for Peace: An International Security Reader.* Cambridge: MIT Press, 1991.
A collection of provocative analyses of why the cold war ended peacefully and what the future might hold for the great powers.

Schelling, Thomas, and Morton Halperin. *Strategy and Arms Control.* 1961; New York: Pergamon-Brassey, 1985.
This is the classic introduction to the possibilities and pitfalls of arms control.

# CHAPTER 5

# Diplomacy, Negotiation, and Peaceful Settlement

## David P. Barash

> Disagreements must be settled, not by force, not by deceit or trickery, but rather in the only manner which is worthy of the dignity of man, i.e., by a mutual assessment of the reasons on both sides of the dispute, by a mature and objective investigation of the situation, and by an equitable reconciliation of differences of opinion.
>
> —Pope John XXIII, *Pacem in Terris*

"War is waged," wrote St. Augustine, "so that peace may prevail. . . . But it is a greater glory to slay war with a word than people with a sword, and to gain peace by means of peace and not by means of war"[1] In this chapter, we shall examine efforts to manage international conflict and gain peace by words and other means of peace. It has been no easy quest. As we shall see, obtaining a good accord often involves far more than agreeing to a simple compromise. The art and science of negotiating and resolving conflicts requires a many-faceted approach.

One way of gaining peace "by means of peace and not by means of war" is for the contending sides in a dispute to reach a mutually acceptable agreement among themselves. When such agreements or understandings are obtained among states, we say that "diplomacy" has taken place. *Diplomacy* may be defined as "the art of resolving disputes between states by highly skilled communication between the trained representatives of governments."[2] The people who practice this art are known as diplomats. There is also a less positive view of diplomats, who have been called "honest men sent abroad to lie for their country."[3]

Peace researcher Anatol Rapaport has made a useful distinction among fights, games, and debates.[4] In a fight, the intent is to defeat the opponent, sometimes even to destroy him or her. Rules may exist, as in a prize-fight, but they may also be ignored—as in a street fight, or a particularly vicious war—and in any event, the means are likely to be violent. In a game, by contrast, each side

---

[1]St.Augustine, *The City of God*. (New York: Modern Library, 1950).

[2]David Zielger, *War, Peace, and International Politics* (Boston: Little Brown, 1977). p. 278

[3]Attributed to British ambassador Sir Henry Wonnon, by Harold Nicholson, *Diplomacy* (New York: Oxford University Press, 1955). p. 119

[4]A. Rapaport, *Fights, Games and Debates*. (Ann Arbor, MI: University of Michigan Press, 1974).

tries to outwit the opponent, playing strictly within the rules. Finally, in a debate, the goal is to persuade the opponent of the justice or correctness of one's cause. The process of conflict resolution, ideally, is closest to a debate, just as wars are fights, although with some aspects of a game as well. However, even diplomacy and negotiations involve the elaborate rules of complex games, not uncommonly backed up by the threat of fighting as well.

Although ways of fighting have changed through history, the basic techniques of negotiation scarcely have. At their most contentious, negotiators have two things they can offer: threats and promises. As we shall see, an important recent insight adds a third option, a shared willingness to identify the problem and engage in creative problem solving. Conflict resolution can be backed up by varying degrees of good or ill will, and a continuum from blind trust to ironclad verification and/or arm-twisting. Negotiations, however, can succeed only if the parties involved want them to; that is, if there is a set of outcomes that each party prefers to reaching no agreement. Even though the participants to a dispute occasionally engage in negotiations just to appear virtuous, there is good reason to think that—in most cases at least—a negotiated settlement is preferred over either a failure to agree or the use of violence to force an outcome. The trick is to find a peaceful settlement that will be acceptable to all sides.

In the course of seeking to achieve agreements and resolve disputes short of violence, contending parties typically try to obtain the most favorable outcome possible for their side. The process of give-and-take and the strategies for succeeding—in reaching an agreement and also getting the best outcome—involve skill at negotiating. This applies both to the direct participants as well as to third parties who are frequently called in to help reach an agreement.

It is important to realize how often we negotiate solutions to conflict, typically on the interpersonal level. Disagreements among children over who gets to play with a particular toy, or within families over what television program to watch, or among coworkers over whether or not to have an office party, or between landlord and tenant over repairs and rent: these disputes are nearly always resolved short of violence. This helps emphasize that there are many routes available for dealing with conflict; it is something we do every day. And yet, one of the most pervasive myths of our current culture of militarism is that war and preparation for war are both somehow "realistic," whereas peace and preparation for peace are hopelessly naive. We are surrounded with subliminal messages to the effect that peacemaking is an impossible dream, whereas warmaking—or at best, deterrence—is the only reality. Hence, it is important to affirm and make visible the peacemaking that happens all around us, most of the time. It is only when international conflict management or peacemaking takes place at the highest government levels, typically involving heads of state, that it receives society's attention.

## A VERY BRIEF HISTORY OF DIPLOMACY

In the past, diplomats were drawn from the same social and economic class and they spoke the same language, not only figuratively but also literally: French. Although there is a long history of monarchs sending ambassadors to the courts of other rulers, it is generally agreed that the current system of diplomatic protocol was established by Cardinal Richelieu, chief minister—some would say, chief manipulator—of Louis XIII, king of France (early seventeenth century).

Although there has always been a peculiar stiffness to official diplomatic discourse and protocol, such formalities have evolved over many years so as to enhance precision of communication, and, whenever possible, reduce the chances that personalities will interfere with formal and serious communication between governments. Historically, ambassadors were the personal representatives of one sovereign to the court of another, and that polite fiction is still maintained, even in the case of democracies. Upon their arrival, ambassadors typically present their credentials to the head of state of the host country. In modern times, electronic communication has largely bypassed the individual diplomat when it comes to the establishment of important international agreements, but as we shall see, the role of person-to-person contact, even at the highest levels, remains important.

Ironically, states communicate with each other least frequently and least clearly during war, precisely when such communication is likely to be the most important. At such times, and occasionally when interactions become severely strained during peacetime, diplomatic relations are broken off, and each state recalls its ambassador. Otherwise, officials are available to correct possible misunderstandings, clarify positions, and, when all else fails, simply to buy time, occasionally in the hope that tense situations will eventually blow over. As we shall see, there have been many cases in which diplomacy has failed; there have also, however, been successes.

*Some Diplomatic Successes*

How well has diplomacy worked in managing or preventing international conflict? We can identify a number of successes. In 1987, Indian military exercises near Pakistan's border alarmed the Pakistanis, whose forces were mobilized in response. Soon, more than three hundred thousand armed men were facing each other across a border that has known substantial violence in the past. Tensions gradually eased, however, via urgent diplomatic exchanges between the two sides; among other things, each agreed (verbally) to refrain from attacking the other's nuclear facilities. Also in 1987, Greece and Turkey exchanged threats over Turkish plans to prospect for oil near several islands in the eastern Aegean that were under Greek ownership but very close to the Turkish mainland. Like India and Pakistan, these two states also have a long history of antagonism and warfare. (Greece was long dominated by Turkey, as part of the Ottoman Empire, and more recently, the two states have engaged in threats as well as fighting over the fate of Greek and Turkish Cypriots.) Once again, tensions were gradually cooled, at least in part because both sides feared to antagonize their NATO ally, the United States, which could lead to a cutoff in military aid.

And once again during 1987, five Central American countries (Costa Rica, El Salvador, Nicaragua, Honduras, and Guatemala) agreed to a peace accord, designed largely by Oscar Arias, president of Costa Rica. The accord called for (1) eliminating all restrictions on political dissent, (2) political amnesty for rebels, (3) national elections under international supervision, (4) a negotiated cease-fire between national governments and all rebel groups, (5) each country forbidding the use of its territory to rebels seeking the overthrow of other countries, and (6) a cutoff in aid provided by outside countries to insurgent groups, meaning U.S. aid to the Nicaraguan contras and Soviet aid to the Salvadoran F.M.L.N. On the strength of his efforts, Arias was awarded the 1987 Nobel Peace

Prize; this represented both a diplomatic success and effective mediation.

During the early 1990s, diplomatic efforts also appear to have resolved violent conflicts in Afghanistan, Angola, Cambodia, and the western Sahara . . . although it must be pointed out that these settlements are tentative—and in some cases, fragile—and that such diplomatic successes have been achieved only after warfare. Although diplomacy is most honored when it prevents violence altogether, we should not lose sight of its value in bringing periods of armed violence to a peaceful conclusion.

*Some Diplomatic Failures*

Unfortunately, history teaches us that diplomacy is an imperfect mechanism for peacemaking. Sometimes, diplomats actually make things worse. They are human beings, after all, and fallible. Moreover, although it is hoped that direct, personal interactions can reduce the likelihood that nations will resort to force in settling their differences, such interactions also provide the opportunity for interpersonal hostility. Perceived slights among rulers and diplomats have, on occasion, endangered the peace. Late in the seventeenth century, France and Spain nearly came to blows when a coach carrying the Spanish ambassador to England cut in front of the French ambassador on a London street. In 1819, the Dey of Algiers—angered about the failure of the French government to make good on a debt—struck the French consul three times with a flyswatter. This insult precipitated a naval blockade by the French and ultimately served as an excuse for what became France's long-term occupation of Algeria.

Even at its best, diplomacy breeds a certain deviousness and social artifice that many people find laughable, if not downright unpleasant. During the protracted negotiations leading to the Treaty of Paris after Napoleon's defeat, Metternich was told that the Russian ambassador had died. The story has it that he responded, "Ah, is that true? I wonder what he meant by that."

**Unintended Consequences.** Efforts at diplomatic clarification sometimes backfire and have the unintended consequence of making things worse for all parties involved in a dispute. For instance, in late July 1914, Sir Edward Grey, the British foreign secretary, warned Kaiser Wilhelm that if a general war occurred, Britain would enter it on the side of France and Russia. Rather than deterring Germany as

Grey had intended, this was seen as a threat. As a result, the kaiser became more belligerent, convinced that a plot against him had been set in motion by the Triple Entente. This misunderstanding may have contributed to the outbreak of World War I.

Sometimes, diplomats' statements intended for domestic consumption have had serious international repercussions. In 1950, for example, Secretary of State Dean Acheson gave a speech in which he outlined the United States' "defense perimeter" in the Pacific; this appeared to exclude Korea, which apparently gave the North Korean government the false impression that the United States would not forcibly resist an invasion of South Korea.

**Increasing Conflict.** Sometimes, ironically, an ongoing war can be made more intense by the fact that diplomats are striving to bring the fighting to a close, as each side seeks to make territorial gains on the battlefield that might influence the ultimate peace settlement. Middle East diplomats noticed that the proposals put forward by Count Bernadotte, the first United Nations negotiator sent to help settle the 1948 war between Israel and the Arab states, closely reflected the immediate battlefield situation; as a result, both sides paid less attention to him and put more effort into achieving military gains so as to influence the negotiations in their favor. During the end stages of the Iran-Iraq War, in late autumn 1988, the Iraqi armies initiated several major offensives, hoping to improve Iraq's bargaining position. Similar intensification of fighting took place about the time that serious peace negotiations were underway at Panmunjom Korea in 1953. For this reason, it is generally recommended that the first step in negotiating peace is to get an immediate ceasefire in place.

**A Tool for War.** On occasion, diplomacy has even been consciously employed by leaders eager to initiate war. The most famous example of this was the Ems telegram, a communication which was craftily abbreviated by German Chancellor Bismarck to make it appear to the French that Kaiser Wilhem had snubbed the French ambassador. In Bismarck's own words, he "waved a red flag in front of the Gallic bull." The bull charged, as Bismarck had calculated, and ran into a Prussian steel wall in the ensuing Franco-Prussian War. In this case, Bismarck wanted to goad the French into appearing to be the aggressor, in order to assure the cooperation of what at the time were the independent South German States of Bavaria, Wurtemberg, Baden, and Hesse, and also to prevent other states (notably Russia and Austria-Hungary) from aiding France. In this case, then, diplomacy was used to create war and to isolate one side.

Sometimes, diplomacy designed to create war between two states has had unintended consequences on a third state. Before the United States entered World War I, Germany tried to induce Mexico to go to war against its northern neighbor, promising return of U.S. territory that had been won during the Mexican-American War. Mexico never took the bait. However, when the "Zimmerman telegram," which contained this inflammatory offer, was made public, it succeeded in further alienating U.S. public opinion toward Germany, hastening U.S. entry into World War I against Germany.

It is also not uncommon for countries to make a show of diplomacy, enabling them to claim that they are seeking nonviolent resolution of a conflict, whereas in fact they are only seriously interested in either capitulation by the other side, or a military showdown. Immediately prior to the 1991 Gulf War, for example, officials within the United States government were reportedly "furious" over last-minute efforts by the Soviet Union to negotiate a partial Iraqi withdrawal from Kuwait; such a withdrawal would almost certainly have undermined widespread support for the subsequent war to which the United States government was apparently already committed.

**European Approach to Diplomacy.**    Classically, European diplomacy served to make peace in ways that avoided excessive humiliation of the loser, so as not to foment grievances that would lead promptly to additional war. Some territory would be transferred, fortresses would be surrendered and frontiers adjusted, indemnities might be required, and reparations exacted, but no one demanded a mortal concession. For example, in 1714, the year after the Peace of Utrecht was signed, France and her neighbors ceased fighting any major battles over the succession to the Spanish and English thrones. The peace in Europe was basically kept for the next few decades by this diplomatic style of mutual concessions and avoidance of humiliation, combined with respect for each other's vital interests.

More recently, however, especially with national wars replacing sovereigns' wars, imposed conditions have often been cause for lasting resentment, which has in turn sowed the seeds of subsequent conflict. Thus, France's loss of Alsace and Lorraine during the Franco-Prussian War—and its national fervor for reclaiming these lost regions—did much to bring about World War I. The German anger and humiliation associated with the Treaty of Versailles (which ended that war) led in part to World War II. By contrast, the diplomatic settlements at the end of World War II, although imperfect, have had greater staying power, at least in part because Germany and Japan were rehabilitated rather than simply punished.

Diplomacy of this sort, however, is not so much an alternative to war, or a means of avoiding it, as an adjunct—or postscript—to national hostilities. As one (admittedly cynical) critic puts it,

> Diplomacy is a disguised war, in which States seek to gain by barter and intrigue, by the cleverness of wits, the objectives which they would have to gain more clumsily by means of war. Diplomacy is used while the States are recuperating from conflicts in which they have exhausted themselves. It is the wheedling and the bargaining of the worn-out bullies as they rise from the ground and slowly restore their strength to begin fighting again. If diplomacy had been a moral equivalent for war, a higher stage in human progress, an inestimable means of making words prevail instead of blows, militarism would have broken down and given place to it. But since it is a mere temporary substitute, a mere appearance of war's energy under another form, a surrogate effect is almost exactly proportioned to the armed force behind it. When it fails, the recourse is immediate to the military technique whose thinly veiled arm it has been.[5]

## DIPLOMACY AND MILITARY FORCE

What is the relationship between diplomacy and military force? According to a common view, diplomacy is only as effective as the military power available to each side; that is, the threats that underwrite courteous diplomatic interchanges. "Diplomacy without armaments," according to Frederick the Great, "is like music without instruments." More recently a former U.S. ambassador and arms control negotiator put it this way, "Diplomacy without force is like baseball without a bat."

---

[5]Randolph S. Bourne, *War and the Intellectuals, Collected Essays 1915–1919.* (1964). p. 60

There have been many examples of diplomatic intimidation, some successful, some not. During the late 1930s, Hitler successfully bluffed and bullied the western democracies into making successive territorial concessions—occupation of the Ruhr Valley, union with Austria, dismemberment and annexation of Czechoslovakia —because Germany had become militarily powerful, and Britain and France, remembering the pointless devastation of World War I, were eager to avert a repetition. On the other hand, during the early 1980s, the USSR sought to intimidate NATO into refusing to deploy Euromissiles by threatening nuclear retaliation against any state that accepted them in the event of war in Europe. This attempt to back up diplomacy with the threat of armed force backfired. By making itself appear more belligerent, the Soviet Union reinforced the arguments of those who proclaimed the need for the Euromissiles in the first place. Subsequently, these missiles were removed via successful bilateral U.S.-Soviet negotiations.

Arguing for the legitimacy—indeed, the necessity—of connecting diplomacy with military force, the renowned political scientist Hans Morgenthau stated that:

> Diplomacy must determine its objectives in the light of the power actually and potentially available for the pursuit of these objectives. Diplomacy must assess the objectives of other nations and the power actually and potentially available for the pursuit of these objectives. Diplomacy must determine to what extent these different objectives are compatible with each other. Diplomacy must employ the means suited to the pursuit of its objectives. Failure in any one of these tasks may jeopardize the success of foreign policy and with it the peace of the world.[6]

Otto von Bismarck, the nineteenth-century chancellor of the German Empire and architect of German unification, was hardly a pacifist. Yet, although he freely employed military force, he also understood its limitations. During the Austro-Prussian War, for example, the Austrians were badly defeated at the battle of Königgrätz, far more soundly than anyone had expected. At this point, political pressure quickly developed within Prussia for a wider victory over Austria, including the dismemberment of the Austrian Empire itself. But Bismarck insisted on limiting Prussian demands to the provinces of Schleswig and Holstein, thereby preventing a

---

[6]Hans Morgenthau, *Politics among Nations*. (New York: Knopf, 1978). p. 171.

wider war—with France and possibly Russia and Britain. As the arch-diplomat Metternich once put it: "Diplomacy is the art of avoiding the appearance of victory."

In contrast to Bismarck's sensitivity to the dangers of pushing one's victories too far, during the Korean War General Douglas MacArthur and President Harry Truman were insensitive to the costs of similarly pressing the North Koreans and Chinese: A very successful surprise landing of U.S. forces at Inchon had resulted in dramatic battlefield gains in the autumn of 1950, after which U.N. (mostly U.S.) troops advanced deeply into North Korea. This led in turn, to large-scale Chinese involvement and massive bloodshed on both sides, ending three years later in a stalemated situation, which could have been achieved with much less suffering had the western leaders shown greater farsightedness. The lesson of Königgrätz— that military restraint can often lead to greater diplomatic and long-term success—had not been learned.

While diplomacy may involve military force, the use of such force may be diminished by so-called tacit bargaining. This involves reaching agreements without actually spelling out the terms of the understanding. During the Korean War a tacit bargain existed: the Chinese would refrain from attacking U.S. aircraft carriers, supply lines, and bases in Japan; the United States would refrain from bombing of North Korean supply lines in China. In the Middle East today, there is another tacit bargain: Israel will not flaunt its secret stockpile of nuclear weapons, and the Arab states will not call attention to it. To some extent, this understanding serves the interests of both sides: the Israelis would rather not acknowledge their nuclear capability, and the Arab states would rather not have to respond publicly to its existence.

## RULES AND GOALS OF DIPLOMACY

In *Poetry and Truth,* the German poet Goethe wrote "If I had to choose between justice and disorder on the one hand, and injustice and order on the other, I would always choose the latter." Many others (notably Metternich in the nineteenth century, and the twentieth century's best-known student of Metternich, Henry Kissinger) have followed suit and made international stability a goal in itself. Diplomacy, in such hands, should not necessarily be seen as an unalloyed good in itself, since regrettable goals, not just stability but also repression and other forms of injustice, can be achieved through diplomacy. Diplomacy and techniques of negotiation in general are of special interest to us insofar as they represent nonviolent ways of resolving conflict. It is a different question, however, whether the end result of diplomacy, or other forms of conflict resolution, is a better world.

Hans Morgenthau, the twentieth century's most influential advocate of "realpolitik" in international relations, proposed nine rules for diplomacy, which he hoped would help states resolve conflicts short of war while also pursuing their own self-interest in international affairs.[7] In summary, Morgenthau's rules are as follows:

1. Do not be a crusader. Avoid "nationalistic universalism," the insistence that the goals of one's own nation warrant being the universal goals of all. As the 19th century French Foreign Minister, Talleyrand, a nineteenth-century French foreign minister put it, "pas trop de zele" (not too much zeal). One case of excessive zeal was the enthusiasm of National Security Council aides to assist the *contra* rebels in Nicaragua during the mid-1980s (the so-called Iran-contra scandal), even at the cost of illegal activities, and ultimately, great harm to U.S. influence and prestige as well as a threat to the constitutional principles within the United States itself.

2. Employ a narrow definition of vital national interests; namely, the survival and maintenance of socioeconomic well-being. Morgenthau emphasized that in the nuclear age, states cannot afford to go to war—or even to risk war—for anything short of their supreme security interests. This implies, among other things, a substantial winding down of international treaty commitments.

3. Be willing to compromise on all national interests that are not truly vital. During negotiations regarding strategic nuclear weapons, the Russian government under Boris Yeltsin made a remarkable series of compromises, agreeing to destroy asymmetrically more weapons than the United States did.

4. Try to see the other side's point of view, recognizing that the opponent will also have vital national interests and should not be pushed into compromising them.

---

[7]Morgenthau, *Politics among Nations.*

5. Distinguish between what is real and what is illusory; do not allow considerations of honor, credibility or prestige to override issues of real national security.

6. Never paint yourself into a corner; always retain avenues of retreat (or advance).

7. Do not allow an ally (especially a vulnerable one) to make decisions for you; as a corollary, do not allow yourself to be drawn into someone else's fight.

8. Always keep military factors subordinate to political ones. Remember that military planners know "nothing of that patient, intricate, and subtle maneuvering of diplomacy, whose main purpose is to avoid the absolutes of victory and defeat and meet the other side in negotiated compromise."

9. "Neither surrender to popular passions nor disregard them."

Following Napoleon's defeat in 1815, the European world entered into a period of relative stability, based in large part on the system established by the victors at the Congress of Vienna. Some of this "success" developed because all the major players accepted the agreed system as legitimate, and everyone felt about equally rewarded and equally slighted by the outcome. Morgenthau's value-free diplomacy can be criticized as being too narrowly state-centered and devoid of any moral basis. A contrasting view suggests that issues of right and wrong lie at the heart of international disputes. Unfortunately, states generally find it easier to look dispassionately at conflicts in which they are not themselves embroiled; once physically involved, the process of moralizing often becomes intense, leaving only victory as a tolerable outcome. President Woodrow Wilson had urged the participants of World War I to seek a "peace without victory" and "a peace between equals" . . . until the United States entered that war. Then, even the American Peace Society declared that "[t]his is not a war of territory, of trade routes or of commercial concerns, but of eternal principles. There can be no end of war until after the collapse of the existing German government."[8]

---

[8]Quoted in Michael Howard, *War and the Liberal Conscience* (Cambridge, Mass.: Harvard University Press).

## MAJOR FORMS OF DIPLOMACY

As a process of communication among major international actors such as states, diplomacy has evolved over time. In today's world diplomacy may take several forms: summitry, so-called Track II diplomacy, and third party involvement.

*Summitry*

Summitry is a special type or form of diplomacy involving a meeting between the leaders of two major groups, usually major states. In ancient times, leaders often were renowned warriors, and occasionally would meet person-to-person to settle their disputes via individual combat. Today leaders at a summit meeting are more likely to be political figures, and their meetings are intended to help establish or cement relationships, or to engage in personal resolution of disputes between their countries while also playing to their domestic constituencies.

Historically, the term *summit* was reserved for meetings between the leaders of the post–World War II superpowers, the United States, and the Soviet Union. It was widely thought that if only the leaders could meet and talk over their disagreements as intelligent and concerned human beings, then peace would reign. Unfortunately, history has not supported this expectation. In some cases, summit meetings have been merely cosmetic, perhaps improving the international atmosphere but offering few if any specific changes, and thereby often disappointing those who had hoped for more. The 1955 summit meeting between Nikita Khrushchev and Dwight Eisenhower falls into this category, along with the 1985 meeting between Mikhail Gorbachev and Ronald Reagan in Geneva.

At other times, minor progress has been achieved, largely by signing agreements that diplomats had laboriously worked out in advance: the 1972 summit between Richard Nixon and Leonid Brezhnev, for example, at which the SALT I agreement was signed, or the 1987 meeting in Washington, D.C., between Mikhail Gorbachev and Ronald Reagan at which an agreement to eliminate intermediate range nuclear missiles in Europe was signed.

A few summit meetings have been highly dramatic. President Nixon's meeting with Chairman Mao Tse-tung in 1972 was especially notable, as was Egyptian president Sadat's journey to Jerusalem and his meeting with Israeli prime minister Begin in 1977. In both these cases, the states involved had previously been bitter enemies, so antagonistic, in fact, that they were not even communicating directly with each other. Hence, the mere fact that political leaders met and talked amicably sent a powerful signal about the possibilities of peaceful coexistence.

Sometimes, however, summit meetings have made things worse, resulting either in feelings of ill will, or dangerous misjudgments by one or both parties. An example of the former is the 1986 summit meeting between Gorbachev and Reagan in Reykjavik, Iceland, which terminated in animosity and subsequent claims by each side that the other misunderstood and/or misrepresented what had transpired. Similarly, a summit meeting between John F. Kennedy and Nikita Khrushchev in Vienna during 1961 appears to have been a personal embarrassment for the younger, less experienced American, and it may have led to Khrushchev's inaccurate estimate that the U.S. president was weak and irresolute, thus setting the stage for the Cuban Missile Crisis the following year. It also appears to have contributed to Kennedy's determination that he would be especially tough in the future, that Khrushchev would not "push him around" again.

Even aside from summits, it is not necessarily true that closer relations and greater communication among world leaders will make war less likely. Kaiser Wilhelm of Germany and Czar Nicholas of Russia, for example, were related and on the very eve of World War I, they sent each other a flurry of telegrams signed "Willy" and "Nicky"! Summit meetings and personal relationships, in short, can be helpful, but they can also cause problems, depending on the issues and the personal dynamic between the leaders. They can also give an illusion of warmth and understanding, even when little or none actually exists.

## Track II Diplomacy

Since the late 1970s, there has been growing interest in what has been called "Track II" diplomacy, also sometimes known as "unofficial" or "encounter group" diplomacy. Track II diplomacy is unofficial in that it need not involve formal negotiations between representatives of different states; rather, it takes place in the course of relatively informal interactions among representatives of opposing groups. It contributes largely to laying the social and political groundwork needed in order for government leaders to act. It also can also represent a way of solving problems independent of the nation-states themselves.

A successful and long-standing example of Track II diplomacy is the annual series of Pugwash Conferences, international meetings that for decades have brought together scientists and students in the interest of diminishing East-West (especially nuclear) hostility. In Track II diplomacy, people are brought together for the purpose of achieving mutual understanding, exploring their commonalities as well as differences, and establishing interpersonal relationships despite the political disagreements between their "home" groups. This has been attempted, often with remarkable success, in groups of Catholics and Protestants from Northern Ireland, Greek and Turkish Cypriots, and Israelis and Palestinians. Typically, the individuals in question are relatively influential in their communities: doctors, lawyers, professors, journalists, mid-range politicians, and military officers. Success is never guaranteed and there is typically substantial distrust and often numerous minor incidents, especially at the outset. Over time, however, most of these "encounter groups" have produced positive results.

The most dramatic example of Track II techniques employed successfully at the highest levels of government occurred during the Camp David meetings in 1977. Hosted by President Jimmy Carter, who served as the facilitator, Israel's Menachem Begin and Egypt's Anwar Sadat spent thirteen days at the rustic presidential retreat in Maryland. Technically, these meetings were examples of mediation; however, they showed characteristics of Track II diplomacy in that they took place without the formalities, protocols, and rigid negotiating procedures characteristic of traditional summit meetings or bargaining sessions. Rather, there was no formal agenda, no intrusive press, and—perhaps as a result—some highly emotional interchanges. Although the Camp David meetings did not solve all Mid-East problems, or even entirely resolve the various Egyptian-Israeli disputes, they did turn out to be highly productive.

Interestingly, just as the meetings were about to end, apparently in failure, because of Prime Minister Begin's refusal to sign any accord, a breakthrough occurred: at the Israeli's request, President Carter was autographing photographs of the three Camp David participants to be given to the Israeli leader's grandchildren. President Carter personalized his autograph, dedicating each photo to one of Prime Minister Begin's grandchildren, by name. Then, as President Carter recalled,

> I handed him the photographs. He took them and thanked me. Then he happened to look down and saw that his granddaughter's name was on the top one. He spoke it aloud and then looked at each photograph individually, repeating the name of the grandchild I had written on it. His lips trembled and tears welled up in his eyes. He told me a little about each child and especially about one who seemed to be his favorite. We were both emotional as we talked quietly for a few moments about grandchildren and about war.[9]

Shortly afterward, Begin indicated his willingness to sign the accords, and the Camp David "process" ended on a strong—even euphoric—note of accommodation, agreement, and mutual respect. (The Egyptians agreed to recognize the state of Israel and to sign a peace treaty; Israel agreed to return the Sinai Peninsula to Egypt.) Although the Middle East remains a region of great tension, desperately in need of creative initiatives, including both formal and Track II diplomacy, the Camp David experience suggests reasons for hope, indicating something of the possibilities when individuals come together on a personal level, with time, goodwill, a skillful facilitator . . . and, perhaps, some luck as well.

*Third-Party Involvement*

Another major form of diplomacy is the involvement of third parties in a conflict. This entails calling in an outside expert to help clarify the issues, resolve misunderstanding, and suggest areas of compromise and common ground. A third party—unbiased and trusted by both sides—can sometimes help reach agreements for which everyone may be grateful, but which, for a variety of reasons, neither party could suggest, or even accept if it was proposed by the other.

Imagine, for example, that two adjacent states—A and B—are disputing the location of the border in a strip of land 100 km wide, between them. If A proposes placing the border right down the middle, giving 50 km to each side, then B might use this "opening" to bargain further, "splitting the difference" between them and

---

[9]Jimmy Carter, *Keeping Faith* (New York: Bantam Books, 1982). p. 104.

proposing a border so that B gets 75 km and A, 25 km. In such a case, the side that first proposes a compromise finds itself at a disadvantage. One obvious solution, therefore, is for a third state, C, to propose independently that A and B agree to 50 km for each. Unfortunately, international disputes are rarely this simple: there are historical considerations, social factors, political passions, military alliances, and economic values of the region in question as well as geographic factors such as marshes, rivers, or mountains, and the like, to take into account. It is also important to bear in mind that disputes always occur on at least two levels: (1) the specific issue under dispute and (2) the underlying question of who wins, who is more powerful—and what this portends for subsequent interactions.

**Acting as Go-Betweens.**    One way third parties can be helpful to disputants is to serve as go-betweens, providing what is known as their "good offices." This may simply involve making a meeting place available on neutral ground. A long-standing dispute between Austria and Italy over control of the Tyrol, a German-speaking region, formerly Austrian but (since World War I) part of Italy, was resolved in 1969 at negotiations held in Denmark. It is typically important that such meetings occur on neutral turf insofar as the disputing parties are concerned. The neutral states of Austria, and particularly Switzerland, have often made themselves available as sites for settlement of international disputes. When in doubt, international diplomats typically meet in Geneva, Switzerland.

During the Falklands/Malvinas War (1982), the United States considered itself allied to both combatants, Argentina and Great Britain. Secretary of State Alexander Haig accordingly sought to interpose himself between the two sides, offering to act as an "honest broker." His efforts were unsuccessful, however, despite numerous trans-Atlantic flights, in part because the United States was perceived to be more supportive of Britain. Similarly, Henry Kissinger engaged in generally unsuccessful "shuttle diplomacy" between Israel and her Arab neighbors during the early and middle 1970s.

As of the early 1990s, no Arab governments—except for that of Egypt—officially recognize the state of Israel, which in turn refuses to negotiate with the Palestine Liberation Organization, thereby making it especially important for third parties to provide a means of communication between the Israelis and Arabs. Of course, when the third party is a high-ranking representative of a major power, he or she presumably does not merely act as a messenger, but also can engage in various forms of arm-twisting such as threatening to cut off economic or military aid unless some proposed compromises are accepted. This suggests why some forms of diplomacy are best conducted in secret: it may be politically unacceptable, for example, for a state to appear to knuckle under to such pressure, although it may be better for everyone concerned if it does so.

During 1967, Greece and Turkey—both U.S. allies and NATO members—were threatening to go to war over Cyprus. The U.S. emissary, Cyrus Vance, eventually succeeded in persuading both sides to step down their military preparations and to accept an expanded role for the United Nations peacekeeping force already on that island. Soviet premier Aleksey Kosygin was similarly successful in inducing India and Pakistan to terminate their second Kashmir War (1966), in part by secret arm-twisting.

**Fact-Finding.**    Third parties, if they have the respect of the contenders, can also serve a valuable role as "fact finders," ascertaining, for example, whether or not a disputed border was crossed, the number of political prisoners in specified jails, the size of military forces, or the economic situation in a particular region. International organizations, notably the United Nations, have been especially helpful in this respect, establishing various "commissions of inquiry" to evaluate conflicting claims. There are certain cases in which basic facts are in dispute, but in others the disagreement is over values—over, not what is true, but what is right.

**Mediation and Arbitration.**    Perhaps the most important role for third parties is to facilitate the use of two key diplomatic processes, in managing international conflict, mediation and arbitration. Mediators make suggestions that might be agreeable to both sides. Like marriage counselors, mediators try to resolve disputes, but adherence to their suggestions is entirely voluntary. By contrast, in the case of arbitration, both sides agree in advance to accept the independent judgement of the arbitrator. Mediation therefore involves less of a threat to sovereignty; it is accordingly less radical and more often acceptable to contending states. A third procedure, adjudication, is also sometimes included here. Adjudication involves making decisions with reference to international law

There is nothing new in the practices of mediation and arbitration. They were especially frequent in Europe during the late Middle Ages, from about the thirteenth century to the fifteenth century. Apparently, this period of successful third-party involvement was due to several factors, some of which at least might be replicated today: family ties among diverse political leaders were common (not uncommonly, heads of state were cousins or even closer—an unlikely situation in the modern world); the economic costs of war were widely recognized to be exceptionally high, and local treasuries often teetered on the edge of bankruptcy; and finally, a powerful third party was available to aid in the settling of disputes, namely, the Catholic Church and its emissaries.

An added advantage to mediation and arbitration in these cases is that a third party can sometimes succeed in fashioning a solution that both contending parties find acceptable, but neither would be willing to propose for fear of being seen as too conciliatory, and thus, weak. Opposing governments often face a dilemma. Even when a compromise is feasible, both sides want to project an image of power. Accordingly, the mediator or arbitrator can suggest something that, privately, both sides want but that neither is willing to propose. President Theodore Roosevelt won a Nobel Peace Prize for his successful mediation between Russia and Japan, which ended the Russo-Japanese War. During the Geneva Conference of 1955—which ended the French occupation of Indochina—Britain, China, and the Soviet Union mediated between France and the Viet Minh. In this case, as with many others, it can certainly be argued that mediation did not resolve the dispute; it only postponed it. At least in the eyes of the North Vietnamese, and many in the south as well, the United States essentially replaced France as colonial occupier of Indochina, leading to the Vietnam War. But as Winston Churchill once noted, "Jaw, jaw, jaw is better than war, war, war." Sometimes, moreover, there can be a real advantage simply in postponing war if, over time, passions cool and peaceful solutions eventually become possible.

At other times, of course, mediation is altogether successful. During the 1980s, the Vatican successfully interceded between Argentina and Chile, for example, defusing a border dispute that threatened to escalate into war. One of the best known cases of binding arbitration, dating to the U.S. Civil War, is that of the so-called *Alabama* claim. This arose after a Confederate warship was purchased (illegally) in Britain, a neutral country, during war. The U.S. government subsequently demanded reparations for the damage done to U.S. shipping by the *Alabama* and other similar ships, and in 1872 both sides consented to arbitration. An independent panel eventually awarded the U.S. more than $15 million in damages, which Britain paid, thereby lowering tensions between the two countries. In fact, the now-close relationship between Britain and the U.S. can be counted as beginning with this successful arbitration.

In 1965, India and Pakistan nearly went to war over the Rann of Kutch, a thirty-five thousand square mile salt marsh. Britain mediated this dispute, getting the two sides to agree to arbitration. A three-member panel was set up: one member was nominated by India, one by Pakistan, and one by the U.N. secretary-general. A decision was made, to which both sides have subsequently abided. (When the two countries later went to war, it was for other reasons.) After Egypt and Israel signed a peace treaty calling for a return of the Sinai to Egypt in exchange for recognition of Israel, the two countries continued to dispute ownership of a small but valuable stretch of beachfront on the Red Sea. They finally agreed to arbitration, and in 1988, a panel gave most of this property to Egypt.

Because of its status and reputation for impartiality, the United Nations has often been asked to act as a third party and mediate or arbitrate disputes among states. U.N. mediators were very active, for example, in arranging for the Soviet withdrawal from Afghanistan and working toward solution of the disputed region of western Sahara, and overseeing peaceful elections in Angola. On the other hand, third party mediation has failed in such cases as the civil war in the former Yugoslavia, in which one side felt that it had more to gain by military force, and the mediator—the United Nations—did not have authority to impose a solution.

## NEGOTIATING TECHNIQUES FOR RESOLVING CONFLICT

There are numerous negotiating techniques available to diplomats engaged in the attempt to manage or end an international dispute. In 1964, Fred Ikle, an American policy analyst, wrote an influential book entitled *How Nations Negotiate*.[10] Ikle argued that if negotiations are to help resolve international conflict, rather than become arenas for yet more conflict, negotiations must be seen as a means whereby contending parties seek to resolve their differences, not to prevail over each other. Put another way, negotiations must be seen as non–zero sum solutions, interactions in which my gain is not necessarily balanced by your loss, or vice versa. Negotiations should aim to achieve "win-win" solutions in which all sides are better off than they were before.

The most obvious, and in some cases the most common, negotiating technique is to seek compromise; that is, to reach an agreement that is midway between the demands of both sides. There are several disadvantages to this, however. For one thing, a compromise may leave both sides dissatisfied. In some cases, this may actually be desirable, so that a "fair" decision may be defined—only somewhat tongue in cheek—as one that leaves everyone equally unhappy. But it may be that, in fact, one side's claim is just and the other's is unjust; in such a case, a compromise simply rewards the unjust side while penalizing the just one. Compromise assumes that both contenders are equally worthy, so that "splitting the difference" between them will produce a fair settlement. But what if state A arbitrarily insists, for example, that it is entitled to impose a 50 percent tariff upon all imports from state B, but refuses to allow B to tax its imports? Clearly a "compromise" that allows a one-sided 25 percent tariff would not be fair and is unlikely to be acceptable—at least, not to state B.

In certain cases, however, one side can "win" without the other "losing." For example, Franco-German relations were bedeviled through the first half of the twentieth century by a dispute over ownership of the Saar region, a rich industrial sector of the Rhineland. Following World War I, occupation and mining rights to the Saar were ceded to France; French control was reasserted after World War II. But the region's population was (and still is) overwhelmingly German, and the governments in Paris and Bonn eventually cooperated to resolve this issue: after a plebiscite in 1955, France permitted the Saar to rejoin West Germany. This negotiated agreement, in which France ostensibly "lost," served everyone

---

[10]Fred Charles Ikle, *How Nations Negotiate* (New York: Harper and Row, 1964).

well, since it proved to be a cornerstone for subsequent Franco-German cooperation and friendship.

## Positional versus Integrative Bargaining

Compromises are often the outcome of what has been called "positional bargaining," in which each side stakes out a position and then holds to it. Positional bargaining does not fit Ikle's criterion that diplomatic negotiations should produce win-win situations, because its very dynamic does not encourage flexibility and reasonable stances or attitudes. Rather, the side that is most intransigent is the one that is rewarded, and willingness to compromise (or even to suggest compromise) is penalized. Thus, in "positional bargaining" the participants are rewarded for staking out a "hard" position and sticking to it, and they are penalized, in turn, for being "soft." As a result, "good" bargainers are those who remain relatively intransigent—that is, who make it difficult or unlikely that an agreement will be reached. Fortunately, there is an alternative approach to negotiating known as "integrative bargaining"[11] or "principled negotiating."[12]

Table 5.1 helps clarify the differences between positional bargaining, with its "hard" and "soft" approaches, and principled negotiating.

Integrative or principled bargaining tries, among other things, to separate the actual dispute from the underlying interests of each side. The goal is to focus on the latter and avoid getting bogged down in the former. As Roger Fisher and William Ury recount, consider the story of two sisters who quarrelled over an orange; they decided, finally, to compromise, each getting one half. One sister then proceeded to squeeze her half for juice while the other used the peel from her portion to flavor a cake. By compromising—restarting to an old and honorable solution—they overlooked the integrative solution of giving one all the peel and the other all the juice.

Or imagine that two states disagree over a boundary. It may be that the real dispute is not over territory as such but rather over one state's desire for access to certain transportation routes and the other's worry that granting such access would diminish its military

---

[11]R. E. Walton and A. B. McKersie, *A Behavioral Theory of Labor Negotiations* (New York: McGraw-Hill, 1965).

[12]R. Fisher and W. Ury, *Getting to Yes.* (Boston: Houghton Mifflin, 1981).

## TABLE 5.1
Approaches to Bargaining

| Positional Bargaining | | Principled Negotiating |
|---|---|---|
| Hard | Soft | |
| Participants are adversaries | Participants are friends | Participants are problem solvers |
| The goal is victory | The goal is an agreement | The goal is a wise outcome |
| Demand concessions to maintain the relationship | Make concessions to cultivate the relationship | Separate the people from the problem |
| Be hard on the problem and on the people | Be soft on the people and on the problem | Be soft on the people, hard on the problem |
| Distrust others | Trust others | Proceed independently of the trust |
| Dig in to your position | Change your position easily | Focus on interests, not positions |
| Make threats | Make offers | Explore interests |
| Mislead as to your bottom line | Disclose your bottom-line | Avoid having a bottom line |
| Demand one-sided gains as the price of agreement | Accept one-sided losses as the price of agreement | Invent options for mutual benefit |
| Search for the one solution *you* will later accept | Search for the one solution *they* will accept | Develop multiple options to choose from |
| Insist on your position | Insist on agreement | Insist on objective criteria |
| Try to win a contest of wills | Try to avoid a contest of wills | Try to reach an agreement based on interests, not wills |
| Apply pressure | Avoid pressure | Yield to principle, not pressure; reason and be open to reasons. |

Source: Modified slightly from R. Fisher and W. Ury, *Getting to Yes* (Boston: Houghton Mifflin, 1981).

security. In such a case, integrative bargaining would seek to identify the underlying issues and solve them directly, perhaps reaching an understanding in which the needs of both sides are integrated into one solution, for example, access to the desired transportation routes for an agreed annual fee, along with a bilateral treaty specifying strict limitations on the nature of the vehicles or number of personnel permitted to travel along them.

There are numerous tactics that may be employed by negotiators seeking to bridge differences between contending sides.[13] They include such things as focussing on the shared interests of all parties rather than the demands as such, diminishing the role of personalities (that is, separating the people from the problem), and "fractionating" the conflict, which is analogous to medical triage, i.e., separating a dispute into intractable components and others that may be resolvable, then working on the latter. The whole process, if successful, contributes to "confidence building," which increases the probability that more difficult issues will be solved in the future. Having made some degree of progress, by building on the easier cases, the disputants are likely to be all the more energetic and optimistic about achieving additional success and, perhaps, less likely to resort to violence in the event of failure.

Certain disputes—such as that in the story of the oranges—have a high "integrative potential" in that they inherently lend themselves to agreements that leave all parties entirely satisfied. Other cases are more difficult, for example, if buyer and seller disagree over the price of a house. Even here, however, there is room for integrative agreements: modifications in the interest rate, the date of occupancy, the amount of principle to be paid off by certain dates, and so forth. In such cases, it may be possible to integrate the interests of both sides, essentially by reaching agreement on other dimensions aside from those initially in dispute (in this case, the purchase price).

## Methods for Integrative Bargaining

Let us now examine five different methods[14] by which integrative agreements might be reached, taking as an example a hypothetical

---

[13]See, for example, Fisher and Ury, *Getting to Yes.*

[14]The methods are derived from Dean G. Pruitt, "Achieving Integrative Agreements in Negotiation," in *Negotiating in Organizations*, ed. M. H. Bazerman and R. J. Lewicki (Beverly Hills: Sage Publications, 1983).

dispute between a husband and wife over where to spend their two-week vacation: the wife wants to go to the seashore, and the husband to the mountains. One solution is to compromise and spend one week at each; they would like, however, to find something better.

**Expanding the Pie.** Sometimes, solutions can be achieved by increasing the amount of a resource in short supply. Perhaps the couple could arrange to take four weeks of vacation, thereby spending two weeks at each location. This is not as utopian as it may seem, since expanding the pie need not necessarily involve getting something for nothing. Thus, if they value their vacations enough, it might be possible to work overtime during the rest of the year to pay for them. For such solutions to work, however, it is necessary that each party not find the other's preferred outcome to be aversive; that is, it could work if each objects to the other's preference, not because of something in the choice itself, but rather because it prevents him or her from doing the other. Specifically, the husband must be able to tolerate going to the seashore, and the wife the mountains. Solutions of this sort are largely based on efforts to help each side get what it wants and to do so by increasing the amount of a limited resource: time, money, land, people, security, hard currency, and so on. (To some extent, the United States has expanded the pie in the Middle East, rewarding both Israel and Egypt for their peaceful behavior by providing generous economic aid to each country.)

**Nonspecific Compensation.** In this case, one party "gives in," but is repaid in some other way. The husband, for example, may agree to go to the seashore, but only if he is relieved of housecleaning chores for the next four months. Or, a country may permit a neighbor to flood its markets with exported goods, if the exporting country agrees to continue providing a certain number of jobs for citizens of the importing country. Solutions of this sort require information about what is particularly valued by both parties and what one party may be able (and willing) to provide to another in return for getting its way. An important factor is whether there exists some form of compensation that may be of low cost to the donor and high value to the recipient: perhaps the wife doesn't particularly mind doing the husband's share of the housecleaning, at least for a few months, and perhaps the exporting country actually needs the labor skills of the importer.

**Logrolling.** If both parties have differing issues within the main ones under dispute, and if they differ in the priorities regarding these issues, then the possibility exists for creative "logrolling," which is in a sense a variant of nonspecific compensation. For example, perhaps the husband-wife disagreement over vacations also involved differences of opinion about the preferred accomodations: let us say that the wife prefers simple, rustic beach cottages, whereas the husband is looking forward to an elegant mountain resort. Perhaps, then, the husband will be quite happy going to the seashore, so long as the wife agrees that they stay in an elegant seaside resort, or alternatively, maybe a rustic cabin—desired by the wife—in the mountains (preferred by the husband). For solutions based on logrolling to be developed, it helps to identify exchangeable concessions and especially to ask, Are some of my low-priority issues of high priority to the other party? or vice versa.

**Cost Cutting.** Solutions based on cost-cutting are those in which one party essentially succeeds in "winning," but the costs to the other party are reduced or eliminated. Thus, cost-cutting solutions are more one-sided than those discussed above, but they are nonetheless feasible and potentially stable if the side that "gives in" truly does not suffer any disadvantage from the agreement. In the case of the husband-wife vacation dispute, perhaps the husband had resisted going to the seashore because he feared being lonely and isolated while his wife was windsurfing; in this case, a cost-cutting solution—and one that could be entirely satisfactory to the husband—might be for the couple to agree to go to the seashore, but to do so along with some of their friends who could provide company for the husband.

Cost-cutting differs from "nonspecific compensation" in that it involves a kind of "specific compensation," a particular kind of recompense directed toward one of the parties, but not really compensation for a painful outcome so much as a way of making the agreement agreeable for the "loser." For cost-cutting to be successful, there must be clarity as to the reasons either side opposes the desires of the other as well as openness (especially on the part of the side giving in) to considering ways in which it might be possible to give in without really losing.

**Bridging.** Bridging occurs when the two parties agree to a solution in which neither side wins or loses: both agree to a different option from the ones each originally favored. This solution must meet the primary interests that actually underlie the specific issues in dispute. Thus, if the husband wanted to go to the mountains to hike, and the wife wanted to go to the seashore for the sun, perhaps it would be possible to find a beach resort near hiking trails (or a vacation site where the mountains are dry and sunny). Successful bridging requires that the parties refocus their negotiations from an insistence on their *positions* to an examination of their underlying *interests*: Why are they pushing for their particular position? Is there some alternative outcome that would meet their actual needs? Is it really the mountains, or the seashore, that you want, or does that site simply provide a means of achieving some other goal?

A fundamental principle underlying all of these diverse solutions is that perceived conflicts of interest may be illusory; in many cases, it is possible to obtain good agreements (i.e., solutions that are beneficial to both sides) without either party having to give in, without there being a winner and a loser, and—most important for our purposes—without violence. Moreover, because such solutions respect the fundamental interests of each side, they also avoid instilling resentment, which so often sows the seeds of violence in the future.

## OTHER FACTORS AFFECTING
## DIPLOMATIC NEGOTIATIONS

Diplomacy is a complex enterprise that can be affected by many factors. For example, apparently trivial details can become surprisingly influential in diplomacy. In some cases, attention to the physical arrangement of participants may be important: thus, it can even be helpful to seat the contenders on the same side of a table—opposite the mediator, whose job is to articulate the disagreement—thereby literally facing the problem together, rather then contentiously facing each other. This sometimes encourages both sides to cooperate rather than compete, to concentrate on defining the problem and then solving it, rather than defeating each other. In other cases, a wise conflict resolver will simply ignore uncooperative statements rather than allow them to derail an agreement; during the Cuban Missile Crisis, for example, the U.S. government received two communications from Soviet premier Nikita Khrushchev, one conciliatory and the other belligerent. At

Robert Kennedy's suggestion, the United States simply ignored the latter and responded to the former.

Clarity is generally a virtue; in some cases, negotiated agreements come unravelled or become a source of irritation when they are interpreted differently by the different parties. For example, Britain and the United States felt that the Soviet Union had agreed at the Yalta Conference toward the end of World War II to allow a pluralistic democracy in postwar Poland. Soviet diplomats (and some U.S. participants as well), on the other hand, recalled the event differently. It is also possible, however, that if the expectations and intentions of each side had been spelled out in detail, an even greater falling out would have occurred. Part of the negotiator's art may therefore include recourse to equivocal and imprecise language. Lester Pearson, a Canadian diplomat who won the Nobel Peace Prize, put it this way:

> I know that there have been occasions, and I have been concerned with one or two, when, as the lesser of two evils, words were used in recording the results of negotiations or discussions whose value lay precisely in the fact that they were imprecise, that they could be interpreted somewhat freely and therefore could be used not so much to record agreement as to conceal a disagreement which it was desired to play down and which, it was hoped, would disappear in time.[15]

In order to avoid misunderstandings, it can be useful for a negotiator to request that each side state, as clearly as it can, the arguments of the other. This can help build empathy, a deeper awareness and appreciation of the other's perspective and of the constraints felt by the other. (In serious disputes, each side is often intensely aware of the limitations on its own behavior, while considering that the opponent has great latitude; failure to reach agreement then seems fairly attributed to the other's intransigence.)

Adequate empathy can lead to another helpful exercise, the "yesable proposition."[16] In this case, each party to a dispute is asked to consider formulating a proposition that the other side is likely to accept. This is a subtle but important shift: in most cases,

---

[15]B. Pearson, *Diplomacy in the Nuclear Age* (Cambridge, Mass.: Harvard University Press, 1949).

[16]R. Fisher, *International Conflict for Beginners* (New York: Harper and Row, 1969).

each side makes demands—indeed, the nature of the negotiating process encourages them to do so—that are likely to be outrageous and unacceptable. In the search for yesable propositions, both sides are more likely to uncover shared interests based on which a mutually acceptable outcome might become clear. Famed negotiator Roger Fisher, for example, recounted that he once asked Egyptian president Gamal Abdel Nasser and Israeli premier Golda Meir what they wanted from the other that the other could conceivably agree to; neither had seriously considered this question.

In the course of seeking an agreement, it can be helpful to make proposals through an intermediary—often a low-ranking one—so that they can be disowned if the other side rejects it out of hand. This avoids the embarrassment that could result from acrimony and ridicule; by being able to deny that any such opening was ever made, either side may be more willing to make an initial attempt. For example, during the Cuban Missile Crisis, Premier Khrushchev chose a low-ranking Soviet embassy official to convey his proposal: removal of Soviet missiles from Cuba in return for a U.S. pledge not to invade that island. In addition, this message was sent via a news broadcaster rather than directly to U.S. officials.

Secrecy can also play a role in diplomatic negotiations. Historically, many of the crucial aspects of diplomacy have been carried out largely in secret. Secrecy was subsequently blamed, by many, for the errors and miscalculations that led to World War I, and President Woodrow Wilson accordingly called for "open covenants openly arrived at." On the other hand, although secret diplomacy sounds inherently unpalatable, especially to a democratic society, it remains true that when conducted in public, negotiating isn't conducive to compromise. Each side fears appearing soft, or a dupe, and is inclined to play to domestic public opinion, making arguments and advancing proposals that may be politically popular, even if it knows that other solutions may be fairer, and even more desirable. So, there is much to be said for diplomacy that is carried out not so much in "secret" as under a mutual understanding that not every offer and counteroffer will be leaked to the waiting world.

There are many additional suggestions. For example: avoid ultimatums, do not impugn the motives of the other side, try to keep from playing to the crowds, be flexible but not spineless, avoid *ad hominem* (personal) attacks, avoid nonnegotiable ploys, and do not be so desperate for agreement that you sacrifice future peace for short-term palliatives. In his inauguration address, President John Kennedy said: "We shall not negotiate out of fear, but we shall never fear to negotiate." The second part sounds just fine, but it is not at all clear why we or anyone else should refrain from negotiating out of fear. It is precisely when fear is greatest—fear that a conflict situation might get out of hand—that serious and creative negotiations are most needed. Ideally, of course, the process would have begun long before a difficult situation becomes a tense, fear-inducing crisis.

What counts, in the long run, is reaching agreements without either side giving in, or resorting to violence. Sometimes it may be possible, even desirable, to paper over disagreements so as to buy time for new events to unfold or for old disputes to grow stale. And of course, there is no guarantee that all disputes can be resolved by negotiations. A positive outcome, for example, requires a degree of good will and a genuine desire to reach an agreement. It also requires willingness to "bargain in good faith," and there have been cases in which good faith was not shown. For example, the Soviet government in 1939 was openly negotiating with Britain and France for a mutual defense pact against Nazi Germany while, at the same time, it secretly organized the now-infamous nonaggression pact that briefly allied Stalin with Hitler and paved the way for Germany's invasion of Poland. Similarly, Japanese diplomats were negotiating with their U.S. counterparts on December 7, 1941, when Japanese forces attacked Pearl Harbor. And when, in 1955, Soviet negotiators accepted U.S. disarmament proposals, complete with international verification procedures, the U.S. delegation put a "reservation" on those proposals—in other words, having been accepted, they were withdrawn!

Nonetheless, there is good reason to believe that such cases are exceptions. The desire for nonviolent resolution of conflicts is, if anything, stronger and more widespread today than at any time in the past. In addition, other factors—domestic opinion, international law, international organizations, the shared costs of violence—combine to make nonviolent conflict resolution an attractive alternative to the use of force, so long as the participants (including the mediator if there is one) is both skillful and persistent.

Ultimately, belief in the feasibility of nonviolent conflict resolution —whether by diplomacy or negotiation, between two parties or with the assistance of a mediator or arbitrator—is just that, an exercise of faith: faith in the underlying good will of people and in their fundamental rationality. Such faith may or may not be warranted. Certainly, the human species has long displayed a penchant for irrational acts, personal as well as collective. But skeptics might consider that the alternative—war—is usually no more rational. And moreover, if it seems unrealistic to rely on the rationality of one's opponents, bear in mind that the fundamental peace-keeping strategy of the nuclear age—deterrence—has long relied precisely on a hefty dose of rationality and mutual dependence. How much better, therefore, to employ these considerations in the pursuit of conflict resolution rather than conflict prolongation or, worse yet, violence as the final arbiter of disputes.

## ANNOTATED BIBLIOGRAPHY

Burton, John. *Conflict and Communication*. London: Macmillan, 1969.
A reasoned analysis of the ways international communication can contribute either to the resolution of conflict or to its prolongation.

Fisher, Roger, and William Ury. *Getting to Yes*. Boston: Houghton Mifflin Co., 1981.
A simple, concise modern classic, describing how creative approaches to problem solving can operate in the interpersonal as well as international realm.

Ikle, Fred Charles. *How Nations Negotiate*. New York: Harper and Row, 1964.
An example of the cold war style of contentious, positional bargaining.

Nicholson, Harold. *Diplomacy*. New York: Oxford University Press, 1955.
The classic historical account and description of diplomacy.

Pruitt, D. G. *Negotiation Behavior*. New York: Academic Press, 1981.
Useful suggestions and examples of techniques in resolving disagreements, with attention to psychological and social processes.

CHAPTER 6

# Economic Cooperation and International Conflict

## Karen Mingst

All states and peoples of today's world have a direct stake in the global economy. Whether rich or poor, large or small, every country tries to find ways to function in the interconnected system of markets that span the globe and to avoid possible conflicts related to economic issues and problems. In this chapter we look at major forms of international cooperation states use to deal with economic issues.

Just what is the relationship between economics and international conflict? Some theorists explain all international conflict with reference to economic forces and suggest that only major economic changes will lead to the elimination of war. For example, Karl Marx posited that conflict arises inevitably from the clash between socioeconomic classes—those controlling the means of production, the capitalists, and those forced into a subservient relationship. To John Hobson, the capitalist classes are faced with the need to reinvest surplus capital abroad—the result being *imperialism*. To Lenin, imperialism was a special advanced stage of capitalism. Lenin argued that the exporters of capital are able to obtain economic advantages based on exploitation. War, then, is a function of capitalist imperialism, necessary—even beneficial to—capitalists. Lenin claimed that war will disappear only when capitalism is destroyed and socialism is triumphant.

Other theorists see the relationship between the economic system and war and peace quite differently. For example, Norman Angell, the 1933 recipient of the Nobel Peace Prize, argued in favor of stimulating free trade among capitalistic states. According to Angell enhanced trade would be in the economic self-interest of all. National differences would vanish due to the world market; interdependence would flourish. Interdependence would lead to economic well-being and eventually world peace, with war becoming an anachronism. And world trade is the mechanism.

Another group, the functionalists, have posited that economic disparity, the gap between the rich and poor, is the major cause of international conflict. David Mitrany, a civil servant working on maritime cooperation between the United States and Great Britain during World War I, proposed that cooperation (for him, world peace) could best be achieved if economic development occurred. Economic differences had to be erased.

In each of these theories, writers suggest that economics and international conflict are closely related. Each finds a solution that will lead to elimination of conflict—for the Marxists, the move to socialism; for the free trade liberals, the promotion of free trade; and for the functionalists, the elimination of economic disparity through economic development. In actuality, the cooperative behaviors emanating from these theoretical perspectives are not as analytically distinct as the theorists would have us believe.

## ECONOMIC CONFLICT
## AND INTERNATIONAL COOPERATION

There are a wide variety of economic problems and disparities, such as balance of trade deficits, that can cause international conflict. How do states in the modern world seek to manage, resolve, and avoid conflict over economic matters? Why would states choose to cooperate on economic matters when there is an absence of a central authority to enforce cooperative agreements? What international cooperative behaviors are especially relevant for dealing with economic issues?

States choose to cooperate for several reasons. First, they do so because of mutuality of interests—cooperation offers more potential gains than expected losses. Second, they do so because of expectations that states will continue to interact in the future; there may be costs to be paid in the future for refusing to cooperate. Third, as the number of states increase, and most issues in global politics involve more than two players, opportunities for cooperation increase.

Once states have decided to cooperate, in what form does cooperation occur? By "cooperation" among states we mean states acting in a conscious way to adjust or change policy in keeping with what they believe is their national interest and consistent with reducing the negative consequences for other states. What actions are taken that can be classified as cooperative behavior? We can identify five cooperative behaviors that are particularly relevant to economic issues. These behaviors form a rough continuum from least to most demanding in terms of the degree of interaction and potential change they require in a state's behavior. They are: participating in international negotiations, policy coordination, developing international regimes, joining formal international governmental organizations, and engaging in regional integration. Table 6.1 presents the typology and cites pertinent examples. In what fol-

TABLE 6.1
Types of Cooperative Behavior

| | |
|---|---|
| International negotiations | New International Economic Order |
| | trade in commodities |
| | debt, foreign aid |
| | technology transfer |
| Policy coordination | Macro-economic summitry |
| | Scandinavian coordination |
| International regimes | Trade (GATT) |
| | Food |
| | Nuclear non-proliferation |
| International organizations | |
| intergovernmental | International Monetary Fund |
| | World Bank |
| | Un Development Program |
| | International Labor Organization |
| | World Health Organization |
| | U.N. Conf. on Trade/Development |
| nongovernmental | CARE |
| | World Catholic Relief |
| | Oxfam European Community |
| Multinational operations | North American Free Trade Agreement |
| and regional integration | Central American Common Market |
| | Economic Community of West African States |

lows we look at how each of these forms of cooperation is used to deal with major international economic issues.

## INTERNATIONAL NEGOTIATIONS

*Negotiation* is the process of discussing or bargaining in order to reach agreement on a subject of common interest. Just as individuals negotiate with family and friends on different issues for many reasons, states negotiate for a variety of different reasons. They may want to perpetuate relationships that already function well, for example, extend tariff agreements. Such negotiations typically involve little conflict. Or they may want to formalize arrangements already tacitly arrived at. States may use negotiation for the purpose of demanding major changes—alterations in economic relationships and enhanced political influence or institutional power. For example, the marathon negotiations in the 1970s and early 1980s over the Law of the Sea brought up many issues that could have altered the economic relations between the technically advanced and technologically developing countries. The mining of the seabed is one such issue—an issue that led the Reagan administration in 1982 to refuse to sign the Law of the Sea Treaty. Such negotiations were intense as power among members was questioned. While different levels of potential conflict are present, it is through the process of negotiation that these conflicts are diffused, contained, managed, or perhaps resolved. Or alternatively, negotiations may break down.

## The Case of the New International Economic Order

The economic gap between the developed countries of the North and the less developed countries of the South has been well documented. Data from 1987 confirm that the large industrialized states had a GNP per capita of $14,670; the low- and middle-income states a GNP per capita of $700. On quality of life indicators, the gap between rich and poor is dramatically exposed. Infant mortality per thousand live births is nine in the developed world and seventy-one in the less developed; life expectancy at birth is seventy-six years in the developed versus sixty-two years in the developing world, and percentage of students enrolled in secondary education (an indicator of future economic potential) is 93 percent in the developed versus 40 percent in the developing countries.

Given these wide economic disparities, it was not surprising that the South has sought dramatic changes in the international economic system, beginning with the establishment of the United Nations Conference on Trade and Development (UNCTAD) and the Group of 77, a coalition of less-developed countries, in 1964. During the late 1960s, this group adopted the Charter of Algiers, advocating global economic change; the group brought their demands of the Sixth Special Session of the United Nations in May 1974 in the "Charter of Economic Rights and Duties of States"—signaling the demand for a *New International Economic Order*.

**Demands by the South.** The South sought changes in six major areas of international economic relations. First and most importantly, they sought changes in international trade, including adjustment in the **terms of trade**—altering (stabilizing and then raising the price of exports from the South including such primary com-modities as coffee, cocoa, bauxite, tin, and sugar—to keep up with the price of capital goods and finished products (e.g., computers, automobiles, machinery) being imported in from the developed world. Change in the unfavorable terms of trade from the perspec-tive of the South could be achieved through indexation, regulation of prices, and the establishment of commodity cartels and multi-lateral commodity agreements, most prominently a common fund. In addition, the North needed to eliminate tariff barriers to prod-ucts from the developing countries in order to stimulate trade.

Second, the Group of 77 demanded greater regulation of *multi-national corporations* (MNCs)—some ten thousand giant cor-porations with upwards of ninety thousand subsidiaries. Accord-ing to their critics, multinationals expropriate local resources; local governments lose control over their economic life and find their political choices circumscribed. Yet MNCs do possess needed technology, and thus the third demand of the South was for better ways for that technology to be transferred. It needed to be cheaper and more appropriate for the population, and new research and development facilities needed to be established in the countries of the South. Since multinational corporations do not fulfill their responsibilities in these areas, governmental arrangements would need to be negotiated.

Fourth, the South was overburdened with debt. Weighted un-der by repayment schedules, countries of the South were unable to use new earnings to reinvest in economic development projects. By the mid1980s, this problem became even more severe. The debt service ratio—the ratio of the principal and interest due on debts to total export earnings- was 47 percent for Latin American states, while African countries and Middle Eastern states had ratios of 27 percent and 26 percent, respectively. The South demanded compre-hensive solutions—restructuring debt burdens, reducing interest rates, and canceling debt. To develop further in light of the eco-nomic deficits, the fifth demand of the South was to receive in-creased foreign aid and to improve the terms and conditions of this aid: grants and untied aid was the preferred method of financial assistance.

Finally, advocates of the NIEO sought changes in international organization structures, specifically the international financial in-stitutions such as the World Bank and the International Monetary

Fund with their *weighted voting schemes*. These suggested changes sought to alter or at least modify the basic power relationships in international affairs.

**Response to the Demands.** During the 1970s and 1980s, there were a whole series of international negotiations—both ad hoc and continuous, some international and others regional—which have attempted to respond to these demands. For example, the Seventh Special Session of the U.N. General Assembly was held in September 1975, the Conference on International Economic Cooperation ran from December 1975 to June 1977, and the Brandt Commission and the Independent Commission on International Development Issues were both held in 1977.

**NIEO Outcomes.**    On some issues, the South has partially achieved its goals, although usually in more limited regional form in and on a unilateral basis. With respect to the commodity trade, in 1975, the Lome Agreements were signed between members of the European Community and a group of countries in the South, the African, Caribbean, and Pacific (ACP) countries, mostly former colonies of European countries. In that agreement, the ACP was given *preferential access* to European markets for both agricultural and manufacturing goods, and a commodity price stabilization system was instituted to meet emergency conditions. To a lesser extent, the United States unilaterally responded with the 1974 Trade Act—a system of preferences for some two thousand goods from poor countries. Similarly, in 1982 the United States responded with the Caribbean Basin Initiative, giving preferential access to American markets to poor countries in the region. But the most sweeping of the South's trading demands—a linked common fund and formally changing the terms of trade—were not met.

Similarly, the demands for controls of multinational corporations and transfer of technology were negotiated in a number of different arenas, mostly at the regional level. For example, in 1976, the Organization for Economic Cooperation and Development (OECD) countries, mostly western developed states, concluded a voluntary code of conduct for multinational corporations, specifically forbidding their participation in host country political activities, but means of enforcement were few. The OECD did establish a Center on Transnational Corporations under the auspices of the United Nations. This center was designed to disseminate information about activities of multinational corporations. Originally the South had something more in mind. Regulation of multinationals has actually come from the South. States have become more selective about which corporations will be permitted. Some, like Nigeria and Mexico, have required certain percentages of local control. States have unilaterally negotiated more lucrative contracts with these corporations—-higher taxes, more reinvestment of profits—-objectives that were to be achieved through multilateral means.

The debt issue was greeted initially during the 1970s negatively by the North; debt cancellation was unacceptable—not subject to negotiation. But during the late 1970s and 1980s, debt restructuring, based on implementation of domestic reforms, became essential. Under the guidance of the International Monetary Fund, negotiations were conducted on a country-by-country basis for debt restructuring with "conditions" imposed. While this did not occur multilaterally as the South preferred, some broad-ranging plans for debt restructuring were initiated. Most visible was Brady Plan, backed by the United States. Several provisions represented innovative approaches to dealing with the problem. Lending institutions were to assist poorer countries with loans to pay off a portion of their debt to commercial banks at a discount. Debt-equity swaps were encouraged—trading the debt owned to a bank for stock in a country's industry. Debt-commodity swaps were developed, with banks forming export companies to export debtors' commodities, retaining some of the profit as repayment. Debt for environmental swaps have been arranged, where debt is used to purchase land set aside for environmental protection. For some of the Latin American countries, these approaches have been successfully implemented, while for the African countries, major problems persist.

Demands for the NIEO have fallen far short in terms of increasing the volume and type of foreign assistance and in reforming international institutions. Only Japan has substantially increased foreign aid allocation from $458 million in 1970, to $3.4 billion in 1980, to $8.9 billion, making it the largest single donor. But Japanese aid has selectively targeted Southeast Asian countries and large industrial projects—the beneficiaries of which are Japanese firms that construct these projects. Nor has the North shown an inclination to negotiate over power within established international organizations. Indeed, the failure of efforts to institutionalize the

NIEO has led some members of the Group of 77 to temper their expectations, recognizing that a new order requires many changes that cannot be forced by a coalition of economically weak states, even though that group commands a majority of votes.

NIEO proposals set the international economic agenda for almost two decades. Negotiations occurred in numerous different forms—compromises were made on the part of both the South and the North. On some issues, such as commodity price stabilization and changes in power in international organizations, negotiations have not led to outcomes satisfactory to both parties. On other issues—the debt—accommodations were reached, or alternative modes of cooperation utilized such as control of MNCs by states themselves. Negotiations provide a forum for parties to explore the possibility of cooperation.

## POLICY COORDINATION

Compared to negotiation, *policy coordination* involves considerably more direct interaction among participants, and more mutual agreement on policy adjustments. To the extent that one actor's policy adjustments are conditioned on other actors' adjustments, this form of cooperation may be a "package deal." Adjustments under this category may also involve changes in national policy to conform or comply with international norms and rules. The consensus is that coordination is more effective when it is a regular and ongoing process.

### The Economic Summits

*Macroeconomic* economic policy coordination among the western developed countries has been achieved through summits—meetings of top leaders. Beginning with a French proposal in 1975, a series of annual summits have been attended by the heads of state of the United States, Britain, German Federal Republic, Italy, Japan, France, Canada, and the president of the European Community Commission. The interaction among a small group of major leaders has led to discussions of both high-level political crises (e.g., the deployment of the intermediate range nuclear force in Europe, Soviet invasion of Afghanistan, and political terrorism) and global economic issues—placing these, therefore, squarely on the political agenda.

Not all the summits have resulted in successful policy coordination. At least nine of the summits have yielded no substantive outcomes, while others have led to coordinated policies. In the 1978 Bonn summit, a comprehensive plan was developed for dealing with global economic recession: the United States pledged to develop a more effective energy policy; France concurred with demands to cut its deficit, while Japan and Germany pledged to expand economically—to provide the engine for global economic recovery. In the summits of the early 1990s, coordination of relief efforts to the former Soviet bloc was organized. In each of these cases, the goals of the participating parties may, indeed, have been divergent, but participants agreed to coordinate policies in the mutual interest.

Other coordination actions were also taken. In 1985, the finance ministers from these same countries agreed in New York to change the value of the Japanese yen and German mark against the U.S. dollar, while the United States agreed to dump dollars for these two currencies. This agreement, known as the "Plaza Accord," was followed by a number of other meetings designed to stabilize currency rates, culminating in a meeting in Paris in which the members agreed to maintain the *exchange rate* among the dollar, yen, and mark within a narrow range. This became known as the "Louvre Accord."

The economic summits and the high-level efforts to coordinate exchange rates among the major industrialized powers are both examples of discretionary policy coordination. Coordination among the Scandinavian countries on a range of economic issues is another example. If the economic summits had not occurred or if the Scandinavians had not met, then national policies would have differed from each other. With policy coordination, however, states have chosen to adjust policies for mutual benefit—to reduce adverse consequences and to reinforce positive consequences for all.

## INTERNATIONAL REGIMES

The term *regime* has been used recently by scholars to include higher levels of cooperation—beyond the willingness to negotiate internationally and to coordinate policy outcomes on a periodic basis. The notion of a regime suggests that states develop implicit or explicit principles about how certain problems should be addressed. Over time, these principles become solidified. Such rules and principles may be explicit—as indeed some international law is when it is codified or these rules and principles may be implicit. Although these principles may or may not be formalized in an organization or in an international treaty, they guide state actions. States agree to participate in regimes out of their own self-interest, but in doing so they help make more information available to governments and create patterns of stable expectations about how different parties should and do operate. Not surprisingly, given the vague definition of the term, there is not always agreement on whether the expectations in a certain issue-area have sufficiently converged to be considered an international regime. However, we examine two issues—trade and food—arguing that international regime may best explain the type of economic cooperation occurring.

## Trade: Economic Cooperation through GATT

In 1948, the victors of World War II proposed the creation of the International Trade Organization as one of the institutions designed to create a *liberal international* monetary and trading *order*. However, for a number of reasons, the formal organization was never created. In its place a multilateral treaty was negotiated—the General Agreement on Trade and Tariffs (GATT); its signatories, the Contracting Parties, were initially the largest developed countries, not including the Eastern bloc or the Soviet Union. Later, the developing states would be included, with the Contracting Parties now consisting of more than hundred states.

**Key Principles of GATT.** The development of a GATT regime began with certain principles being enshrined in the original agreement: (1) support of trade liberalization—trade is seen as the engine for economic development; (2) nondiscrimination in trade—most-favored-nation treatment—when states agree to give the same treatment to trading partners as they give to their best, most favored, trading partner; (3) reciprocity; and (4) designation of tariffs as the only devices acceptable for protecting home markets.

Procedures were also incorporated in the original GATT agreement: (1) disputes between countries are to be resolved through consultation; (2) negotiations are to be conducted among those sharing major interests in the issue (major suppliers and consumers of a product); (3) the agreement reached by the major interested parties is to be subsequently multilateralized to all Contracting Parties; (4) provisions for "safeguarding" (protecting domestic interests), including the option of countervailing duties, are to be permitted.

These principles and procedures have been modified to meet changing international imperatives. Most importantly, beginning in the 1960s, under pressure from many developing countries, norms of nondiscrimination and reciprocity were modified to permit preferential treatment for less-developed countries. Preferential access to the markets of the developed world was seen as a necessary stimulus to economic development. So regimes are flexible—the norms may change. By 1967, it was estimated that 80 percent of world trade was covered by GATT agreements.

**Multilateral Negotiations.** The heart of the GATT are periodic multilateral negotiations—called "rounds"—designed to reduce trade barriers. There have been eight so-called rounds. Those in the 1960s, the Dillon Round (1960–61) and Kennedy Round (1962), were primarily concerned with adapting the GATT system to the European Community (EC). Although the EC's Common Agricultural Policy proved to be an intractable issue, the Kennedy Round led to tariff reductions covering eight times as much trade as included in the Dillon Rounds. Between 1973 and 1979, the Tokyo Round resulted in still deeper tariff cuts, better treatment for the less-developed countries, and agreements leading to the elimination of subsidies and countervailing duties.

In addition, during the Tokyo round other issues were discussed and agreement reached on government procurement, customs valuation, and technical barriers and standards. During this round GATT's broad rules and principles became enshrined in detailed regulations. These regulations enhanced the orderliness of the trading system, and international trading arrangements became fairer from the perspective of the less developed countries, even though protectionism was not reduced.

Finally, in the current Uruguay Round beginning in 1986, still more issues have entered the negotiations—trade in services (e.g. insurance), agriculture, high technology, and intellectual property (e.g. patents). Particularly troublesome have been the efforts to reduce agricultural subsidies to farmers in the developed states—

the EC, Japan, and the United States. Domestic economic and political constituencies have sought protection for the vital agricultural sector—directly counter to the norms and principles of GATT. Equally troubling has been the problem of textiles.

The GATT serves as the centerpiece of the international trading regime: perhaps 50 percent of world trade is covered under the rules and principles. Although the percentage of trade covered may have declined, GATT remains central; it has served as the forum for multilateral trade negotiations, a forum in which specific principles are firmly embedded. Conflicts over specific policies continue—in what one commentator has referred to as "an unfinished symphony"—but the importance of the forum remains. There is no preferred alternative.

### The Case of Food

Another issue area of economic policy that has been described as having an international regime is international food policy. Formal organizations are an important part of the international food regime, including six United Nations-based organizations, the Food and Agriculture Organization (FAO), the World Food Program (WFP), the International Fund for Agricultural Development (IFAD), the Consultative Group on International Agricultural Research (CGIAR), the World Food Council and the less well known International Wheat Council (IWC). Other organizations have specific interests and responsibilities; these groups include the OECD and its committees on Agriculture and Development Assistance, the GATT, and the World Health Organization with expertise in nutrition and food standards.

Organizations and standards for food issues have developed incrementally. Between 1944 and 1960, the thrust was toward harmonizing agricultural policies with free trade principles. Between 1960 and 1973, the emphasis moved to economic development in the South through the transfer of agricultural technology —both financial resources and technical expertise. In addition, during this time, the norms of multilateral food aid became established, as did the mechanism for the distribution of such aid, the World Food Program. During much of the 1970s, the North-South struggle dominated the food regime, as the less developed countries sought greater influence in controlling the organizations in order to reshape regime principles.

The principles of the food regime have not been uniformly achieved, despite annual spending of the major organizations of more than $2.5 billion dollars. For example, the first principle—freer trade in agriculture—has not been achieved, as agricultural crops continue to enjoy protected status in most states. On the other hand, the principle of multilateral food aid has become firmly embedded in the food regime, partly as a response to a series of international crisis situations in Africa in the 1970s.

**Nongovernmental Organizations.**    An integral part of the food regime are the nongovernmental organizations (NGOs). For example, in Somali during 1991 and 1992, the NGO sector, including the International Committee of the Red Cross (ICRC), CARE, and Medicines sans Frontiers ran emergency food programs, child and mother health clinics, and supplementary food programs. The ICRC alone organized five hundred communal kitchens and fed more than six hundred thousand people a day. They provided technical advisors for the health and agricultural sectors. The cooperation between the international governmental organizations (IGOs) (UN-based) and these NGOs is close—CARE, for instance, is in charge of distributing the food brought in by the World Food Program.

Another success of the regime has been the establishment of the CGIAR system. CGIAR's forty donors support to the tune of $400 million annually seventeen international research centers, with a staff of seventeen hundred scientists. Technical research is aimed at improving agricultural productivity; new varieties of cereals and legumes specifically suited to the environment of less-developed countries, have been created. Research on pest control has targeted the special needs of the tropics. Centers like the International Rice Research Institute and similar ones for wheat and maize have continued to be vital conduits for the transfer of agricultural technology. Their main goal is sustainable development with agriculture as the centerpiece.

In both trade and food issues, the concept of regime is a useful means for evaluating cooperation. In each, there is a web of organizations, some global, some regional, some general purpose, many very specialized, which are engaged in activities. Most importantly, these various actors operate within sets of explicit principles, norms, and procedures with respect to trade issues, and with respect to implicit principles in agricultural issues. In each case, the regime has evolved—with principles changing to meet new international demands and responsibilities. The regime concept provides a way that scholars and decisionmakers can think about another level of cooperation—one evolving out of self-interest and which may or may not lead to formal institutional commitment.

## International Organizations

States have chosen for centuries to associate in more formal organizations for a variety of reasons. **International governmental organizations** (IGOs), as shown above, may play key roles in the creation and maintenance of international regimes. Their charters incorporate principles, norms, rules, decision-making processes, and functions for the organizations that formalize these aspects of a regime. Through regularized processes of information gathering and analysis, IGOs bring governments into continuing interaction with one another; they foster habits of cooperation through the repetition of patterns of behavior over time. States become socialized by regular involvement in the activities of IGOs and related processes of multilateral interaction and policy coordination. Formal organizations are particularly important in the formation and stability of habits of cooperation: they institutionalize regular meetings, processes of information gathering and analysis and of dispute settlement, and operational activities. Thus, formal organizations provide a durable means of managing conflicts and addressing the expanding agenda of international problems.

Today more than one thousand IGOs exist; and according to one estimate just over 50 percent of these organizations, most of them highly specialized and possessing specific mandates, have responsibilities related to economic issues. And, most important to the goal of fostering cooperation, inside such organizations, more than 85 percent of state behavior is cooperative.

### The World Bank

The World Bank and the International Monetary Fund (IMF) are two prominent international organizations that have played key roles in managing international economic relations. Both institutions, founded at the 1944 Bretton Woods Conference, have become part of the organizational foundation for the liberal international economic order. The World Bank was designed originally to stimulate reconstruction in post–World War II Europe. The IMF was created to promote economic stability and development by regulating monetary policy.

Today the purpose of the World Bank is to generate capital by borrowing from state members and the international financial markets. Like all banks, its purpose is to loan these funds, with interest, to states proposing major economic development projects. And indeed, over the years, a high portion of the funding has gone to construction of large infrastructure: hydroelectric projects, basic transportation (bridges, highways), and agribusiness projects. In 1956, the International Finance Corporation (IFC) and the International Development Association (IDA) joined the World Bank group of organizations. The task of the latter is to provide capital to the poorest countries, usually in the form of no-interest loans; repayment schedules of fifty years allow the least-developed countries more time to reach takeoff, sustain profitability, and hence develop economically. Such funds have to be continually "replenished"— added to—by major donor countries. The former, the IFC, is aimed at providing loans to private enterprises to invest in the private sector in the developing countries.

The priorities of the World Bank group have changed over time: from rehabilitation in war-torn Europe to targeting of the developing world; from an infrastructure orientation to a movement in the 1970s toward provision of what World Bank president Robert McNamara called "basic needs" (i.e., health, food, housing, and water); and in the 1980s and 1990s to a renewed emphasis on the private sector as the engine of economic growth, to increased use of conditionalities put on borrowing countries to cut government involvement in economic life, and more recently, to adoption of democracy. In fact, in 1980 the bank introduced a new program, Structural Adjustment Lending—lending to alleviate medium-term *balance of payments* problems, while maintaining the level and rate of economic growth at as high a rate as possible.

These changes in World Bank priorities coincide closely with the orientation of the major western donors, particularly the United States. Indeed, many have viewed the bank as merely an appendage of the U.S. government. A weighted voting structure, which guarantees major donors voting power commensurate with economic contributions, guarantees conformity of policies to the wishes of the developed countries. Although the United States itself does not command a majority of votes, tradition dictates that the president of the institution be an American approved by the U.S. government. What the developing countries sought under the rubric of the new international economic order was, in fact, alterations in this weighted voting structure. Yet, upon closer examination, the relationship between the bank and its donors suggests less direct influence than one of mutual influence and congruent interests. The large bank bureaucracy, composed mostly of economists trained in western countries in the same liberal economic tradition in which U.S. decision makers have been trained, exerts a great deal of independent autonomy. Most of the time the economic orientation of this allegedly apolitical bureaucracy has coincided with the orientation of the United States.

## The International Monetary Fund

The IMF was designed to stabilize exchange rates by providing short-term loans for member states confronted by "temporary" balance of payments difficulties. With a weighted system similar to that of the World Bank, approval by the United States of the country programs—size of the loans and conditions attached to them—was essential.

**Original Mission.** Upon its creation, the fund sought to establish a system of fixed monetary exchange rates and currency convertibility. From the 1940s to the 1970s the United States guaranteed the stability of this system by fixing the value of the dollar against gold at $35 an ounce. However, this system collapsed in 1971, with the United States announcing it would no longer guarantee a system of fixed exchange rates; the dollar was decoupled from the gold standard. So exchange rates floated. To cope with this change, a regional effort was undertaken in 1978 to stabilize currencies for the European states under the European Monetary System (EMS). Its purpose is to recreate a system of predictable exchange rates among the smaller group of participants in order to foster trade and better compete against the United States. In fact, a new currency unit was created from a "basket" (group) of European currencies: the European Currency Unit (ECU). This alternative approach to the IMF has until very recently provided some monetary stability in Europe, even though it has been frought with problems, including the fact that some states have refused to join the system.

**Role in Less-Developed States.** The IMF itself plays an increasingly key role in less-developed countries plagued by persistent deficits. Expanding from its short-term loan function, the IMF provides longer-term loans and the "international stamp of approval" for other multilateral and bilateral lenders as well as for private banks. Such loans are increasingly contingent upon high *conditionality:* the IMF requires that a country design a specific set of measures approved and monitored by them in order to eliminate fundamental economic problems before loans are granted. The country may be required to make both internal adjustments (following deflationary fiscal and monetary policies) and external adjustments (eliminating import controls and exchange restrictions, and devaluing its currency). Once a strategy is negotiated, the IMF monitors the adjustment programs and determines whether performance criteria have been met. Virtually all forms of external assistance, multilateral as well as bilateral foreign aid, come with some "conditions" attached, conditions that the donors believe will enhance the value of the aid.

As the IMF does this job, the clear-cut distinction between the fund and the bank is blurred. Both play key roles in structural adjustment lending. And both, particularly the IMF, have been subject to intense criticism, especially in Latin America and Africa. Critics charge the institutions with providing too little aid, at interest rates that are too high, only slightly below market rates. In addition, criticisms have arisen against the content and timing of the conditionality imposed. Finally, critics have noted that debt rescheduling is dependent upon conclusion of an agreement with the IMF.

As the tasks of the bank and the fund become less distinct, and as the level of direct involvement in national governments by these two institutions increases, the institutions are faced with difficult problems. Consistency of policy advice and uniformity of policy dialogue toward any one country by these institutions may be increasingly difficult to maintain; distributing inconsistent advice is clearly counterproductive. Hence, these institutions emphasize the criticality of increased cooperation, not only between the institutions themselves, but between the international organizations and the countries.

*The Unique Role of Nongovernmental Organizations.*

International cooperation may also be achieved through international nongovernmental organizations. These are organizations composed of private individuals and/or groups from different countries. NGOs outnumber IGOs, and while some, like the International Committee of the Red Cross or World Catholic Services, have earned an international reputation, many, like the African Organization of Technology Transfer, labor in relative obscurity.

Many of these NGOs participate in economic development activities in the developing countries and in local projects, working with individuals, states, and even IGOs. Increasingly, for example, economic development projects in Africa are carried out by both IGOs and NGOs. Interorganization cooperation not only increases the flow of resources but also enhances the possibility of more effective implementation with strong ties to the grass roots.

NGOs have also been effective critics of international organizations. In particular, NGOs have been critical of structural adjustment programs of the World Bank and IMF, believing that these organizations have ignored principles of grassroots participation and often supported antidemocratic regimes. Coalitions of NGOs like the Forum for African Voluntary Development Organizations have been instrumental in launching their own grassroots program with local input into policy formulation.

Joining and participating in international organizations, either governmental or nongovernmental, clearly does not ensure that cooperation will be easy to achieve or that conflict will be eliminated. However, with regularized procedures for consultation and with supposedly "neutral" bureaucracy intervening, international cooperation is more likely to occur.

## REGIONAL INTEGRATION

Membership in international organizations like the United Nations, the World Bank, or the International Monetary Fund does not directly undermine national sovereignty. States join these organizations assured that sovereignty is affirmed and that interference in their internal affairs is minimized. The World Bank's and International Monetary Fund's excursions into conditionality that constrains national economic choices have been controversial precisely because they threaten national sovereignty. Yet, in a few cases, states have chosen a mode of intense cooperation called "regional integration," which may lead to an actual diminution of national sovereignty and to the establishment of a new supranational entity to which states are subordinated.

*Regional integration* is the process by which states attempt to combine separate national economies into large economic regions. Two changes typically occur. First, states choose to invest decision-making power in *supranational* authorities, forming new institutions to make decisions on the allocation of scarce resources. Second, people's loyalties are to shift—moving from primary loyalty to the state to affective identification with the larger supranational unit. These changes occur over long periods of time—for some, that process occurs inevitably. Once integration begins, it proceeds toward supranationality. For others, key political decisions need to be made along the way; the process is not inevitable; "progress" may be in "fits and starts."

The theory that best explains why and how integration occurs is *functionalism*. Functionalists believe that economic disparities can best be erased by concentrating technical cooperation in specific sectors. Elites working on supposedly noncontroversial economic problems should work together in order to achieve economic development by sectors. As these functional elites work together, they would establish "habits" of cooperation. And eventually, inevitably, other elites working on other issues, social, political, and even security, would find such cooperation beneficial. "Habits" of cooperating in the economic sector would "spill over" to cooperation on social issues; social issues would "spill over" to political and security questions. The state as we know it would no longer have purpose. Sovereignty would effectively be transferred to the new functional supranational elites.

## The Case of European Unification

The idea of a united Europe goes back centuries. Plans presented by Immanuel Kant (*Perpetual Peace*), William Penn (*Essay Toward the Present and Future Peace of Europe*), Abbe de St. Pierre (*A Project for Making Peace Perpetual in Europe*), and Jean-Jacques

Rousseau (*A Lasting Peace through the Federation of Europe*) were filled with ideas about both the goal of a united Europe and the mechanism through which it could be achieved. Theorists writing after World War I were particularly enamored with the idea that a united Europe might have forestalled the conflagration caused by the war. World War II only intensified these sentiments. Hence after the war, some theorists and political leaders themselves began reviving discussions about a united Europe.

**European Defense Community.**   One proposal called for the creation of the European Defense Community (EDC). The EDC would have represented a *federalist* approach, in contrast to the functionalist approach. Federalism, direct institutional devolution of authority to a supranational government, attacks head-on the major question of security. The EDC would have touched on the core of national sovereignty. Security of all would have been entrusted to a supranational body. However, the French legislature rejected the treaty establishing the European Defense Community; they clung to gradualist proposals. The EDC failed in 1954.

**European Coal and Steel Community.**   Others argued that European cooperation could best be achieved through a gradual functionalist approach, beginning with cooperation among elites in limited economic areas. The establishment of the European Coal and Steel Community and its supranational High Authority in 1951 was the first institutional manifestation of functionalism. In that arrangement, two major European antagonists of the war, France and Germany, agreed to harmonize and eventually unify the coal and steel sectors—-two sectors essential for postwar European economic reconstruction. And the High Authority could make decisions for its economic agents in each country without approaching the respective governments. In 1955 another sectoral project was initiated, the Atomic Energy Community, later Euratom.

**The Common Market.**   The Treaty of Rome signed in 1957 established the framework for the broader economic union—eventually to be a *common market*. A common economic market is achieved when internal tariff barriers among member states are eliminated and there are uniform external barriers. Under the Rome Treaty, there was to be a long transition period—tariff barriers would be gradually reduced over a twelve- to fifteen-year transition period. The core of the community was to be the goal of removing all internal tariffs and quotas. Yet, the EC treaty provided for more than the free movement of goods across national borders, but also envisioned free movement of workers, enterprises, capital, agriculture, and transportation. According to liberal economic theory, the economic welfare of the community was to be enhanced, with the establishment of the EC. The larger economic market would permit economies of scale and benefits of specialization; opportunities for investment would be enhanced and competition and innovation stimulated.

Until the mid-1960s, the program was achieved more quickly than anticipated: functional theory seemed to be succeeding. However, between the mid-1960s and the mid-1980s, stagnation set in. It was clear that functionalism would not inevitability lead toward more integration. Specific political actions needed to be taken by the leadership to "push" the process. Those recognizing the need for such intervention by political leaders are referred to as *neofunctionalists*.

Some actions were taken. New members joined the original six. France, Belgium, Netherlands, Luxembourg, Italy, and Germany were joined by Denmark, the Irish Republic, and Great Britain in 1973; Greece in 1981; and Portugal and Spain in 1986. In 1979, the European Monetary System was established, and the European Parliament became directly elected, the expectation being that elections of representatives would positively affect the loyalties of people behind the new Europe.

In 1986, the critical next step was taken to further the integration process. The passage of the Single European Act made some institutional changes to insure more speedy decisions; new environmental and technological issues were added to the agenda; the objective of a monetary union was outlined, and the commission's white paper listed three thousand specific measures that needed to be taken for completing the single market. The deadline for full economic union was 1992. Political decision makers had taken direct steps to push the process in the neofunctionalist mold.

**The Maastricht Treaty.**   In December 1991, EC leaders concluded in a summit meeting what is known as the "Maastricht Treaty," committing themselves by the year 2000 to closer political and economic unity, including the establishment of common foreign and defense policies, a single currency, and a regional central bank.

Scrupulously avoiding the "F-word"—federalism—the treaty was characterized as a "new stage in the process creating an even closer union." But the Maastricht Treaty met with stiff opposition, even during its negotiation. The British were allowed to "opt out" of the monetary union and some social commitments. In a June 1992 referendum, the Danish public rejected the treaty, while the French electorate approved the treaty by a slim margin in September 1992. These referendums have signaled to the European leaders, those who negotiated Maastricht with little public consultation, that while members of the European public support the idea of international cooperation, they have a strong fear of diminution of national sovereignty—losing their national currencies—and a reluctance to lose their democratic rights by placing more power at the hands of functional nonelected elites.

Other problems are far from being resolved. Cooperation in agricultural trade has met with serious obstacles. The high cost of these subsidies—the amount taken from the EC budget to sustain subsidization—remains controversial. And of course, since the Single European Act was drafted, major changes in Eastern Europe and the Soviet Union have completely altered the map of Europe. Germany has been reunited—a process that has led to economic and social disruptions, cautious reminders of historic Germany. Eastern European countries are struggling toward democracy, and many, like Poland and Hungary, have expressed interest in joining the EC. The so-called neutrals of Europe—those countries who have not previously joined the EC—are likewise seeking admission: Austria, Sweden, and Finland have applied; Switzerland, Norway, Iceland, and Liechtenstein are leaning that way. All these major political changes and increasing membership suggest a state of gridlock for the near future.

*The North American Free Trade Agreement: Integration in the Making?*

Not all regional trading agreements—or even free trade areas— may have as their goal economic integration. The North American Free Trade Agreement (NAFTA) is one example. The free trade area negotiated by the United States, Canada, and Mexico differs substantially from the EC and other regional schemes. There is one dominant economy (U.S.) and two dependent ones: Mexico's and Canada's combined economic strength is one-tenth of that of the United States. The driving force behind NAFTA is not political elites but multinational corporations that seek larger market shares than their international competition, the Japanese and Europeans. The agreement phases out many restrictions on foreign investment and most tariff and nontariff barriers. This has allowed the multinationals to shift production to low-wage labor centers in Mexico, and to gain economies of scale through mergers and acquisitions.

However, the social, political, and security dimension is absent from NAFTA. Functional cooperation in trade and investment is not to lead to free movement of labor—quite the opposite: the United States expects that Mexican labor will not seek employment in the United States since economic development in their own country will provide employment opportunities. And economic cooperation does not mean political integration in this case, nor is it anticipated to lead in such a direction. Public questioning of the Maastericht Treaty suggests that even Europe may not be ready for this final step in regional integration. And the question has not been broached in the North American context. Economic integration is to remain just that—confined to specific economic sectors.

## COOPERATION AND CONFLICT

Cooperation—the normal state of affairs in international relations —describes states consciously changing or adjusting policies. But cooperation occurs at different levels. This essay has introduced five levels of international cooperation particularly relevant to global economic issues: negotiation, coordination, international regimes, international organizations, and regional integration. These are core concepts for understanding a variety of economic interactions—from NIEO, to summit diplomacy, to cooperation in trade and food issues, to the World Bank, IMF, and NGO interactions, to the EC and NAFTA.

If cooperation occurs in these areas and economic development is enhanced in the South through more equitable trade arrangements, technology transfers, control over multinational corporations, and more effective foreign aid, trade should be stimulated, thereby creating greater interdependence among states. In such an event, both liberals and functionalists contend that important roots of international conflict will be largely eliminated. Yet, clearly, achieving economic development, even economic well-being, will not eliminate tensions among states over specific economic issues. These different types of cooperation represent ways that states have to manage these tensions in a mutually satisfactory way.

## ANNOTATED BIBLIOGRAPHY

Gilpin, Robert. *The Political Economy of International Relations.* Princeton: Princeton University Press. 1987.
This comprehensive treatment of the subject integrates the ideologies of political economy with specific issues.

*Finance and Development.*
This quarterly magazine of the International Monetary Fund and the World Bank contains excellent articles on economic issues.

Krasner, Stephen D. *Structural Conflict: The Third World against Global Liberalism.* Berkeley and Los Angeles: University of Calif. Press, 1985.
This sophisticated treatment on North-South relations emphasizes that the conflicts are rooted in profound asymmetries of power, international financial institutions, multinational corporations, transportation, and the global commons.

Lairson, Thomas D., and David Skidmore. *International Political Economy: The Struggle for Power and Wealth.* Fort Worth, TX: Harcourt Brace Jovanovich, 1993.
In this up-to-date introductory text, the students are introduced to basic economic and political terms.

Mortimer, Robert. *The Third World Coalition in International Politics.* Boulder: Westview Press. 1984.
This is a detailed history of the rise and fall of the South in the quest for the New International Economic Order.

Nugent, Neill. *The Government and Politics of the European Community.* 2nd ed. Durham: Duke University Press. 1991.
In this thorough introduction to the European Community, the author examines the origins and historical development, the powers of the major institutions, and community policy interests and processes.

Putnam, Robert, and Nicholas Bayne. *Hanging Together: Cooperation and Conflict in the Seven Power Summits.* Cambridge: Harvard University Press. 1987.
This is the best study of cooperation relating to macroeconomic coordination.

Spero, Joan Edelman. *The Politics of International Economic Relations.* 4th ed. New York: St. Martin's Press. 1990.

This popular book covers the western system (emphasis on trade and monetary system), the North-South relationship, multinational corporations, and the East-West system.

Riggs, Robert E., and Jack C. Plano. *The United Nations: International Organization and World Politics.* Pacific Grove, CA: Brooks/Cole, 1988. This introductory college textbook on international organizations covers not only the United Nations, but the economic organizations in terms of historical origins, functions, and decision making.

World Bank. *World Development Report.* New York: Oxford University Press.

Issued annually, these reports contain essential information of various aspects of southern economies.

CHAPTER 7

# Human Rights
## and International Conflict

## David P. Forsythe

243

Human rights, according to the United Nations, are a principal foundation of international and national peace. The United Nations Charter, similar to a world constitution, states in Article 55: "With a view to the creation of conditions of stability and well-being which are necessary for peaceful and friendly relations among nations . . . , the United Nations shall promote . . . universal respect for, and observance of, human rights and fundamental freedoms for all." The Universal Declaration of Human Rights, a U.N. General Assembly resolution from 1948, expands on the charter by stating: "recognition of the inherent dignity and of the equal and inalienable rights of all members of the human family is the foundation of freedom, justice and peace in the world; . . . it is essential, if man is not to be compelled to have recourse, as a last resort, to rebellion against tyranny and oppression, that human rights should be protected by the rule of law."

## THE LINKAGE BETWEEN HUMAN RIGHTS AND CONFLICT

It is difficult to know for sure what was in the minds of those who created the basic rules of world affairs after World War II. It is possible that those who drafted the U.N. Charter in 1945 and who negotiated the Universal Declaration of Human Rights three years later genuinely believed that practicing human rights prevented international and civil wars. After all, it has been believed by some, like Woodrow Wilson and Ronald Reagan, that democracies (which practice civil and political rights) are inherently peaceful. And some believe those same democracies are immune from civil war. The first push for new international law on human rights in the 1940s came before the full awareness of the atrocities carried out by the fascist powers. So those demanding more laws and action on human rights must have believed that there was a real linkage between practicing rights and peace.

On the other hand, it is possible that many political leaders after the mid-1940s were morally outraged by the atrocities committed by, particularly, Germany and Japan during the Second World War. They even accepted a new term for part of what had happened: *genocide,* defined as the attempt to destroy a "national, ethnic, racial, or religious group." In this view, political leaders were morally appalled especially at the German "Holocaust" whereby approximately six million Jews, Gypsies, homosexuals, and other "undesirables" were held in concentration camps and then murdered. Japan, like Germany, engaged in pseudomedical experiments constituting torture of persons, and it also forced Korean "comfort women" into serving as sexual objects for Japanese troops. Thus, according to this second view, there was a focus on human rights after 1945, not because they were really linked to peace, but because of this moral outrage at past atrocities. After all, if one traces the history of intellectual discourse about human rights (see below), the primary concern was to improve human dignity, not chart a path to peace.

## Relationship to International Conflict

The exact linkage between the practice of human rights and international conflict management is very complex. On the one hand there is considerable evidence that democracies, meaning those states implementing civil and political rights to great degree, do not war with each other. In the last three hundred years of the state system, there has been no clear example of two democracies engaging in major war. In the war of 1812, Britain was not yet fully democratic, having still a powerful monarch; whereas the United States had established a representative, constitutional democracy although women, slaves, and Native Americans did not participate in the voting processes of the time. Likewise during World War I, Imperial Germany had widespread voting, but its parliament lacked any real authority to check the hereditary kaiser and his advisors. Democracies are not inherently peaceful, because powerful ones like Britain, France, and the United States have been among the most war-prone of any states across time. Yet recent research in international relations clearly demonstrates that stable democracies do not engage in armed conflict among themselves.

On the other hand, concern for human rights may be a pretext or a genuine motivation for international armed conflict. Hitler cited the plight of the German minority in Czechoslovakia in the 1930s to try to justify his military move into that country. Ronald Reagan and George Bush claimed to be acting in the name of human rights, at least in part, when invading Grenada and Panama, respectively. The Great Powers in the last century claimed to be acting for humanitarian reasons when using military force in places like Turkey and Lebanon. Short of the use of armed force, it is certainly true that a concern for human rights abroad can generate conflict, as demonstrated by U.S. concern for human rights in places like contemporary China.

Moreover, it should be recalled that during the cold war the democratic United States used the threat or application of force (including promises of support for those actually using force) to overthrow or pressure several elected governments in developing countries: Iran (1953), Guatemala (1954), Indonesia (from 1955), Brazil (early 1960s), Chile (1973), Nicaragua (1980s).

*Linkage to Domestic Conflict*

The relationship between human rights violations and political rebellion *within* countries is also complex, with much debate over the available scientific evidence. At least sometimes it is clear that violations of human rights within countries can generate violent reactions. In South Africa, the denial of many human rights to the black majority there led to repeated instances of violence inside the country. There was also cross-border violence between states and by nonstate groups operating from foreign state territory. In 1977 the U.N. Security Council imposed a mandatory arms embargo on South Africa because of apartheid. Only when there is some agreement on human rights for all South Africans will there be much prospect for genuine peace there.

*Current International Conflicts and Human Rights*

Thus, we can see there is a complex relationship between human rights and conflict management at both the national and international levels. Nevertheless, in recent years the United Nations has seemingly moved to establish a clear connection between human rights and conflict resolution. This is shown by events in both Iraq and Somalia during the 1990s.

In 1990, the U.N. Security Council authorized states to use "all necessary means," which included military force, to undo

Iraqi aggression against Kuwait. After the liberation of Kuwait by Desert Storm in early 1991, the Security Council explicitly declared (in Resolution 688) that Iraq's violation of the human rights of its citizens constituted a threat to international peace. At that time Iraqi repression caused the flight of thousands of its citizens into both Turkey and Iran. Several states subsequently used military force in the north and south of Iraq, in both 1991 and 1992, presumably to protect the rights of Iraqi citizens. So we see that in United Nations' dealings with Iraq in the 1990s, the issue of human rights has been intertwined with the question of international and internal conflict.

Likewise in Somalia during 1992–93, the U.N. Security Council declared (in Resolution 794) "that the magnitude of the human tragedy caused by the conflict in Somalia, further exacerbated by the obstacles being created to the distribution of humanitarian assistance, constitutes a threat to international peace and security." In that same resolution, the council authorized "all necessary means to establish . . . a secure environment for humanitarian relief." Under this permission, the United States and a few other states sent tens of thousands of military personnel into Somalia, primarily to deliver food to starving civilians. Thus, conflict in Somalia led to gross violations of human rights, which finally merited a militarized response by the international community.

## THE ROOTS OF UNIVERSAL HUMAN RIGHTS

The idea that recognizing the fundamental rights of persons is a good way to advance human dignity (and perhaps achieve national and international peace) was originally a western idea. Other parts of the world, and sometimes parts of the West as well, stressed other means to the end of improved human dignity, or perhaps justice and well-being. Some believed in reliance on a philosopher-king (Mao Tse-tung in China), or a benevolent dictator or father figure (the emperor in Japan), or in rule by a priestly class following religious principles (Ayatollah Ruholla Khomeini in Iran).

### The Western Origin of Human Rights

But first in Greece and Rome on a limited basis, then in Western European intellectual circles, then through the American (1776) and French (1789) political revolutions, the idea took hold that people had fundamental rights by the very nature of being human. The idea developed that governments had to respect those fundamental rights that were essential to a worthwhile life. Indeed, democratic theory holds that the fundamental reason a government exists is to secure individual rights.

Of course, ironies abound in this evolutionary process. The American Founding Fathers declared that all men were created free and equal. But they obviously did not mean to include nonwhite men, since many of the Founding Fathers were slave owners. Thomas Jefferson, the author of the American Declaration of Independence, never freed his slaves. The Founding Fathers certainly, in the eighteenth century, did not intend to include women as equals. It was only later in the United States, and in other nations as well, that racial and gender discrimination was legally corrected, so that universal human rights did indeed pertain to all. By 1945 the U.N. Charter spoke of human rights "without distinction as to race, sex, language, or religion."

## Global Diffusion of the Human Rights Idea

Particularly after about 1800, as western societies began to prosper and dominate world affairs, their practice of rights was progressively accepted by most other nations—at least in the abstract. Western societies based on rights were emulated around the world. The basic notion of human rights became internationalized in the same way that other ideas like the territorial state and state sovereignty, originating in the West, became accepted as the way of doing things in the nonwestern world. This was very clear as formal colonialism came to an end during the middle of the twentieth century (about 1945–75). The former colonies in Africa and Asia not only accepted the idea of territorial states supposedly possessing state sovereignty but also proclaimed their acceptance of human rights (however much they might violate them in reality). Their national constitutions frequently endorsed the 1948 Universal Declaration of Human Rights.

By the 1990s only very few states, like Saudi Arabia, openly rejected the basic idea of human rights. As European communism collapsed (during 1989–91), the new or newly independent states in the old Soviet sphere of influence proclaimed their acceptance of the idea of human rights. Some of these countries—Czechoslovakia,

Hungary, and Poland—made remarkably good progress in institutionalizing the practice of rights. Some others, especially areas of the former Yugoslavia and southern parts of the former Soviet Union, saw major human rights violations. Others fell between these extremes. But none rejected human rights as a central notion in law and policy. The Commonwealth of Independent States, the confederation replacing the Soviet Union, stated in Article 2 of its basic document: "Each of the agreeing parties guarantees citizens of other parties and also people without citizenship who reside on its territory, regardless of nationality or other differences, civil, political, social, economic and cultural rights and freedoms in accordance with common international norms on human rights."

Even The People's Republic of China, still officially communist with a single ruling political party, claimed to accept the idea of human rights. The Chinese party-state officials, however, then said it was up to each country to determine which rights to implement first and how to do so. Chinese practice clearly indicated the practical absence of many civil and almost all political rights, as officials stressed the need for Chinese national economic growth, population control, and order.

## A Legitimate Topic for International Relations

It was thought for a long time that because human rights involved a sensitive relationship between persons and their national government, such rights were not a proper subject matter for interstate relations. In short, scholars and policymakers alike believed that human rights were an internal matter and that the concept of 'sovereignty' meant that no country had a right to interfere in any way with the internal politics of any other country. This is still the position of several countries.

Particularly since 1945, however, attitudes toward the role of human rights in the conduct of international relations and foreign policy have been changing. Most nations today officially accept the notion of universal human rights, and many states genuinely endorse that idea. It is now generally accepted that human rights is a routine part of international relations or world affairs. States regularly discuss other states' human rights behavior at meetings of the United Nations and other international organizations. Countries regularly circulate the reports of private groups, like Amnesty International, in international meetings. Some states adjust their foreign assistance because of human rights behavior in recipient countries. States, singularly or collectively, apply various sanctions because of rights performance. For example, the Organization of American States (OAS) voted economic sanctions on Haiti in the early 1990s after a military coup overthrew the elected president. The U.N. Security Council voted to use "all means necessary," which is diplomatic language for military force, in August 1992 in order to get food to starving civilians in Bosnia, then under attack by Serbian forces.

## The Historical Process

This internationalization of human rights has been a long and slow process. It is still an incomplete one. From about the middle of the nineteenth century, the international community focused on slavery and the slave trade and on victims of war. Slavery and the slave trade were made international crimes, and the idea of universal jurisdiction was attached to treaties outlawing them. This meant that the British navy, or any other party, could arrest slave traders on the high seas and punish them in British, or any other, courts. Likewise, violations of the laws of war were made war crimes. Universal jurisdiction attached to treaties composing the laws of war meant that someone who abused prisoners or attacked civilians could be seized in international areas and tried in court regardless of nationality or place of crime. The Nuremberg trials of 1945 were based on this idea, and most German leaders convicted and punished through these trials were war criminals. There were similar trials in Tokyo. In 1992, the U.N. Security Council voted to create a war crimes commission to investigate violations of human rights in the Balkans, the former Yugoslavia. In 1993, it created a war crimes tribunal.

During the time of the League of Nations, the International Labor Organization was created to draft laws on rights of laborers and also to supervise state implementation of those laws. There was also international attention to the rights of foreigners (aliens) in another state.

These four categories—slaves, victims of war, laborers, and aliens—made up the meager background of international attention to human rights prior to the explosion of human rights activity during the United Nations era.

## INTERNATIONALLY RECOGNIZED HUMAN RIGHTS

Nothing better illustrates the internationalization of human rights than the proliferation of agreements on the subject since 1945. Supposedly sovereign states have consented to numerous documents that not only define universal and regional human rights, which states are supposed to respect, but also create agencies to supervise state behavior under the treaties.

### International Bill of Rights

There is an international bill of rights. It is made up of the 1948 Declaration of Human Rights, the 1966 U.N. Covenant on Civil and Political Rights, and the 1966 U.N. Covenant on Economic, Social, and Cultural Rights. The universal declaration, while not a treaty, contains thirty principles that have been widely endorsed. These principles cover: the first generation or negative rights blocking governmental intrusion into personal lives (e.g., freedom from arbitrary arrest, torture, unreasonable search and seizure); the second generation or positive rights mandating governmental action to do things for persons (e.g., provide adequate food, clothing, shelter); and the third generation or solidarity rights providing broad collective rights (e.g., an international order in which the other rights could be achieved).

The 1966 UN Covenant (or convention, meaning "multilateral treaty") on Civil-Political Rights not only reaffirms the rights familiar to the American Bill of Rights (the first ten amendments to the U.S. Constitution) on the international level but also creates a Human Rights Committee of individual experts, not governmental representatives, to whom a person can complain if he or she thinks the rights covered in the treaty have been violated (if the person's state has consented to the treaty and to the jurisdiction and authority of the committee). This UN Human Rights Committee also reviews reports from states, covering their steps to apply the treaty. While this Human Rights Committee is not a court, it can generate some diplomatic pressure on an offending state through questions and ultimately negative publicity.

The Covenant on Socio-Economic Cultural Rights affirms rights to such "goods" as adequate nutrition and health care, among others. About one hundred states have consented to its terms, a number similar to the Covenant on Civil and Political Rights.

Among the democracies, only the United States, believing historically that human rights are only civil and political has refused to
accept it. This treaty, too, now has a committee of independent
experts to supervise state behavior and make suggestions for improved practice.

*Growth of Rules and Public Watchdogs*

Beyond this international bill of rights, there are global treaties on
other matters related directly to various aspects of human rights
including: genocide, racial discrimination, treatment of refugees,
discrimination against women, use of torture, rights of children,
political rights of women, slavery, forced labor, victims of war,
apartheid, and certain labor rights. In addition, the International
Court of Justice, or World Court, which is technically part of the
United Nations, sometimes pronounces on human rights matters
when handling legal cases brought to it by countries. The court sits
at The Hague in the Netherlands and has dealt, for example, with
human rights in armed conflict and the rights of children. Individuals and private groups, however, do not have standing to sue in
this court, and its impact on the development of international
human rights law has been slight. Some of the more interesting
developments concerning international human rights have occurred on a regional basis.

**European Developments.**    The European Convention on Human
Rights and Fundamental Freedoms now has twenty-seven signatory states. The treaty not only specifies civil and political rights
but also creates a conciliation commission and a court. The European Commission on Human Rights tries to promote an out-of-
court settlement of disputes arising under the treaty. It accepts
well-founded complaints from persons as well as from states. The
European Court on Human Rights is given ultimate authority to
make a legally binding judgment about the meaning of the treaty.
Since the mid-1950s the court has ruled more than four hundred
times that states have violated the terms of the treaty. All states
involved were democracies, and all voluntarily implemented this
court's decisions. Thus, in a process normally starting with individual complaints, an international court of individual experts
makes the final decision about whether "sovereign" states are ob-
eying international law on human rights.

In Europe, there is also a regional treaty against torture, with a
supervising committee; and there is a regional treaty to promote

social and economic rights, with a separate system of supervision. This latter process deals mainly with labor questions.

Also in Europe broadly defined, there is the Conference on Security and Cooperation in Europe (CSCE) process. This process of interstate negotiation produced the Helsinki Accord in 1975. This document reaffirmed various human rights and established humanitarian principles that were to be implemented by the original thirty-five states ranging from Canada to, at the time, the Soviet Union. Pressure from the western states in support of these human rights and humanitarian standards, when linked to human rights groups inside European communist states, pushed these latter states into human rights reforms. Between 1975 and 1991, therefore, the Helsinki process generated considerable influence in support of human rights reform within European communism. Since 1991 and the disintegration of the Soviet Union, the CSCE, now expanded to include more than fifty states, has not yet found the same degree of influence in an unstable Europe, compared to the days of the cold war.

**The Western Hemisphere.**   Likewise under the OAS in the Western Hemisphere, there is the American Convention on Human Rights, dealing mostly with civil and political rights, supported by a commission and a court. The InterAmerican Court on Human Rights has been given jurisdiction to exercise ultimate authority as to the meaning of the treaty by only about a dozen states. Thus, it has had less impact on the Western Hemisphere than the European Court of Human Rights has had on Europe. The United States has not ratified the American convention and therefore has not had to deal with consent to the jurisdiction of the court.

**Africa.**   Finally, there has been some progress on human rights in Africa, where the Organization of African Unity has sponsored the African Charter on Human and People's Rights. This treaty tries to combine individual with collective rights. It has also created a commission to oversee implementation, but the commission has little authority.

*Implementation and Enforcement*

Overall, contemporary international relations show a veritable explosion of international standards on human rights, both globally and regionally. A number of innovative steps have been tried concerning the monitoring or supervision of state behavior under the agreements. The most impressive have been in Europe. There is now routinized and almost constant international collective diplomacy in behalf of human rights, in addition to whatever countries might do for rights through their unilateral foreign policies. We still live in a world where territorial states are the most important actors, but these states are not completely free to treat persons as they wish. Legally, most states are obligated to treat persons in accord with internationally recognized human rights. Politically, they are pressured to act in accordance with those rights' standards. This is the process of implementation. Sometimes states are ordered by courts or the U.N. Security Council to change their policies. This is the process of enforcement. It represents a remarkable transformation from the situation prior to 1945.

*Human Rights and Democracy*

From an international perspective, the idea of human rights is much broader than the idea of democracy. *Democracy* has been defined in various ways, but fundamentally it refers to the process in which, people govern themselves through competitive elections resulting in a real impact on who governs. Thus, democracy refers to the political right to participation in government; this political right necessitates a series of civil rights such as freedom of speech and assembly and organization.

But the international definition of human rights goes beyond democracy, mandating that governments, speaking for states, guarantee a minimal living standard by promoting so-called positive rights, dealing with such socioeconomic matters as nutrition, clothing, shelter, and health care. Thus, it is possible for a nondemocratic state like Cuba to meet some international human rights standards pertaining to health care and education while violating other human rights standards of a civil and political nature. Likewise, it is clear that the United States, while meeting very high standards on civil and political rights, fails to meet fully some of the broader international standards pertaining to socioeconomic rights. This is the primary reason why the United States became a party to the U.N. Convention on Civil and Political Rights during 1992 but did not accept the U.N. Convention of Social, Economic, and Cultural Rights.

Relatedly, it is important to note that democracies do violate human rights. We have just noted that the United States does not accept international standards on most socioeconomic or positive rights. It is also true that the European Court on Human Rights has found West European democracies in violation of the European Convention on Human Rights numerous times. It is obvious that in India—according to Amnesty International, among other organizations—one can find genuine free elections side by side with ill-treatment of prisoners and child labor (not to mention child marriages for money). This fact strengthens the case for those who call for international supervision of rights practices, not just for authoritarian governments, but for democracies as well.

## SIGNIFICANT CONTROVERSIES

The subject matter of international human rights presents a central paradox. Never before in world history has there been so much official consensus in support of the abstract idea of human rights. On the other hand, despite this formal agreement, there are numerous controversies both about the definition of human rights and about their application. Three issues concerning the meaning of human rights are especially important.

### *Interpreting Vague Principles*

First, there are debates over how to interpret broad principles that have been accepted. For example, everyone agrees on a right to life. But under this general principle, where does the practice of abortion fit; should one be pro-life or pro-choice? Legally speaking, does human life begin at conception, or only at some later point when "human" characteristics are distinct? Do national governments such as The People's Republic of China have the right to force women to have abortions in the name of population control? Under the same principle, should the death penalty be applied to so-called common crimes like armed robbery or aggravated assault? Should the death penalty be applied to those under eighteen years of age?

Both U.N. Conventions on Civil-Political and Socio-Economic rights have a common article one codifying the right of peoples to self-determination. This is a collective rather than individual human right. But who is the "self" in self-determination? Or, who is a "people" with a right to some degree of self-rule? Do the Basques in Spain have a right to statehood? The Ossetians in the former

Soviet Republic of Georgia? The Scots in the United Kingdom? The people of Northern Somalia? Indeed, controversy over national self-determination may prove to be the most disruptive issue in international affairs after the cold war.

## Relative Priorities

Second, there are debates about the importance of the different types of rights that have been recognized in various international documents and meetings. The U.N. General Assembly, the debate forum of the world, has passed resolutions saying all human rights are equal and interdependent, but this has not resolved the issue. In general, western countries like the United States have given priority to civil and political rights. Even those western states accepting the validity of positive rights dealing with economic and social conditions have said that such rights should be realized over time and without court judgments. On the other hand, socialist states, especially those in Eastern Europe up until 1989, gave priority, at least in rhetoric, to economic and social rights and downplayed civil and political rights. China and some other states still follow this pattern. From their legal independence until about 1990, most developing countries have also emphasized in their public statements economic, social and cultural rights.

## Are There Too Many Rights?

Third, there is debate over the wisdom of adding new rights to the list of internationally recognized rights. For the United States, this debate is still at the stage of deciding whether it should be obligated under international law to provide adequate food, clothing, shelter, and health care to those who cannot purchase these "goods" in private markets. For most of the rest of the world, since they accept both civil-political and economic-social-cultural rights already, the debate has moved to new, third generation rights of solidarity: Should there be formal recognition of collective rights to development, peace, a healthy environment, and the vague common heritage of mankind? For example, should the supposed riches of the international seabed or Antarctica be made available to the poor of the world? There is also debate about whether there should be a new treaty to protect the rights of indigenous or aboriginal peoples. This latter type of debate, for example, has affected Canada's deliberations over a new national constitution in the 1990s.

*Beyond Definition To Action*

Even if we set aside debates about definition, we find ample debates about what action can be taken in behalf of the human rights that have apparently been agreed to in international laws and international organizations. Five kinds of debates over application of human rights standards give us the flavor of the controversy.

**Humanitarian Intervention.** First, there is controversy over collective use of force for human rights. Noted above was the example of the U.N. Security Council's response to Iraq's repression of its citizens after 1990. When the council voted to declare these human rights violations a threat to the peace, several states abstained in the voting. Thereafter, when military force was used by the United States and others, some states complained that such action violated both the council resolution and the terms of the U.N. Charter. Even when the council voted to authorize military force in Somalia, some states were fearful that this would lead to the overriding of state sovereignty in other places like Mozambique or the Sudan.

Also in the 1990s, a number of people, including Margaret Thatcher, the former prime minister of Britain, called for the use of force to stop violations of human rights in the Balkans. But the United States and most other states hesitated, fearing another Vietnam-like situation in which outside military forces would become ensnared in a long and unclear irregular war.

**Nonforcible Sanctions.** Second, there is controversy over collective nonforcible sanctions for human rights. When the U.N. Security Council voted legally binding economic sanctions on the breakaway, white minority government in Rhodesia, the U.S. Congress passed a law permitting trade with Rhodesia. Other states, like South Africa, openly refused to cooperate with the sanctioning effort, and still other states, like communist Bulgaria, covertly tried to make money by trading with Rhodesia "under the table." So while it is true to say there was official and broad support for economic sanctions in the name of self-determination and majority rule in Rhodesia, now Zimbabwe, there was unofficial and sizable support for the racist government there. This was true of part of the American business community.

**Multilateral Diplomacy.** Thirdly, there is controversy over collective diplomacy and political pressure for human rights. The U.N.

Human Rights Commission, the "hub" in the "wheel" of U.N. diplomacy for human rights, is made up of countries. A coalition of western and developing countries has created a number of useful techniques for the advancement of human rights. For example, individuals have been appointed to study human rights issues in specific states such as Guatemala. This puts the diplomatic spotlight on the targeted state. In the case of Guatemala, the army has killed tens of thousands of Guatemalans over the past decades; the victims were mostly indigenous Indians. The winner of the 1992 Nobel Peace Prize, Rigoberta Menchu, was a Guatemalan Indian. Special working groups have been appointed to study specific problems such as disappeared persons: people held and sometimes tortured or killed by the state but without the state's acknowledging that it ever detained the person. These working groups have also generated pressure to stop violations of human rights. But in the 1990s, several developing states tried to slow down or stop these activities by the U.N. Human Rights Commission. They seemed afraid that the human rights spotlight might be directed on them next.

A North-South conflict may replace the East-West conflict as a major brake on international action for human rights. At the 1993 UN Conference on Human Rights, held at Vienna, Austria, however, most southern or developing states accepted the reaffirmation of universal human rights, valid for all countries and cultures.

**State Foreign Policy.**    Fourth, political controversies often arise within a country over what the country should do unilaterally to advance human rights internationally. The U.S. Congress, for example, several times passed legislation that would have placed U.S. economic sanctions on China for its human rights violations after the massacre in 1989 at Tiananmen Square. But the Bush administration vetoed the legislation, saying that it was not an appropriate and timely way to advance the practice of rights in China. At the time, U.S. foreign policy sought the cooperation of China on a number of international issues: arms sales to the Middle East, a political solution to disorder in Cambodia, various votes in the U.N. Security Council. How to link U.S. concern for human rights in China with these other concerns was obviously a matter on which the Democrat-controlled Congress and the Republican-controlled White House disagreed.

The U.S. unilaterally used force in Panama in 1989 and essentially in Grenada in 1983, claiming that one of the reasons for the use of force was to correct both civil and political human rights violations in those countries. While the invasion was a success from the standpoint of the U.S. government and American people, the U.N. General Assembly and the OAS condemned the action in Panama as a violation of international law. Essentially the same could be said about the U.S. operation in Grenada.

**National Courts in International Perspective.**   Fifth, there is controversy over the role of national courts in protecting rights in international context. In an oft-cited case stemming from California (*Sei Fuji*), the state supreme court there said that one could not use the U.N. Charter (a treaty) and its provisions on human rights as a basis for resolving legal disputes within California. Since the U.S. Supreme Court has never reviewed this judgment, its logic presumably extends to the other forty-nine states. On the other hand, in the 1980s and 1990s a series of federal courts in the United States held that one could use international customary law in order for one private person to sue another private person for torture committed abroad, even though neither person was a U.S. citizen. The overall situation was complex, with much ambiguity about the proper role of courts within a state in relation to international human rights.

It is easy to see, therefore, that despite a broad and formal global consensus in support of human rights principles, there are still ongoing controversies about international human rights and their proper definition and application. But we should not forget that one of the central arguments has been resolved. It used to be debated whether human rights was a proper subject matter of international relations. Many countries used to argue that human rights fell under the sovereignty and domestic jurisdiction of the nation-state. This argument has largely been put aside in favor of the view that there are internationally recognized human rights and that at least diplomatic action to apply them is permitted. There is no doubt that some international action, such as debating and passing resolutions about a state's human rights performance, is quite permissible. On that point there are only a few countries that still object, and their objections are overridden by the majority of contemporary states.

## SIGNIFICANT ACHIEVEMENTS

There is much that is wrong with the international effort to define and apply human rights standards. States still, all too often, elevate self-serving and dubious concerns over the value of persons. They pursue status, military advantage, and wealth at the expense of the dignity of human beings, more than could be wished. There is much posturing and paying of lip service to human rights values. But international agencies working for human rights are usually underfunded, and they often lack the authority to compel states to change their repressive and exploitative policies. Nevertheless, the international human rights movement (represented mostly by non-governmental organizations discussed below) can claim a number of significant achievements to its credit, especially if one takes a long-term or historical view. The following factors are interlocking, without necessarily a clear cause-and-effect relationship; most of them are mutually reinforcing.

### Public Action

The subject matter of human rights has been firmly placed on international and foreign policy agendas. It is there to stay. This is to say that most public authorities have accepted a responsibility to deal with human rights on a transnational basis.

About one-third of the resolutions adopted each year by the U.N. General Assembly pertain to human rights. There is a Human Rights and Humanitarian Affairs Bureau headed by an assistant secretary of state in the U.S. Department of State. A similar office exists in most of the major states.

Human rights is now one of the major issue-areas in world affairs, along with security, economics, and ecology. There are now too many laws, too many international governmental agencies, too many state offices for the issue to be placed back where it was in previous times—namely, as a domestic issue protected by the claim of state sovereignty. This major change at least creates the opportunity for more action in defense of human rights on the part of states and various international agencies.

*Private Action*

Over time private groups for human rights have increased their numbers, activism, funding, and political and legal sophistication. These nongovernmental organizations (NGOs) focus on human rights issues full time, and thus keep pressure on public authorities as well as journalists to pay consistent attention to violations of these rights. Some of these groups, such as Anti-Slavery International (London) and the International Committee of the Red Cross (Geneva), have a long, proud record of effectiveness. Others, like Amnesty International (London) founded in 1961, are of more recent vintage but have also accomplished good things. Starting with Helsinki Watch (1975), the Watch Groups (New York) now cover the Americas, Africa, the Middle East, and Asia.

In congressional hearings on human rights, some groups like the Lawyers Committee for Human Rights (New York) regularly contest executive versions of events. At the United Nations, groups like the International Commission of Jurists (Geneva) or the League for Human Rights (New York) keep a watchful eye on governmental rhetoric and real policy. Groups like Doctors without Borders (Paris) and Physicians for Human Rights (Boston) focus on some internationally recognized positive rights dealing with hunger, health care and the like. Groups like Oxfam (Oxford) have also proven valuable in delivering international relief in order to meet standards for socioeconomic rights. Groups representing indigenous peoples have had an impact in pushing for new norms to protect vulnerable tribal peoples.

This is not to say that these groups always have a significant impact on policy. But it is to say that at both the national and international level of policy making, private groups for human rights are more numerous and active than ever before in world history and that they make a definite contribution to placing and keeping human rights concerns in policy debate. More than one thousand human rights NGOs attended the 1993 UN conference on rights in Vienna. Because they normally act through or with public officials, it is usually difficult to specify their exact degree of influence on a policy or situation.

*World Public Opinion*

Stemming from both more public and private action, there is more awareness of human rights in most places of the world. Newspapers and magazines, radio, and television cover human rights issues more frequently, and more broadly, than in the past. Political leaders, such as U.S. presidential candidates, feel the need to adopt positions on human rights questions. This was not an accepted practice as recently as 1975.

As reports of private human rights groups are given more prominence in the communications media, governments find it more difficult to summarily reject their criticisms. In fact, public concern about human rights pushed western governments into doing something about the plight of Iraqi Kurds in the spring of 1991. Again in the summer and fall of 1992, public concern about gross violations of human rights in the Balkans—especially in Serbia, Croatia, and then Bosnia—pushed the United States and other governments into at least doing more than had been done until that time. Especially students, but others as well, have demonstrated for human rights in places like China and Thailand—nonwestern states without a strong rights tradition. Today such actions are often publicized worldwide via cable television networks such as CNN.

## Collapse of European Communism

The collapse of European communism has also aided the human rights movement. That collapse was partly a response to human rights concerns, especially articulated through the CSCE or Helsinki process, as noted above.

It is certainly true that communism in places like the old Soviet Union failed in a material sense. Mikhail Gorbachev felt the need to make fundamental changes in the USSR because the economic situation was desperate. There was slow growth, a lack of innovation, and a further falling behind other great powers. The Soviet Union had global ambitions, but it had engaged in "imperial overstretch." Its foreign commitments exceeded its ability to pay, because its domestic economy was so weak.

But European communism also failed morally or spiritually or psychologically. Particularly by comparison with western democracies, the USSR and its allies repressed and exploited people. This was certainly known by the people. In addition to all the other international agreements on human rights, after 1975 there was the Helsinki Accord, which the USSR and its allies had freely signed pledging serious attention to human rights. A number of

dissidents in communist countries, like Vaclav Havel in Czechoslovakia, demanded that their governments live up to their promises.
They were supported by the west. This process centering on human
rights contributed to the collapse of European communism.

And this collapse sent shock waves around the world. There
was a "domino" effect. Dictators and one-party states in Africa
and Asia were under increased pressure to pay more attention to
human rights. If repression could be ended in European communist states, why not elsewhere? Even apparently popular father
figures like Kenneth Kauda in Zambia felt compelled to allow free
elections and a multiparty political system. And in several Islamic
countries, not known for a human rights tradition, ruling circles
like the al-Sabah family in Kuwait faced more activism for human
rights. In 1992, opposition groups in Kuwait dominated the first
parliamentary elections held there since 1986.

## Status of State Sovereignty

The appeal of state sovereignty has been generally reduced by comparison with advancing human rights, and nowhere more clearly
than in Western Europe. Under the auspices of the Council of
Europe, the European Court of Human Rights, a grouping of
about thirty democratic states, makes the ultimate decision about
the practice of civil and political rights under authority granted by
the European Convention on Human Rights.

Moreover, under the Common Market or European Community, a separate grouping of twelve states for economic advancement, the European Court of Justice also makes supreme human
rights judgments. Hence, in Western Europe, countries have used
their sovereignty initially to restrict their own sovereignty ultimately. Thus, Western European countries have consented to rules
and courts that make the state only an intermediate, not an ultimate, authority in matters of human rights. The result is impressive
international systems of decision making for the benefit of improved human rights.

Of course, the territorial state has not disappeared. The Council of Europe and the Common Market still consist of largely
sovereign states. Their consent remains necessary for these international systems to function. In some parts of the world, like the
Balkans, the rabid push for collective pride, linked to the establishment of new states, has largely eclipsed respect for individual hu-

man rights. Serbian nationalism is driving gross violations of human rights against Bosnian Muslims, for example. Nevertheless, state sovereignty is no longer absolute, especially in Western Europe; it is limited for the benefit of the rights of persons. And even though all states in the council and the EC are democracies, there is still a need for international rules, agencies, and courts to see that individual countries do not find it convenient to violate the human rights of their citizens.

## THE FUTURE OF HUMAN RIGHTS

What will happen to human rights in the future? The social sciences are not especially good at predicting the future. Personalities, for example, can make dramatic and often unpredictable differences whether for better (e.g., Gorbachev, Havel) or for worse (e.g., Hitler, Stalin). Both Anwar Sadat of Egypt and Harry Truman of the United States behaved differently in office than predicted. Chief Justice Earl Warren of the U.S. Supreme Court was appointed by President Eisenhower in the expectation that he would be conservative. However, particularly on human rights matters such as the right to equal education, Warren turned out to be very liberal.

In addition, some situations are made up of competing tendencies, and it is rarely clear which tendency will prevail in the future. By 1990 in the Western Hemisphere, for instance, elected governments had developed in almost all countries except Cuba, despite the continued presence of nondemocratic elements. By 1993, elected governments had been overthrown, suspended, or attacked in Haiti, Peru, and Venezuela; and such governments exercised only limited influence elsewhere, as in El Salvador, Guatemala, and Argentina. Thus, it has been very difficult to predict the future of political rights in the Western Hemisphere.

### The Chances for Progress

In general, however, we can state with some confidence that increased attention to human rights around the world will continue. As noted already, there are too many laws and agencies focusing on the subject for the effects of the last half-century to be undone. Too many people now have raised expectations about human rights for the subject to fade away.

With the end of the cold war, the U.N. Security Council is able to take more action for human rights. One does not have to worry so much about a Soviet veto. Russia has cooperated on human rights matters. China has abstained rather than veto resolutions it dislikes. The Council has acted in exceptional ways for human rights in Iraq, Somalia, Haiti, and the Balkans, in particular. It may do so in other situations in the future.

There are more democracies than ever before in the U.N. General Assembly and Human Rights Commission. There are more votes for human rights matters. But we shall have to wait and see if a North-South conflict intensifies to hamper human rights activities by these parts of the United Nations. A number of southern or developing states are still not enthusiastic about international review of their rights performance. At the U.N. Vienna Conference on Human Rights in 1993, there was clearly a handful of states like Syria, Iraq, Iran, Vietnam, Malaysia, Indonesia, China, and a few others who were opposed to further attention to human rights through international diplomacy.

In Europe several states like Bulgaria, the Czech Republic, Slovakia, Hungary, and Poland have gained admission to the Council of Europe, with its stringent human rights standards. More are likely to join in the future. Some may eventually join the Common Market and become further integrated into democratic Europe.

In Asia, there is some discussion of creating a regional human rights charter and organization. But it must be recognized that a number of Asian states, including large and important ones like China and Indonesia, do not support further attention to international human rights.

In Africa, especially since the end of the cold war, there has been growing sentiment that African governments must pay more attention to the various rights of their peoples rather than blame poor situations on colonialism or imperialism. There is growing unhappiness with the record of rule by the generation of political leaders that achieved state independence. The African Charter on Human Rights, while generally not as strong a document as the European Convention on Human Rights, does require all signatory states to teach human rights principles.

The World Bank should also be mentioned. By the 1990s the bank, officially the International Bank for Reconstruction and Development, based in Washington, was tying its development loans to "good government." Part of the meaning of "good government" was certainly the right to participate in the making of public policy, and occasionally the bank suspended loan activity because of serious violations of civil rights. For example, after the Tiananmen Square massacre of June 1989, the bank suspended its operations in China for a time.

These trends, which illustrate continued or even increased action on human rights, should not imply an easy and linear progress on human rights. While there has been progress, it has been uneven.

## Challenges to Continued Progress

Some areas —for example, Saudi Arabia, Indonesia, and most (but not all) Islamic countries in general—have not progressed very far, if at all. (Algeria showed an interesting but complicated record on human rights matters. It moved toward free elections and a multiparty system that might have led to victory for a fundamentalist Islamic party that probably would have violated a number of rights. Increased democracy was therefore stopped by the army.) The appeal of Islamic fundamentalism, especially as practiced by governments in Iran and the Sudan, has proven inhospitable to many human rights.

Some areas may even show a regression on rights matters. Many people were clearly worse off after the disintegration of communist Yugoslavia, even though Marshall Tito, its dictator, was never committed to broad civil and political rights. Military attacks on civilians and "ethnic cleansing" is relatively worse than the "routine repression" in the former Yugoslavia. Students in China are clearly worse off after the Tiananmen Square massacre than they were before it.

While the end of the cold war may allow some states more room to maneuver for human rights—since they do not have to worry so much about their traditional security concerns—these same states may actually have less motivation to act for human rights around the world. Once the United States was not worried about Soviet advances in the horn of Africa; Washington was very slow to act for human rights in Somalia, Ethiopia, and the Sudan—much less in other distant places like Mozambique.

And most of the western-style democracies had domestic problems that worried voters and leaders. The United States, Germany, and Japan all manifested serious economic problems, albeit for different reasons. Their citizens were not always happy about spending money and time on human rights problems abroad. Japan, in particular, seemed disinclined to link its growing foreign assistance and investment to human rights performance in foreign states.

Thus, from an international perspective, progress on protecting human rights will be sporadic as it has been in the past. Overall, however, the trend is encouraging. In historical terms there has been revolutionary change in favor of human rights. The world in 1995 or 2000 will be far different from that of 1945, much less that of 1900. Yet, particular persons, unfortunately, will still be the victims of political murder, torture, starvation, inadequate health care, and insufficient education. Still more unfortunate is the fact that sometimes these deprivations of internationally recognized human rights will occur on a national or regional basis. The challenge for the future is to build on the remarkable changes of the past to guarantee the protection of rights for all without regard to nationality, ethnicity, gender, and color.

## ANNOTATED BIBLIOGRAPHY

Claude, Richard P., and Burns H. Weston, eds. *Human Rights in the World Community.* 2nd ed. Philadelphia: University of Pennsylvania Press, 1992.
   The best reader on international human rights, with broad coverage of many good essays by leading authorities. Attention to basic standards and different approaches to implementing them.

Donnelly, Jack. *Human Rights and International Relations.* Boulder: Westview Press, 1993.
   A readable introduction covering basic theory and practice. Sections on political philosophy as well as national and international practice. Broad coverage by one of the best American thinkers on this subject.

Forsythe, David P. *Human Rights and World Politics.* Rev. ed. Lincoln: University of Nebraska Press, 1989.
   A readable introduction, with cartoons. Special attention to U.S. foreign policy and private American groups lobbying for human rights in Washington.

———. *Human Rights and Peace.* Lincoln: University of Nebraska Press, 1993.

A discussion of how human rights relates to overt international war, covert force in foreign policy, and domestic violence. Much attention to democracy and international war, United States overthrow of elected governments during the cold war, and case studies of revolution in Sri Lanka, Liberia, and Romania.

Lauren, Paul Gordon. *Power and Prejudice.* Boulder: Westview Press, 1988.
A readable history of international efforts to deal with racial discrimination. Attention to slavery and the slave trade, racist thinking in the 1930s, the end of colonialism, and contemporary issues in the United Nations. Many good historical examples of both racism and progress in overcoming it.

Timerman, Jacobo. *Prisoner without a Name, Cell without a Number.* New York: Knopf, 1981.
First-person account by the dynamic journalist of his experience as a political prisoner and disappeared person in Argentina during military rule. Griping accounts of torture, anti-Semitism, and efforts by the Carter administration to secure his release.

Vincent, R. J. *Human Rights and International Relations.* Cambridge: Cambridge University Press, 1986.
A brief introduction by the late British scholar. Particularly good on philosophy and human rights. Also good on theories of international relations and human rights.

Wechsler, Lawrence. *A Miracle, a Universe.* New York: Viking/Penguin, 1991.
Moving account of repression in Uruguay and Argentina and of efforts by various human rights organizations to improve the situation.

## WORKS CONSULTED

Blaustein, Albert P. et. al., eds. *Human Rights Sourcebook.* New York: Paragon House, 1987.
Brownlie, Ian. *Basic Documents on Human Rights.* 2nd ed. New York: Oxford University Press, 1991.
U.S. House Committee on Foreign Affairs. *Human Rights Documents.* Committee Print. Washington: Government Printing Office, 1983.

# CHAPTER 8

# Self-Determination

# Dov Ronen

Over the years, many struggles for self-determination in different parts of the world have resulted in bloody conflicts and sometimes threatened world peace. There is no simple answer as to how to end, or prevent, such conflicts. Should one engage in, or advocate, the forceful repression of those engaged in the struggle arguing that the already independent state is the terminal outcome of the exercise of this right? Or, should one support the right of specific "legitimate" claims, thus possibly limiting the number, or reducing the intensity, of conflicts? A third option could be to insist on granting the right to self-determination to all those who struggle for it.

Each of these options (and others) has its advocates and opponents. For some, self-determination is no more than an empty slogan used by "revolutionaries," "terrorists," or disenchanted elites in their striving for political power, hence the struggle should be forcefully repressed. Others argue that the right to self-determination is only a right to overthrow colonial or other foreign rule, and does not apply to groups within legally constituted, independent countries. Proponents of one or the other option may also be associated with a specific political view or political status. Liberals and conservatives, for example, may be assumed to have different views of self-determination. Further, political actors in power are likely to have different views from those seeking power.

## WHAT IS SELF-DETERMINATION?

All these and other positions in regards to self-determination are possible, because there is no consensus among scholars, political actors, and observers on what self-determination means, and little agreement on the likely consequences of self-determination for the stability of the international system.

### The Meaning of "Self" and "Determination"

Defining self-determination first requires that one think about the meaning of "self." The Charter of the United Nations, for example, recognizes the self-determination of "peoples," thus implying that "peoples" are the legitimate selves. But it is not made clear in the Charter what group of human beings constitutes a "people." Some scholars, referring to the Charter and various other documents, speak of self-determination of "peoples and nations." But, the addition of "nations" does not help to clarify the issue. What group of human beings constitutes a "nation" having such a right? Is the numerical size of a "nation" or a "people" an appropriate criterion? Or might "people" be defined in terms of a common culture or in terms of economic viability? And, in any case, who is to decide which legitimate "self" has a legitimate "right"?

"Determination" is similarly difficult to define. Although that difficulty is often "solved" by assuming that the right to self-determination is a right to independent statehood. This assumption stems largely from the fact that the term *self-determination* is most immediately associated in our minds with the struggle of colonized peoples for freedom from their colonial masters in the post–World War II era. Since colonized peoples became citizens in independent states through the exercise of the right to self-determination, a clear-cut link has been formed in many minds between the exercise of that right and independent statehood.

## The Consequences of Self-Determination

Scholars and policymakers do not agree on the likely consequences of granting self-determination to all groups who struggle for it. Many observers, however, are concerned that unrestricted self-determination might lead to a world of hundreds, perhaps thousands, of additional states. Consequently, even those who, in theory, would be sympathetic to the right to self-determination for groups within independent states hesitate in practice to subscribe to unlimited self-determination for fear of a resulting world disorder and the probable mushrooming of conflicts.

## Moral versus Legal Bases: The Key Distinction

To understand self-determination better, we must distinguish between the legal and moral bases of self-determination, and the connections between the two. Legal bases for self-determination may be found in the Charter of the United Nations and in various other international documents. Among the moral bases of self-determination one could list ethical values, norms of behavior, philosophical ideas, religious beliefs, and, probably in the future, scientific evidence on human nature as well.

The framers of the Charter of the United Nations and other international documents attempted to codify the moral principle of self-determination and officially recognize it as a right. It is, however, an open question as to whether or not such legal documents have succeeded in capturing the essence of the moral right and in delineating the forms of its expression accordingly. In any case, if the moral basis of self-determination preceded the legal principles, then human beings probably struggle for self-determination not because it is a legal right but because it is a moral right.

This chapter examines the legal and the moral bases separately. I will argue that ongoing struggles for self-determination may best be understood as struggles waged on moral grounds of self-determination. Consequently, the resolution of conflicts stemming from the struggle for self-determination should also be based on moral rather than legal principles. To use an analogy, "thou shall not kill," a moral principle, precedes the legal prohibitions of murder and should be the fundamental reason for respecting the sanctity of human life. The legal ban "do not kill" codifies the moral principle and can assist in reinforcing the moral ban "thou shall not kill."

Further, in this chapter I will explore the following proposition: without the free exercise of the moral right to self-determination there can be no end to conflicts stemming from this right, nor lasting peace in the world. Therefore, for the sake of peace, the moral right to self-determination should be supported and granted. In my judgement, the realization of self-determination on the basis of moral principles is practical. It is likely to lead not to hundreds or thousands of new independent states but, more likely, toward a new global order that will not be based on a state system.

## THE LEGAL BASIS FOR SELF-DETERMINATION

The Charter of the United Nations is the primary source for legal interpretations of self-determination in the post–World War II era. All subsequent international legal documents containing references to self-determination may be seen as elaborations, clarifications, and reinterpretations of the principles found in the UN Charter. Further, most if not all political statements and declarations by governments and nongovernmental political leaders refer to the principles found in the Charter.

### Self-Determination in the U.N. Charter

The Charter of the United Nations was signed by delegates of fifty-one states on June 26, 1945, before the end of the Second World War in September 1945, and before the "outbreak" of the cold war. People hoped the United Nations would become a truly global organization dedicated to the preservation of peace. In order to promote world peace, the United Nations was committed to promoting human rights, social and economic progress, and self-government for people in "non-self-governing territories."

The phrase "self-determination" appears twice in the UN Charter, in chapter 1 (Article 1, paragraph 2) and Chapter 9 (Article 55). However, neither reference provides a definition of the concept nor specifies a "right" to self-determination.

Chapter 1, Article 1, lists the "Purposes of the United Nations." It states that these include: "To develop friendly relations among nations based on respect for the principle of equal rights and self-determination of peoples, and to take other appropriate measures to strengthen universal peace." Chapter IX is devoted to "International Economic and Social Cooperation." Article 55 mentions "respect for equal rights and self-determination of peoples." In addition, the U.N. Charter contains two other phrases that have come to connote self-determination. These phrases appear in Chapters 11 and 12 of the Charter. One is "self-government"; the other, "independence."

## Self-Government and Independence

Article 73 of Chapter 11 presents a "Declaration Regarding Non-Self-Governing Territories." This declaration refers to "territories whose peoples have not yet attained a full measure of *self-government*." It asks "[m]embers of the United Nations which have or assume responsibilities for the administration of territories whose peoples have not yet attained a full measure of self-government . . . to develop self-government, to take due account of the political aspirations of the peoples, and to assist them in the progressive development of their free political institutions . . ."

Chapter 12, on the "International Trusteeship System," establishes a new system for overseeing former colonies of the Central Powers that had been freed at the end of World War I. These former colonies were called "Mandates" under the system created by the League of Nations. Chapter 12 states that the objective of the new system should be "to promote the political, economic, social, and educational advancement of the inhabitants of the Trust Territories, and their progressive development towards self-government or independence." Thus, Chapter 12 refers not to colonized peoples at large but only to the inhabitants of "Trust territories," which were relatively few in number. In addition, in Chapter 12 *self-government* is not used synonymously with *independence,* and self-determination is not mentioned.

## Self-Determination and Decolonization

While the Charter of the United Nations did not intend to give rights to colonized peoples to rise against colonial rule, the Charter came to be seen by many groups as providing justification for their efforts at self-determination. From the early 1950s on, members of the United Nations began to make a direct connection between three ideas: self-government, non-self-governing peoples, and the right of self-determination.

**Key U.N. Resolutions in the 1950s.**   The first steps in this process involved the U.N. Commission on Human Rights. In 1952, the commission was requested "to study ways and means which would ensure the rights of *peoples and nations* to self-determination." The first result of this study was included in General Assembly Resolution 648 (7), of December 10, 1952, which stated that a territory may attain a full measure of self-government in one of three ways: (1) "the attainment of independence"; (2) "the attainment of other separate system of self-government"; or (3) "the free association of a territory with other component parts of the metropolitan or other country." In 1953, General Assembly Resolution 742 (8) added that a full measure of self-government may be attained "primarily through independence." This resolution and subsequent discussions in the United Nations in the 1950s may be primarily responsible for the subsequent synonymous use of the three concepts: 'self-government,' 'self-determination,' and 'independence.'

**The 1960 Declaration of Independence.**   On December 14, 1960, the United Nations formally recognized decolonization as a right in the "Declaration on the Granting of Independence to Colonial Countries and Peoples" (General Assembly Resolution 15514[15]). It declared that, "All peoples have the right of self-determination; by virtue of that right they freely determine their political status and freely pursue their economic, social and cultural development." Further, it stated that the "Inadequacy of political, economic, social or educational preparedness should never serve as a pretext for delaying independence." Significantly for the future evolution of the notion of self-determination, the declaration also contained the statement that, "Any attempt aimed at the partial or total disruption of the national unity and the territorial integrity of a country is incompatible with the principles of the Charter of the United Nations."

Some of the founders of the United Nations in 1945 may have intended the new international organization to be concerned with decolonization, but this intent was not explicitly translated into basic principles in the Charter. Decolonization became a "higher law" in 1960, because the colonized, often through self-appointed representatives of "their" peoples, pressed against colonial rule and lobbied successfully for support within the United Nations.

**Human Rights and Self-Determination.**    Additional legal support for the right to self-determination came in 1966 when the United Nations enacted the International Covenants on Human Rights. Both the Covenant of Economic, Social, and Cultural Rights and the Covenant on Civil and Political Rights contain in their Article 1 the same statement: "All peoples have the right to self-determination. By virtue of that right, they freely determine their political status and freely pursue their economic, social, and cultural development." Further reference to self-determination is found in the African Charter on Human and People's Rights (1986), which states that protection of human rights "enshrines the people's right to self-determination."

*Self-Determination in Newly Independent States*

By the late 1960's most, though not all, overseas colonies in Africa, Asia and the Caribbean, had become independent states. A few minor boundary changes were effected—for example, Pakistan became independent from India—but most boundaries were inherited colonial boundaries. The colonial boundaries, in turn, were carved out by colonial rulers without regard to the variety of "peoples," "ethnic groups," or "nations" enclosed within them. The new independent states were successors to entities created by colonialism, thus the successors of nationally or ethnically diverse entities. Among the several hundred groups that composed the population of Nigeria, for example, there are several that had independent existence long before the colonizers arrived. Nigeria may not be typical because of the size of its population, which today is estimated to be some eighty or ninety million, but it is far from unique in this respect. The cultural, linguistic, often religious distinctions among ethnic groups or nations within newly independent states are often so deep, and the resulting social *and* spacial separations so pronounced, that in certain circumstances, self-perception of being a separate "nation" or a distinct "ethnic group" can be more meaningful to members than can being designated as members of a plural society.

The governments of the newly independent states accepted the old colonial boundaries, which became internationally recognized boundaries safeguarded by the U.N. commitment to the territorial integrity of the new states. No group within these states had been considered as having the right to self-determination. Secession was out of question. The citizens of newly independent states constituted the nation. In order to consolidate that nation, and to attain a sense of nationhood processes of "national integration" were launched as part and parcel of modernization.

Nevertheless, there have been numerous attempted secessions, that is, the attempted breaking away of a population and territory from an independent state. Notable among them over the years were the attempted secessions of the eastern part of Nigeria from Nigeria under the name Biafra, southern Sudan from Sudan in Africa, and the Tamils from Sri Lanka in Asia. The only successful secession from a newly independent state was that of Bangladesh from Pakistan. In addition, Eritrea successfully seceded in 1992 from Ethiopia, after decades of struggle.

## Self-determination in Older Independent States

Not only newly independent states but most other states in the world are marked by major cultural, linguistic, religious, or ethnic distinctions. As a result, secessionist attempts, or struggles for self-determination falling short of secession, have been made in the western, noncolonized world as well, at least since the late 1960s. For example, some French speakers in Quebec have long demanded linguistic autonomy, others secession from Canada—and thus independence for Quebec. Similarly, there have been secessionist demands in western Europe by Basques and Catalans in Spain, in Brittany and Corsica from France; and in Northern Ireland, Scotland, and Wales in the United Kingdom. Struggles for self-determination have been waged by German-speaking Swiss in the Jura region of Switzerland and the Flemish in Belgium.

The number and intensity of struggles for self-determination have fluctuated over the years since the end of World War II. In several newly independent states, such as Uganda, military regimes have suppressed or neutralized the exercise of most, if not all, rights. In addition, struggles for self-determination by the Bosnians in the former Yugoslavia, the Tamils in Sri Lanka, and the Eritreans in Ethiopia have continued up to the present. Eventually, some western European states' governments made concessions to various groups seeking self-determination. The Basques and Catalans received a degree of political and cultural autonomy in Spain. Concessions were also made in Belgium to Flammands and to French speakers in Quebec.

In some other instances, demands were satisfied to a sufficient degree through the political process. Politically active Bretons, many of whom were members of the French Socialist party, could pay attention to the grievances of Bretons in Brittany once the Socialist party gained electoral power and formed the French government. Similarly, Scottish demands for sovereign independence tended to decline when the Labour Party, in which many politically active Scots are members, came to power and represented Scottish interests in Parliament.

## *The Legal Bases for Self-Determination and the State*

Do the legal grounds for self-determination provide clear guidance to determine who has the right to self-determination and what that right entails? If the legal bases were unequivocal, then we could assume that some, most, or possibly all conflicts stemming from the exercise of that right could be ended or prevented. To use an analogy, if the minimum age for marriage were legally set, clearly stated and widely published, then it would be evident who is allowed to get married and who is not. This would not prevent some illegal marriages, but at least it would allow parents and authorities to prevent the marriage of underage persons who claim to be "in love." Essentially, such a law would provide clear, unequivocal guidance for preventing or resolving certain kinds of conflict within the families.

Our review indicates that since World War II the right to self-determination has been recognized in legal documents, but it has not been defined unequivocally. Thus, it remains unclear who exactly has the right, in what circumstances, and what it might entail in practice. However, from the available historical evidence it appears that among the various interpretations of self-determination one has gained greater validity than any other. It is that self-determination applies to the right of independent *states* to continue to exist, and to groups of people deemed to be inhabitants of "illegal" states, such as colonial holdings or the satellites of the communist ruled empires. Two phrases might help us understand why this interpretation has gained validity. One is *territorial integrity*, the other *nation-state*.

**Territorial Integrity.**    Secessionist movements become entangled with the legal concept of territoriality because Article 2 of the U.N. Charter recognizes the right of states to protect their "territorial integrity" in case of external threats to the state. Consequently, many governments when faced with internal secessionist movements claim that such movements are aided and abated by foreign powers, often a neighbor, and thus an external threat to their territorial integrity. For example, the attempted secession of Kashmir is claimed by the Indian government, rightly or wrongly, to be aided by neighboring Pakistan.

The idea of "national interest," while not mentioned in the U.N. Charter, has reinforced the importance of the idea of territorial integrity. National interest is perceived by diplomats, policymakers, and other political actors in the international system to have legal basis. Thus, if exercise of self-determination would affect the territorial integrity of my state, it could be legitimately opposed on the basis of "national interest." Inversely, the exercise of the right of self-determination and its effect on the territorial integrity of another state would be acceptable, if the boundaries of that other state were deemed illegal by my state, such as those of the former Soviet Union or those of present day Iraq after its invasion of Kuwait.

**Nation-State.**    The other phrase that helped this interpretation to gain validity is the term *nation-state*. The territory of a state is inhabited by a population that is more commonly referred to as "the nation." In fact, the state, as legal entity, has two dimensions and has been interchangeably regarded as both territorial state and nation-state (or, at times, national state). Secession from a state would therefore involve the breaking away of both territory and the inhabitants, the nation, living on it. "Territorial integrity," then, safeguards not only the territorial domain of the state but also its national domain. The U.N. Charter, in fact, uses the terms *state* and *nation* interchangeably. The problem is that the term *nation-state* does not readily apply to many countries in the world. Most countries are multination states. In fact, human beings struggling for self-determination within independent states consider themselves to be a nation and aspire to form their own, more genuine, nation-state. The prevailing interpretation of the legal bases of self-determination denies the right to self-determination to any part of the nation, which is defined by the territorial extent, the boundaries, of the state.

## THE MORAL BASIS OF SELF-DETERMINATION

Moral or ethical principles may serve as a better guide for understanding the struggle for self-determination, because they have influenced the concept of 'self-determination' as defined in legal documents. Exploring the moral aspects of self-determination is therefore an exploration of the very sources from which the legal principle emanates.

*Moral* is defined by most dictionaries as implying conformity with the generally accepted standards of goodness or rightness in conduct, or character. "*Ethical* by most dictionaries means conformity with an elaborated, ideal code of moral principles." If a self's aspiration for freedom from being "determined" by an "other" conforms with "generally accepted standard of goodness or rightness in conduct, or character," then self-determination is on a moral basis because, to be free from unfreedom is moral and ethical. Hence the unhindered exercise of self-determination is a moral and ethical right.

Who has that right? What is the unit whose freedom is referred to? Does it not refer to the individual human being? It seems clear from history that the right was exercised by groups of human beings. In legal documents the right is granted to the "people" or "nation." However, the aspiration exists within the individual human being. It is the human being that aspires, or does not, to freedom from unfreedom. Thus, the relevant moral standards pertain, at least a priori, to the individual person.

The personal aspiration for self-determination has probably existed from the early days of human history. There have been innumerable manifestations of this aspiration *through* slave rebellions and opposition to rule inflicted after military conquests and to tyrannical rule. The recognition of the morality of this aspiration and its propagation as a right is more recent. There could have been no recognition of the right to self-determination, a sense that one is entitled to be free from being subject to an external will, before a long process of secularization, which had taken place in Europe since about the sixteenth century. The period from the sixteenth century to the incorporation of the right in international documents may be regarded as the centuries-long evolution of the moral right to self-determination.

Important stages along this long evolutionary process were the American and French Revolutions, attempts at national and proletarian revolutions in the nineteenth century, agitations of human beings as members of "minorities" and "nationalities" before the First World War, and between the two world wars. The Wilsonian principle of self-determination and various decisions of the League of Nations also stemmed from moral principles.

## The American and French Revolutions

The recognition of the human right to freedom *from* various conditions of unfreedom emerged with the process of secularization in western Europe. This process culminated in the Enlightenment. The ideas of the Enlightenment greatly influenced the American and French Revolutions. Thus, the resolution of the Continental Congress on July 4, 1776, stated that "these united colonies are, and of right ought to be, free and independent States." This resolution referred to the right of political freedom from British rule. Subsequently, Jefferson and the other Founding Fathers were concerned with individual rights and freedoms within the thirteen states.

So were the revolutionaries of the French Revolution. However, the important transformation from *personal* freedom to *national* freedom occurred in Europe after the French Revolution. More precisely, individual rights, gestating through hundreds of years of secularization, recognized in the Constitution of the United States and implied by the French *Declaration of the Rights of Man and the Citizen* eventually appeared as *national* rights in Europe. In France, the emphasis of individual rights led to the 1791 and 1792 *plebiscites* (from the Latin *plebs* [people] and *scitum* [decree], itself from the root *scire,* "to know," i.e., the will of the people) to find out whether or not the people of the papal enclaves, Avignon, Venaisssin, Savoy, and Nice wanted to be part of France. As most "peoples" or "nations" in the nineteenth century were under the sway of large empires—among them the Holy Roman, Hapsburg, Russian, Spanish, and Ottoman Empires—the idea of freedom prompted *national* awakenings there too.

Many thinkers and political actors became excited by the newly recognized moral right of human beings. They demanded political rights, the rights of free speech and organization. They also demanded and became the proponents of *national* freedom.

## National and Class Self-Determination

While the American and French Revolutions prompted *national* movements for political rights and freedoms another revolution, the Industrial Revolution, brought about the socialist/communist movement or, more accurately, the proletarian-*class* movement.

As national liberation movements emerged in the mid-nineteenth century, Marx proposed that the core problem throughout human history was not lack of freedom of *nations* but the economic deprivation of the *class* of workers. Marx proposed the deprived proletariat as the preeminent "self" identity instead of the nation.

Marx's idea was as ingenious as it was innovative. While most inheritors of the American and French Revolutionary ideas were preoccupied with political rights, political freedoms, and social justice, Marx addressed economic issues: ownership and distribution of resources. While nationalists fought for *national* self-determination against monarchs, empires, absolute rulers, and foreign rule; communists fought for *class* self-determination against capitalist rule. While the nationalists aggregated around a national, linguistic, shared historical, or religious identity; the communists aggregated, or were supposed to have aggregated around their shared consciousness of their unbearable economic condition.

The nationalists wanted primarily to attain *political* power in order to control their lives; the communists wanted primarily to attain *economic* power in order to establish a new political order. The communists wanted to change the world; the nationalists wanted changes in and of their country. And, significantly, communists moved against the middle class, the bourgeoisie, the urban dwellers; the nationalists were the middle class, fought for middle class values of education, history, language, and democracy.

Thus, in the nineteenth century two schools of thought, two rival and seemingly unreconcilable interpretations of the individual's moral right had emerged, two different types of movements stemming from the very same moral principle at the same time. National revolutions erupted in 1848, the same year that Marx and Engels's *Communist Manifesto* was published.

Curiously enough, the European socialist movement was the first to raise the issue of national self-determination. The apparently first explicit use of the term *self-determination* in a formal document was in the resolution of the 1896 International Socialist congress in London, which stated that the Congress "upholds the full rights of the self-determination of all *nations*." In 1903, the Second Congress of the Russian Social-Democratic Labor Party adopted "the right to self-determination for all nations forming part of the state." In 1913 in his "Postulates on the National Question" Lenin restated "the right of every nation to self-determination and even to secession from Russia." In January 1915, the Socialist Conference of Denmark, Holland, Norway, and Sweden also called for the "recognition of the self-determination of nations."

How could that happen? It was not because socialists and communists underwent a change of heart. Marxists did not doubt that proletarian demands were more "correct," or at least that the historically proven economic exploitation obliges the priority of economic demands. They just had to deal with the historic reality of the growing effectiveness of *national* demands. The fact was that in the nineteenth century, the Poles and the Irish, to cite only two examples, demanded rights *as* Poles and *as* Irish rather than as proletarians. In the eyes of the socialists, and later communists, persistent *national* demands for self-determination threatened to diminish the effectiveness of *proletarian* demands for the same. It seemed to them tactically useful to support the former in order to enhance the effectiveness of the latter.

## Self-Determination during and after World War I

The French Revolutionary idea that human beings have a right to be free spread, and in spite of the failure of most European nationalist movements to attain that freedom in 1848, the aspiration for freedom from repressive rulers intensified. The Great War started, in a very real sense, because of a struggle for self-determination. Archduke Franz Ferdinand's assassin was a Serbian nationalist protesting Austria-Hungary's annexation of Bosnia-Herzegovina. The Austrians, fearful of the influence of nationalism within their borders, decided to go to war with the state of Serbia, which was backing the rebels in Bosnia-Herzegovina. Russia distrusted Austrian motives and wanted to increase its own influence in the Balkans—partly out of a sense of pan-Slavic nationalism. When Austria declared war on Serbia, Russia declared war on Austria, and the conflagration began.

This in not to say, however, that the European powers fought the First World War over the principle of self-determination. Each was concerned with its own position in the state system; the concerns of peoples like the Serbians or the Belgians, while providing good material for propaganda, were secondary. In October 1915, for example, Arthur Balfour, a member of the British cabinet, circulated a memorandum on war aims that received wide acceptance and generally reflected public opinion. Among other things, this statement called for "rearranging the map of Europe in closer agreement with what we rather vaguely call 'the principle of nationality.'" From the rest of the document, however, one can tell that Balfour was more concerned with maintaining a balance of power than with promoting self-determination. Meanwhile, the Germans were considering changing some borders themselves, but they did not even feign concern for other nationalities. Their aim was to gain more territory for Germany.

**Wilson's Self-Determination.**    Historians disagree over Woodrow Wilson's commitment to self-determination during and after the First World War. Many of his public declarations, including his War Message and the Fourteen Points, indicate that he considered self-determination to be an important principle. He obviously favored democracy (which he associated with Germany and Austria-Hungary). He apparently believed that he, as an eminently qualified representative of the United States, had a mission to reform the world political system. However, his policies often fell short of his ideals. Willingly or not, he had to recognize the limits of his power.

For the first two and one-half years that the Great War raged in Europe, American interests remained fixed on freedom of the seas and the rights of neutrals. Wilson may have believed that a victory by the Central Powers would destroy his hopes of reforming the world order, but if so, he hid his feelings well. In his actions, he was careful to maintain at least the appearance of neutrality. He offered to mediate an end to the conflict, but he based his offers upon the idea that the European powers should return to the prewar status quo; apparently, the ideal of self-determination had no place in his proposals.

When Wilson gave his War Message to Congress on April 2, 1917, he spoke of a war for democracy, for the right of peoples to have a say in their own government, and for the rights of small nations. However, practical concerns took precedence over ideals, at least initially. The most obvious candidate for territorial reform among the Central Powers was Austria-Hungary, but Wilson's primary concern was to maintain stability in the region. Therefore, Wilson concentrated on separating Austria-Hungary. In truth, however, Wilson held onto his earlier policy until well into the summer. Only a series of national rebellions in the Austria-Hungarian Empire, combined with the obvious inability of the Habsburgs to act independently of Germany, persuaded Wilson and his advisors to change course.

This example notwithstanding, the Fourteen Points stands out as a significant departure from past diplomatic practice. It represented liberals' most fervently held hopes; they clung to the idea that national self-determination, combined with a mechanism for settling international disputes (the League of Nations), offered the best chance of creating a lasting peace. Eight of the Fourteen Points dictate the adjustment of borders, either in order to create new nation-states or to give territory to old ones along lines of nationality; point number fourteen calls for the establishment of the League. However, applying the liberals' lofty ideals to the real world of international diplomacy would prove difficult. In both their birth and their application, the Fourteen Points would highlight the complex interaction between idealism and power politics.

There can be little doubt that the Fourteen Points reflect Wilson's intentions concerning the postwar world, since he sought little advice in drafting them. Indeed, the document was not born of international cooperation or even consultation. It was Wilson's reaction to the challenge of the Bolshevik Revolution and a unilateral attempt on his part to influence Allied war aims.

The Bolshevik Party took control of Russia in November 1917. It immediately pressed the Allies for a peace based on the principle of "no indemnities or annexations." Wilson's foremost advisor, Colonel House, had just arrived in London for an interallied conference. He asked Britain and France for a statement of liberal war aims, as a way of keeping Russia in the war, but was unsuccessful. Then, in mid-December the Bolsheviks, pressing their appeal for a general peace and desiring to demonstrate the degenerate nature of the capitalist states, published all the secret treaties entered into by the Entente powers before the war. The Austrian foreign minister followed this up by stating that the Central Powers would consider a peace without annexations. A political uproar followed among liberals and socialists in Britain and America, who believed these offers deserved a response. Wilson felt he had to act, to keep Russia in the war, to try to move the Central Powers toward a settlement, and to compete with Bolshevism as a political philosophy. The Fourteen Points were his response.

The reaction from the Germans and Austrians was positive, though they were evasive on some specific points. Wilson warned them in an address on February 11, 1918, that peace could not be made by old methods or standards. He went on to define four principles upon which the belligerents must agree if talks were to continue. Three of these directly addressed the idea that national self-determination must be the basis of all territorial settlements. Here was Wilson at his most powerful and idealistic.

Reality intruded on March 3, when the Germans forced the Russians to accept the Treaty of Brest-Litovsk, which included enormous territorial annexations. The true extent of German interest in self-determination and a moderate peace suddenly became obvious. Wilson, in despair, accepted the fact that Germany would have to be defeated militarily before he could hope to implement his program. He now pinned his hopes on the peace conference that would follow the war. He expected that the United States' contribution to the war effort would give him the power to hold his allies' ambitions in check.

When military necessity forced the Germans to sue for peace in the autumn of 1918, they did so on the basis of the Fourteen Points. Britain and France also accepted the points as the basis for an armistice, though with some important reservations. The Peace Conference of 1919 would show whether or not Wilson's program could resist the power politics of the Old World.

**The Peace Conferences.** Wilson went to the Paris Peace Conference of 1919 with high hopes, hopes that mirrored those of thousands of liberals and millions of nationalists. Self-determination would be one of the key elements of his program; it would, so he thought, allow democracy to flourish, ridding the world of autocracy and exploitation. But the principle of self-determination had no legal standing at the Paris Peace Conferences; the other participants were not obliged to pay it any heed. Moreover, powerful forces were ranged against it: racism, imperialism, economic and political self-interest, and a thirst for revenge built up over four years of brutal warfare. The intransigence of the other allied leaders, exacerbated by the feelings of their constituents, denied Wilson much of his new world order.

The most positive way in which the conferees applied self-determination concerned the new political entities of eastern Europe, including Poland, Yugoslavia, Hungary, and Czechoslovakia. The Paris conferences created these states from territories formerly controlled by the Central Powers and Russia (the latter, having opted out of the war, was not allowed to participate). Teams of experts from Britain and the United States pored over maps in an effort to draw boundaries according to nationality. In the end, peoples who had been subject to outside rule gained their independence, with one important caveat: many of the new nation-states contained minorities that would eventually voice their own nationalistic ambitions. Still, the established powers could look upon the independence of these new nations in a positive light, for idealistic as well as practical reasons.

Elsewhere in the various treaties, the principle of self-determination was more obvious by its absence than its application. Germany and Austria both lost territory in which ethnic Germans constituted the majority of the population; later, the two nations would be denied the option of unification. Apparently, self-determination applied only to the victors and their friends. It also applied only to white people. Territories removed from Turkish control were made "mandates" of the victorious powers—little more than colonies, actually. The same happened to Germany's colonies in Africa, Asia, and the Pacific; the British, French, Italians, and Japanese divided them up among themselves. Representatives from many small countries—such as Ho Chi Minh from French Indochina—came to Paris, hoping that they would be given some say in their own affairs by these high-minded Europeans. They left with nothing to show for their efforts; frustrated, many of them returned to their homelands to foment rebellion.

The Paris Peace Conference certainly cannot be considered an unqualified success for the principle of self-determination. And yet, it represented an important step forward. The hopes of liberals and nationalists had not been completely fulfilled, but the issue was out in the open. For the first time, self-determination had become a foundation for international agreements. More than ever before, it would be a rallying cry for peoples all over the world.

## Self-Determination between the World Wars

The problem of self-determination was not solved after the end of the First World War. A variety of groups of people were again enclosed in independent states whose governments now attempted to create national unity within them. The League of Nations attempted to guarantee minority rights by forcing the governments of the newly created states of Poland, Czechoslovakia, and Romania to sign minorities treaties. These were to protect minorities from forced assimilation and discrimination. But this attempt did not work; the governments of small states were no more willing to accept intervention in their internal affairs than were the governments of large countries. In any case, minorities could be guaranteed only their civil rights, which fell far short of the right to self-determination they hoped to attain. By safeguarding their civil rights but negating the right of minorities to self-determination in the form of autonomy or independent statehood, the commission of the League of Nations responsible for minorities in fact safeguarded the rights of governments to consolidate their states. The League did not recognize the right of secession.

Then, there were cases of minorities whose homelands were in neighboring states. These minorities came under the care of the concerned governments. Thus, German and Polish governments were concerned with Germans in Poland, and similar relations existed between Greece and Turkey, Poland and Lithuania, Greece and Bulgaria, Albania and Greece, and Hungary and Romania. None of these measures solved what were labeled "minority problems."

The issue of minorities was not limited to the new European states emerging from defeated Austria-Hungary and the Ottoman

Empire. There were "minority problems" in the British Empire (Egypt, India, Iraq) and in the French Empire (in the Middle East and Africa). There were nationalist insurrections in Wales, Brittany, Flanders, Alsace, and Scotland. In Spain, Catalans and Basques rebelled. The Aaland Islands dispute illustrates the dilemma faced by the League of Nations after World War I.

**The Aaland Island Case.**    These islands, located next to Finland, "belonged" to Sweden. In 1809, Sweden ceded them to Russia, which also ruled over Finland. In 1917, Finland declared independence. The Swedes on the islands, more than 90 percent of the inhabitants, wanted the Aaland Islands to be attached to Sweden. Finland objected, arguing that they inherited the islands from Russia. The Swedish government proposed a plebiscite on the islands, to which Finland objected. There was an impasse.

Britain, afraid of war breaking out between Sweden and Finland, brought the issue to the Council of the League of Nations under Article 11 of the Covenant. Finland objected to discussion of the issue by the League because, according to Article 15 "domestic jurisdiction" was not an affair of the council. The matter was referred to Commission of Jurists, who came out with a complex and interesting decision. The commission distinguished between external and internal self-determination. So far as external self-determination was concerned—that is, the international status of the islands—the territorial dimension counted: the territory would belong to Finland. As far as internal self-determination was concerned—that is, the internal constitutional arrangements—the inhabitants were granted considerable autonomy. Whether or not this dualism might have application elsewhere was an open question. It is significant, however, that, in this case, the distinction between external and internal self-determination settled a problem and probably prevented war.

**Successes and Failures of the League.**    The First World War, as its name indicates, involved virtually all states of the world. The carnage was so great and the desire for peace so intense, that ideas were seriously entertained to change the system, the international state system, in which such a war was possible. However, after World War I, the French delegation, and it alone, was willing to renounce the principle of national sovereignty for the purpose of creating a new international order. The French were ready to transform the League of Nations into a military security organization to which the various states would transfer some of their sovereign rights. No other delegation was ready to go along. National sovereignty gained the upper hand in its competition with the principle of self-determination. Claims and struggles for self-determination continued. Twenty years after the League of Nations was founded another world war broke out. Could it have been prevented if the moral principle of self-determination had been more faithfully adhered to?

## IS THE MORAL BASIS OF
## SELF-DETERMINATION PRACTICAL?

Permitting the unrestricted realization of self-determination on the basis of moral principles seems an attractive response to the human aspiration for freedom. But is it practical; would this approach really reduce conflicts in the world? Many observers of international politics argue that this approach might actually lead to chaos because it would result in the birth of hundreds of tiny new states that would destabilize the international system.

In my judgement, such concerns are not warranted. The exercise of self-determination on the basis of moral principles need not lead to independent statehood but rather could lead to other forms of autonomy achieved, for instance, through various types of federal arrangements. The United States is one example of a federal arrangement in which each of the fifty states, and within them various local levels, have a degree of autonomy from national government control.

Even if the widespread exercise of the moral right to self-determination did lead to independent statehood for many groups, this would not necessarily mean chaos. These small and economically weak states would form various types of confederation arrangements with other, similar states. I believe it reasonable to hypothesize that the greater the political disintegration of existing states under the pressure of the struggle for self-determination, the greater will be the need to develop such confederation arrangements. This, in turn, could lead to a different world order of various types of confederations, themselves composed of possibly scores of ever changing number of autonomous communities. In other words, the recognition and exercise of the moral right to self-determination is likely to hasten the end of the international system of independent states as we know it today and with it the end of a centuries-old pattern of inter-state conflict and violence.

## SELF-DETERMINATION DURING THE COLD WAR AND AFTER

During the cold war did western governments advocate the self-determination of peoples behind the Iron Curtain either on legal or moral grounds? The struggle for self-determination in the Communist world was clearly encouraged by exiled groups in the West, by the Voice of America broadcasts, and through other governmental, public and private efforts. On the other hand, a close examination of the stated *foreign policies* of United States and other western governments seems to show that the encouragement of that struggle for self-determination was not their priority. Instead, priority was given to nuclear and strategic considerations, limitation of the Soviet Union's foreign influence, democratization of regimes, and other issues emerging from time to time, all within the framework of superpower confrontation.

Western governments supported and aimed to export democracy, just as Woodraw Wilson had decades earlier. However, unlike Wilson, western statesmen did not hide democracy behind the noble slogan of self-determination during the cold war. Just the opposite. Strategic, political, and economic aims were hidden under the noble slogan of democracy. The term *self-determination* was referred to by western powers during the cold war only if a struggle could be cast, in some way, in the context of decolonization. Among such struggles were those in Namibia and South Africa and, at times, by Palestinians. During the cold war, self-determination in countries behind the Iron Curtain was not a major issue for the West on either a legal or a moral basis.

For that reason or another, the frequency, intensity, and spread of the struggle for self-determination *within* the Soviet Union and Yugoslavia during the cold war are far from clear. The Baltic states broke away from the Soviet Union as expected with the *end* of the cold war and, after the cold war, unexpectedly, other Soviet Union republics did so as well. Yugoslavia also fell apart after the end of the cold war, and "ethnic conflicts" broke out. Czechoslovakia broke peacefully apart into its Czech and Slovak components. The processes have not stopped there. In the now independent Russia, for example, the government of the Checheno-Ingush Autonomous Republic declared independence in March 1992, and some of Russia's other fifteen autonomous republics' governments are still contemplating following suit.

Some of these outcomes were welcomed by the West, others less so. None of the outcomes were the products of western insistence on the right to self-determination. It seems that after the cold war, western-supported democratization has brought about struggles for self-determination. What we seem to be faced with in the post–cold war era is the rather unintended reversal of the Wilsonian pattern. The Wilsonian message of self-determination hid democracy; the post–cold war message of democracy is hiding self-determination.

The end of the cold war seems to have revitalized the struggle for self-determination outside the former Communist world as well. The struggle of the Kurds both in Iraq and Turkey continues, so has that of the Sikhs and others in India, southern Sudanese in the Sudan, the Palestinians, and the blacks in South Africa. Furthermore, the issue of Quebec and the Native Peoples in Canada has not been settled, nor for that matter that of Native Americans in the United States. In Northern Italy, there is a separatist movement that appears to be gaining strength in spite of the supposed unifying influence of Italy's membership in the European Community. Although rarely mentioned in the media, the struggle for self-determination of various groups in Afghanistan continues as well.

## ANNOTATED BIBLIOGRAPHY

Buchheit, Lee C. *Secession: The Legitimacy of Self-Determination.* New Haven: Yale University Press, 1978.
    Probably the best in-depth study of secession.

Cobban, Alfred. *The Nation State and National Self-Determination.* New York: Thomas Y. Crowell, 1969.
    A classic.

Emerson, Rupert. *Self Determination Revisited in the Era of Decolonization.* CFIA Occasional Papers, no. 9. Cambridge: Center for International Affairs, Harvard University, 1964.
    An assessment of decolonization during decolonization.

Jackson, Robert H. "Juridical statehood in Sub-Saharan Africa." *Journal of International Affairs* 46, no. 1 (summer 1992): 1–16.
Argues that boundaries of African states are "violating tribal and ethnic boundaries" and advocates changes of the "juridical statehood" in Africa.

Kohr, Leopold. *The Breakdown of Nations.* New York: Reinhart, 1957 (and subsequent editions).
A book that some would regard as visionary.

Anthony D. Smith. "Conflict and Collective Identity: Class, *Ethnie* and Nation." In *International Conflict Resolution, Theory and Practice,* ed. Edward E. Azar and John W. Burton. Boulder: Lynne Rienner, 1986.
Calls for the recognition of communal identities within states for "a more just and more stable world."

Rigo Sureda. *The Evolution of the Right to Self-Determination: A Study of United Nations Practice.* Leiden: A. W. Sijthoff, 1973.
A close examination of several cases from a critical perspective.

Ronen, Dov. *The Quest for Self-Determination.* New Haven: Yale University Press, 1979.
An early version of the author's view.

Rupesinghe, Kumar, ed. *Ethnicity and International Conflict in a Post-Communist World: The Soviet Union, Eastern Europe and China.* London: Macmillan, St. Martin's Press, 1992.
Papers, mostly case studies, presented at the International Peace Research Association's (IPRA) thirteenth general conference, July 1990.

Umozurike, Umozurike Oji. *Self-Determination in International Law,* Hamden, CT: Archon Books, 1972.
A close examination of cases.

CHAPTER 9

# Resolving Conflict over the Use of Global Environment

## Marvin S. Soroos

The United Nations Conference on Environment and Development, held in Rio de Janeiro in June 1992, testifies to the rise of the environment to a prominent position on the global agenda. The official conference, more commonly known as the "Earth Summit," drew representatives from 172 countries, including 106 heads of state, making it the largest gathering of world leaders in history. In addition, more than seven thousand nongovernmental organizations took part in the informal '92 Global Forum that was held in downtown Rio in conjunction with the Earth Summit. These events in Rio were a response to increasingly ominous warnings from the international scientific community that human activities are causing fundamental changes in the physical environment, including atmospheric warming, depletion of the ozone layer, destruction of tropical forests, spread of deserts, and loss of biodiversity.

Environmental problems were once primarily local in geographical scope and thus confined within the boundaries of states. However, with several decades of rapid growth in the world's population, energy consumption, and industrial production, humanity's assault on the environment has taken on international and global proportions and involves realms that either transcend or are outside the jurisdictions of individual states. Accordingly, environmental issues have become a growing source of international conflict as states seek to maximize their share of the limited natural resources of the planet and to preserve the quality of their environments in the face of threats originating beyond their borders.

Many of the world's most serious environmental problems involve the overuse and misuse of global commons, in particular the oceans and seabed, the atmosphere, outer space, Antarctica, and the electromagnetic spectrum. Use of all of these commons has intensified, leading to greater international competition for access to their resources and, in some cases, to their deterioration or destruction, which becomes another source of international conflict. The international community faces the challenge of managing these commons in ways that will maintain their usefulness and resolve peacefully the conflicts that inevitably arise among those who use them.

## WHAT IS A COMMONS?

### Hardin's Parable

Biologist Garrett Hardin has popularized the concept of the 'commons' in a widely read article that appeared in 1968.[1] He asks us to visualize an old English village that has a pasture available to all the residents to graze their privately owned cattle. The products and profit from these cattle enrich the individual villagers who own them. Hardin refers to such an arrangement as a commons.

The commons system can work well as long as the number of cattle is small, relative to the capacity of the pasture to nourish them. However, as the villagers prosper, they are tempted to add to the cattle they graze in order to increase their incomes. Eventually, the "carrying capacity" of the pasture is reached, and any additional cattle will cause overgrazing and a deterioration of the pasture. Will the villagers then act in a personally responsible way and refrain from adding further cattle to the pasture in the interests of preserving the resource upon which they depend? Hardin warns that the villagers are more likely to continue adding cattle to the pasture, even if they are aware of the inevitable consequences of overgrazing. The typical villager will calculate there is more to gain from adding cattle as long as the profits go exclusively to him, while the resulting environmental costs caused by overgrazing are shared by the entire community. Other villagers can be expected to act on the same logic and also add cattle to the pasture.

Thus, the stage is set for a "tragedy of the commons" to occur. The pasture is increasingly overgrazed, its carrying capacity declines sharply, and eventually its value to the community as a place to graze its cattle is lost. Paradoxically, what appears to be the

---

[1]Hardin, Garret, "The Tragedy of the Commons," *Science* 168, no. 3859 (December 13, 1968): 1243–48.

most rational course of action for the individual villagers seeking to maximize their personal profits has a disastrous outcome for the community as a whole.

## Definition of a Commons

A commons is resource domain that has the following two characteristics: (1) a group of actors is entitled to make use of it and (2) the benefits from using it accrue to them as individuals.

Ownership of the resource domain is a separate but related issue. In Hardin's story, the pasture could be owned by a wealthy lord, who permits it to be used by the residents of the village because he has no immediate need for it. Alternatively, it could be the property of the villagers collectively, as in the case of city parklands. Finally, the pasture could be owned by nobody, with the users refusing to recognize the legitimacy of exclusive claims that any of them might make. All of these types of ownership are compatible with a commons arrangement as long as the resource domain is available to multiple users for their private gain.

## The Primary Global Commons

Several resource domains have traditionally been treated as global commons in that they are available to parties from any nation to use for their own benefit. States have occasionally asserted exclusive rights to parts of these domains, but in most cases, other states have refused to recognize these claims. This section identifies the major global commons and briefly reviews the history of their use.

**Oceans and Seabed.**   The oceans, which cover approximately 70 percent of the Earth's surface, have been used by human civilizations for navigation and fishing for millennia. While the living resources of the oceans were once vast in comparison with the scale of human harvesting of them, a mushrooming world population and revolutionary changes in the technology of fishing since the Second World War have greatly increased the world's catch, resulting in the depletion of many once highly productive fisheries. Populations of whales and other marine mammals have also been decimated by overharvesting.

The cornerstone of modern international ocean law has been the doctrine of the "freedom of the seas," which can be traced to *Mare Liberum* (1609), a treatise written by Dutch jurist Hugo

Grotius. Under this doctrine, all states have the right to navigate the world's oceans and to help themselves to its bounty. There has also been, however, a long tradition of coastal states claiming parts of the oceans, most commonly a narrow area off their shores known as "territorial waters." For several centuries, international customary law recognized a three-mile zone of territorial waters in which coastal states could exercise most prerogatives of state sovereignty. After the Second World War, a succession of coastal states asserted national claims to ocean areas out to two hundred nautical miles in order to keep other countries from exploiting marine resources in these areas.

The seabed has been treated as a distinct issue in international ocean law. The principal seabed resources are oil and natural gas found in the continental shelves and potato-sized nodules rich in copper, manganese, cobalt, and nickel lying on the floor of the deep seas. Numerous coastal states, including Mexico, Norway, United Kingdom, and United States, have developed fossil fuel resources in adjacent continental shelves. Companies from several countries have developed technologies for mining the deep-sea nodules, but commercial operations are on hold due to depressed mineral prices.

The 150 countries participating in the third United Nations Conference on the Law of the Sea (UNCLOS III), held intermittently from 1973 to 1982, addressed the full range of legal issues pertaining to use of the oceans and seabed. The resulting Law of the Sea Treaty broadens the territorial waters of coastal states from three to twelve nautical miles. Beyond that, it defines an exclusive economic zone (EEZ) extending out to two hundred nautical miles in which the adjacent coastal state has the primary rights to the resources of the oceans and continental shelf. The new ocean law will resolve many of the conflicting claims that have posed a threat to international peace.

**Antarctica.**    Antarctica is the only land mass that has been treated as a global commons. The continent, which is as large as the United States and Mexico combined, was first sighted in 1820, and only in 1911 did the first explorers reach the South Pole. Thus far, the principal activity on Antarctica has been scientific research conducted by a gradually increasing number of countries. Very little has been learned about Antarctica's natural resources, primarily because 98 percent of the continent is covered by ice averaging one mile in thickness.

Antarctica's status as a commons is not clear in view of the territorial claims of seven nations (Argentina, Australia, Chile, France, New Zealand, Norway, and the United Kingdom), which collectively cover 85 percent of the continent. These claims were staked between 1903 and 1943 on grounds such as first exploration, geographic proximity, and the contiguity of the terrain of the South America. The overlapping claims of Argentina, Chile, and the United Kingdom have been a source of conflict between the three countries. The United States, the former Soviet Union, and Japan have been actively involved in Antarctic research, but they have not made territorial claims and refuse to recognize the claims of others.

The entire Antarctic region south of 60 degrees south latitude is currently governed by the Antarctic Treaty, which was adopted by the twelve countries that were active in the region at the time. The treaty does not resolve the issue of previous territorial claims in that it neither recognizes nor denies them, while prohibiting new ones. The entire continent is to be open to scientific research, but all military activities, including nuclear tests, are prohibited. Additional agreements may be adopted by a consensus of the Antarctic Treaty Consultative Parties, a group that has grown to twenty-six states that fulfill the membership criteria of operating a permanent research station on the continent.

**The Atmosphere.**   The atmosphere is a different type of resource domain in that it is a gaseous substance (comprising primarily nitrogen and oxygen) that circulates around the planet Earth without regard to political boundaries. The atmosphere is essential to all life on the planet, not only as a source of chemicals that fuel biological processes, but also as a moderator of climate. Humanity has long used the atmosphere as a convenient medium for disposing of pollutants with few negative consequences until well into the twentieth century, the primary exception being health-threatening smogs occurring over European cities, which for London became a serious problem as early as the thirteenth century.

In recent decades, air pollution has become increasingly both a transboundary and a global problem. By the 1960s, Scandinavian scientists were presenting evidence that the atmosphere not only transports pollutants over great distances but also is a medium in which sulphur and nitrogen oxides are transformed into acidic substances that have been linked to the disappearance of aquatic life in lakes and rivers, widespread damage to forests, and deterioration of stone and metal structures. Evidence mounted in the 1980s that pollutants such as CFCs and carbon dioxide are destroying the stratospheric ozone layer and contributing to climate change.

International law empowers states to exercise jurisdiction over the "air space" above their territory, but no similar division of the continually circulating atmosphere is possible. No negotiations have been held to draw up a general international law of the atmosphere comparable to the one that was adopted for the oceans. However, more narrowly defined international treaties address specific atmospheric problems, including nuclear testing, acid deposition, depletion of the ozone layer, and climate change.

**Outer Space.** Outer space became a significant international legal issue when the Soviet Union launched its first Sputnik in 1957. Since then a growing group of nations, now numbering more than twenty, have actively used outer space for purposes such as remote scanning, weather forecasting, and telecommunications. While outer space is vast in relation to the number of satellites that have been launched, there are regions, such as the geostationary orbit at an altitude of 22,300 miles in which satellites stay above the same location on the planet. This orbit is much more useful than others and thus has become congested with satellites. Furthermore, space debris that can seriously damage or interfere with operating satellites is accumulating at a disturbing rate.

No international agreement specifies the altitude that officially divides air space over which nations have jurisdiction from outer space which is not subject to national claims. It is simply understood that the altitudes at which planes fly are in the realm of air space, while the orbits of satellites are in outer space. Outer space does not lend itself to national claims, because the region of outer space above each country is constantly changing as the planet rotates. The only possible exception is the geostationary orbit, parts of which have been claimed by the equatorial states located below them, but without the recognition of the advanced space countries that make heavy use of the orbit.

The Outer Space Treaty of 1967 is the principal international agreement governing the use of outer space as a global commons. It declares that outer space is the "province of all mankind" and that all space activities be carried out "for the benefit of mankind." All countries are free to explore outer space "on the basis of equity." No country may claim sovereignty over any part of outer space, nor may nuclear weapons or other weapons of mass destruction be stationed in outer space. Similar principles and rules are incorporated into a 1979 treaty that regulates human activities on the moon and other celestial bodies.

**Electromagnetic Spectrum.** Perhaps the most unusual of the resource domains that are treated as a global commons is the electromagnetic spectrum, or what is more commonly known as "radio waves" or "airwaves." The spectrum comprises frequencies ranging from 3 Hz in the extremely low band to 300 Hz in the extremely high band, which are used to transmit a variety of types of communication services, including telephone, AM and FM radio, shortwave broadcasts, UHF and VHF television, air and marine navigation, radar, radio astronomy, meteorology, data transmission, and electronic mail.[2] The spectrum is also used to transmit signals to and from satellites.

The airwaves are a very useful medium for telecommunications as long as multiple parties don't make simultaneous use of the same frequencies for transmissions in overlapping regions. With the information and communication revolutions of the twentieth century, use of spectrum has grown dramatically, making it necessary to manage the resource to avoid interference among competing users that would seriously diminish its value to them. The problem is inherently an international one, because transmissions cannot be kept from crossing over political boundaries and encroaching on use of the spectrum in neighboring jurisdictions.

International rules on use of the electromagnetic spectrum are made in the International Telecommunications Union (ITU), a specialized agency of the United Nations. The spectrum has historically been available for all countries to use, but they are not allowed to stake permanent claims to any segment of it. However, it

---

[2]$Hz$ is the abbreviation for hertz, which is the number of cycles that pass a fixed point within one second. $GHz$ is the abbreviation for gigahertz, or one billion hertz.

is generally recognized that the first users of a frequency in a given geographical area have a right to continue using it, or what has been called "squatter's rights." The ITU registers these uses and informs other would-be users that the frequency is already occupied. Use of the spectrum is also governed by allocation schemes of the ITU, which assign ranges of frequencies known as "bands" to various types of telecommunication services.

## ACTORS

In Hardin's English village, the only actors are the villagers, the cattle, and possibly a village government. A much more extensive array of actors is involved in the use and management of global commons. The 170 sovereign states are the counterparts of the villagers. The world's population that individually or corporately uses global commons is akin to the cattle that consume the pasture's grass. Finally, international institutions are the analog of the village government. Nongovernmental organizations, which are increasingly important actors on the international stage, do not have an equivalent in Hardin's story.

Despite repeated forecasts of the demise of nation-states in an increasingly interdependent world, they continue to be the most important actors in the international system. The governments of states are legally empowered not only to license their people to use global commons but also to impose rules and limits on their exploitation of the resources in these domains. Sovereign governments negotiate among themselves to draft up international treaties that apply to their activities in global commons. Once states sign and ratify a treaty, they are expected to take measures to ensure that all actors under their jurisdiction comply with the regulations contained in the treaty. Governments are not obliged to comply with the provisions of treaties that they have not accepted, although they are bound by the generally recognized tenets of international customary law.

The users of global commons are a much more diverse lot. At one extreme are individual motorists whose vehicles emit hydrocarbons and nitrogen oxides into the atmosphere and artisan fishermen who work coastal waters for a day's catch, as their ancestors have done for centuries. At the other extreme are large energy-producing utilities and smelting operations that release large quantities of sulphur and carbon dioxide into the atmosphere, as well as corporate conglomerates that operate communication satellites in the geostationary orbit and depend upon clear frequencies to transmit signals. A majority of users operate privately, although many stateowned enterprises also use global commons intensively, examples being the national space agencies such as the National Aeronautics and Space Administration of the United States.

The United Nations is the preeminent international institution concerned with the management of global commons. It sponsored the UNCLOS meetings where the 1982 Law of the Sea Treaty was negotiated; this provided for the establishment of an International Seabed Authority. Specialized agencies and committees within the United Nations system are the loci for managing other commons; examples include the Food and Agricultural Organization (FAO), which deals with fisheries; the Committee on the Peaceful Uses of Outer Space, which addresses most issues pertaining to outer space, and the previously mentioned ITU, which oversees the electromagnetic spectrum and the geostationary orbit. The principal role of these international institutions is to facilitate cooperation among the sovereign states that have created them. Most lack the authority and the resources to impose and enforce rules, although some are charged with monitoring the compliance of states with certain international rules or standards.

A profusion of nongovernmental organizations (NGOs), ranging from global to local in their membership and purpose, perform a variety of critical roles in international policy processes. Scientific organizations such as the International Council of Scientific Unions (ICSU) are important sources of knowledge about the impact of human activities on the global commons and are sometimes invited to participate in the drafting and implementation of international policies. International advocacy groups such as Greenpeace are active in calling attention to environmental problems, informing and mobilizing public opinion, lobbying national delegates to United Nations conferences, publicizing violations of international rules, and even organizing consumer boycotts to put pressure on the worst violators of international environmental treaties. Opposing perspectives are offered by NGOs that represent industries in such fields as electric power, chemicals, automobiles, fishing, and telecommunications that make intensive use of commons and are thus affected by international rules.

## CONFLICTS ARISING OVER THE USE
## OF GLOBAL COMMONS

The potential for conflict increases with the rising use of a resource domain, which has been the case with the principal global commons. The following are several types of conflict that may arise among multiple users of a commons.

*Competitive Uses*

Conflicts inevitably occur when a commons contains a resource that two or more parties desire and, once it is taken by one user, is no longer available to others. Thus, in Hardin's story, a clump of grass eaten by one villager's cow cannot be consumed by the cattle of other villagers. Mutually exclusive consumption is not a serious problem as long as the resource is plentiful enough to satisfy the ambitions of all parties. However, when demand exceeds the productive capacity of the resource, users compete to maximize their shares at the expense of others. For resources that may be degraded or destroyed by overuse, the consequence of competitive harvesting may be a disastrous "tragedy of the commons" for all who depend on the resource.

This type of conflict frequently arises over fishing in the oceans. A fish caught by a boat of one country will never appear in the nets of other countries, which puts a premium upon harvesting the resource as soon as possible. Thus, nations have greatly expanded their fishing fleets in hopes of increasing, or even merely maintaining, their shares of the world's catch, resulting in a wasteful surplus of boats and badly depleted fisheries. Bluefin tuna, halibut, cod, haddock, herring, flounder, Peruvian anchovy, California sardine, salmon, and swordfish are among the species whose stocks have dramatically declined due to overfishing.

*Interfering Uses*

Interference occurs when various parties hinder each other's use of a common resource, as when vehicle congestion slows down traffic on urban streets. An example of interference among users of a global commons is static on the airwaves, which is most severe on the frequency bands that can be used to transmit signals over great distances with relatively inexpensive equipment. Thus, the HF (high frequency) bands used for shortwave radio have been especially congested. Without regulations limiting use of frequencies within given areas, the airwaves become useless to all. However, unlike other resources that are destroyed when consumed, the electromagnetic spectrum immediately returns to its original state when the users stop beaming signals.

## Incompatible Uses

Conflicts can also arise when one party makes use of a commons in ways that preclude other activities. If one resident in Hardin's English village plows up part of the pasture to grow crops, others cannot graze cattle on that part of the commons. Use of the oceans as a sink for a myriad of pollutants has contaminated numerous fisheries, rendering the catch unfit for human consumption. Large scale mining activities on Antarctica would be incompatible with scientific research that seeks to take advantage of the otherwise pristine quality of the Antarctic environment.

## Collateral Damage

Use of a commons is also problematical when it causes damage or harm to others. For example, cattle grazing the village pasture may contaminate the local source of drinking water or become a public nuisance. Such has been the case with the transboundary movement of pollution causing acid precipitation, which has been a serious problem for Europe and North America. Countries with land-based mining operations have expressed concern that seabed mining may create a glut of minerals on international markets that would depress prices, causing serious harm to their economies.

## Infringement on Sovereignty

Finally, certain uses of global commons trigger international conflict because they encroach on what some governments consider to be their sovereign prerogatives. For example, the airwaves have been used extensively to beam propaganda to the radios of the citizens of foreign countries against the wishes of their governments. Likewise, direct broadcast satellites that can transmit television signals to home receivers over large areas threaten to undermine public television monopolies that numerous national governments have sought to maintain. Some states have raised the sovereignty issue in objecting to another country's use of remote-sensing satellites to take detailed pictures of their territories, which they fear could be used to their disadvantage.

Certain uses of commons may be viewed as a threat to national security, as in the case of naval vessels or submarines of hostile countries navigating nearby coastal waters or the stationing of weapons of mass destruction in outer space.

## STRATEGIES FOR AVOIDING OR MANAGING CONFLICTS

Conflicts over the use of commons can be avoided or resolved in a variety of ways, including some that retain the commons arrangement and others that discard it. In the case of the village pasture threatened by overgrazing, each of the residents could voluntarily refrain from adding additional cattle. If the overgrazing problem persists because some do not exercise restraint, the town council could impose and enforce limits on the number of cattle each villager could graze on the pasture or levy taxes to discourage additional cattle. Alternatively, the pasture could be divided into sections that are assigned to individual villagers for their exclusive use. Finally, the village council could purchase all the cattle and operate a community herd with profits being distributed to the residents according to a specified formula. Let us consider the applicability of each of these strategies to the global commons.

### Voluntary Restraint

The simplest strategy to implement is to urge all users of a commons to limit their activities voluntarily to avoid overuse and competition for limited resources. This approach is most likely to succeed in small communities where there is a high level of social cohesion and the implicit threat of being ostracized deters irresponsible behavior. Hardin contends this strategy will usually fail because self-serving parties will enrich themselves by taking advantage of the restraint of the others. The presence of even one such "resource pirate" undermines the willingness of all others to act in the interests of the larger community.

Calls for voluntary restraint are a common first step in efforts to limit use of global commons. They are often written into framework treaties that establish the groundwork for international efforts to address a problem. For example, the Convention on Long-Range Transboundary Air Pollution (known as the LRTAP

Convention) of 1979 calls upon states to "endeavor to limit and, as far as possible, gradually reduce and prevent air pollution" and to "use the best available technology that is economically feasible."

Voluntary restraint is generally regarded as an ineffective and inadequate strategy for reducing use of global commons. It clearly has not worked in the case of marine fisheries, where pirate operators have been all too willing to harvest the fish that others pass up. Neither will the problems of ozone depletion or climate change be effectively mitigated by appeals to global environmental responsibility. It is encouraging, however, that a number of developed countries have announced unilaterally their intention to reduce emissions of such pollutants as sulphur dioxide, CFCs, and carbon dioxide well beyond any previous treaty requirements. These unilateral declarations are usually made to set an example for other countries and in some cases are contingent on others following their lead.

*Regulations on the Use of Commons*

Hardin maintains that coercive measures will usually be necessary if use of a commons is to be limited. Several forms of regulations may be adopted and enforced. States may be required to limit or even reduce their use by a certain date. For example, protocols appended to the 1979 LRTAP Convention require ratifiers to reduce emissions of $SO_2$ by 30 percent from 1980 levels by 1993 and not to allow emissions of $NO_x$ to exceed 1987 levels after 1994.

International fishery commissions have adopted rules to limit catches below a sustainable level known as the "total allowable catch." Examples include limitations on the length of fishing seasons, quotas on the catch of each country, and rules pertaining to equipment such as the minimum size of the mesh of nets. In some cases there have been outright prohibitions on harvesting a species, such as the moratorium on commercial whaling that was imposed by the International Whaling Commission in 1986.

The success of international regulations depends on the availability and effectiveness of mechanisms for monitoring and enforcing compliance. Detecting violations of regulations by the large number of fishing vessels from many lands has been a problem, although some of the fishery commissions provide for on-board inspectors. The LRTAP Convention is backed by an extensive atmospheric monitoring network that regularly reports on emissions and transboundary flows of the principal air pollutants. International institutions generally do not have the power to enforce international regulations, but depend upon individual states to put pressure on violators. For example, the United States significantly reduces access to its coastal fishing zone to countries that refuse to abide by international rules regulations on the harvesting of marine mammals, including those of the International Whaling Commission.

## Market Incentives

In recent years, national governments are relying more on market incentives or disincentives that make it less profitable to use scarce resources wastefully or to engage in environmentally destructive behaviors. An example is carbon taxes that some countries are imposing on the burning of fossil fuels in proportion to the amount of $CO_2$ the fuel generates. Another is the introduction of a system of tradeable permits to pollute, which may be bought or sold by companies that respectively exceed or do not use up their quotas of permissible emissions. Gradual reductions could be made in the number of permits made available each year to achieve a targeted cutback.

Taxes and other market incentives have been used rarely at the international level because they are looked upon as infringements on national sovereignty. Nevertheless, internationally applied market incentives may warrant serious consideration as an alternative to regulations, which can be cumbersome and inefficient, especially if environmental problems such as climate change become more severe. An international system of tradable permits to emit $CO_2$ would enable less developed countries to generate income for sustainable development by selling unneeded permits to countries that account for far more than an equitable share of total global emissions, most notably the United States and Canada.

## Exclusive Sections

Another of Hardin's preferred solutions is to discard the commons system and divide the resource into sections that are assigned permanently to individual members of the community for their exclusive use. The "owners" will have a strong incentive for conserving their sections because not only do they receive all of the profits from using them, but they also bear all the costs of poor environmental stewardship. Segregating the users of the resource into their own sections also avoids many of the conflicts that arise when they competitively exploit the same resources in a commons.

The 1982 Law of the Sea Treaty divides the most productive regions of the oceans into sections in the form of the two-hundred-mile EEZs, over which the coastal states have almost exclusive rights. Approximately 90 percent of the world's catch of fish comes from the zones, as does virtually all of the oil and natural gas that is produced from continental shelves. Ironically, the EEZ system has not been very effective in conserving ocean fisheries, because coastal states have failed to restrain the fishing activities of their nationals. Moreover, some countries license foreign vessels to fish in their EEZs as a source of income.

The physical characteristics of some common resources preclude division into exclusive sections, making it necessary to adopt one of the other management schemes. Such is the case with highly migratory species of fish, such as skipjack tuna, which move through several countries' EEZs and also live part of their lives on the high seas, where they may be harvested by any country. Another example is the atmosphere, which is constantly in motion, so that the portion that is over a specific country is always changing. Likewise, it is difficult to conceive how outer space could be divided into exclusive sections, with the exception of positions in the geostationary orbit, which could be linked to locations on the Earth's surface beneath them.

*Public Monopoly*

The final strategy would also discontinue the commons arrangement, but in this case by closing the resource to private users. All use of the resource would be the prerogative of a public enterprise that would divide its profits among the entire community. Communist ideology maintains that public enterprises are better stewards of natural resources because they eliminate the motivation for private profit, which it contends is the primary cause of environmental degradation. Public managers, it posits, will be more inclined to balance economic and environmental priorities. Furthermore, exclusive public use avoids the conflicts that inevitably arise among private users of a common resource. In actual practice, the environment fared poorly under the Communist regimes of the Soviet bloc because resources and the environment were grossly undervalued in their push for economic growth and military might.

Sovereign states and the private interests they represent can hardly be expected to defer exploitation of global commons to international public monopolies. It is difficult to envision a global fishing enterprise that would have exclusive rights to harvest the living resources of the oceans. It is even less imaginable that states would relinquish all rights to pollute the atmosphere. However, the less-developed countries did propose at UNCLOS that mining of the deep seabed should be the exclusive right of an international public enterprise, which would distribute its profits broadly, possibly as a new form of international development assistance. The countries with deep-sea mining interests rejected this proposal, but most were willing to compromise on a "parallel system" of mining. The Law of the Sea Treaty provides for an international enterprise that will operate alongside nationally based mining firms. The national firms are expected to sell their technology to the international enterprise at reasonable prices and to assist it in locating prospective mining sites.

## COMPLICATING FACTORS

Reaching agreement among a diverse group of states on how to manage global commons is inevitably a complicated and often frustrating process, which may take many years and even decades to complete. The conflicting positions that states often take in international negotiations reflect characteristics such as their level of economic and technological development, geographical location, established policies, and historical circumstances. The following are some of the types of circumstances that can make it more difficult to achieve international agreements that will effectively regulate the principal global commons.

### Scientific Uncertainties

A decisive international response to an environmental problem presumes a broad-based consensus on its seriousness. Inevitably, some states will refrain from making commitments requiring costly action if there is any doubt that they are needed. The United States shunned repeated appeals from Canada during the 1980s for reductions of acid-forming pollutants on the grounds that the relationship between the pollutants and damage to lakes and forests had not been adequately established. Likewise, at the 1992 Earth Summit, the United States insisted that a timetable for limiting or reducing $CO_2$ emissions was premature given that scientists still disagree on the inevitability of significant global warming. Most other developed countries subscribed to the "precautionary principle," which dictates taking the first steps to prevent a potentially catastrophic turn of events until it can be proven that it is not going to occur.

### Economic Circumstances

The impetus for most of the rules and standards on the use of global commons comes from the highly developed countries, which have the economic and technological resources to invest in complying with them. Alternatively, the dominant priority of poorer countries, many of which are saddled with heavy international debt, is economic development for their impoverished people. Thus, less developed countries are reluctant to commit to international standards proposed by the advanced countries, which will require expensive technologies that they cannot afford to import unless they are assured of compensating economic and technical assistance.

This type of issue arose in the ITU during the late 1970s when less developed countries objected to the proposals of the technologically advanced ITU members to require more expensive telecommunications equipment that would permit more efficient use of the radio waves. It was also a sticking point in international negotiations over the past decade on preserving the ozone layer; this was finally resolved by the creation of a fund to assist less-developed countries adopt substitutes for the substances being phased out.

### Access to Technologies

Benefiting from the use of several of the global commons, in particular outer space and the mineral-rich deep seabed, requires advanced technologies that a small minority of states posses. Third World countries, caucusing in a number of international forums as the Group of 77, have argued that these realms are the "common heritage of mankind," which implies ownership by the world community of states. They have argued further that it is unfair that only the technologically advanced countries should profit from use of these commonly owned resources. Thus, provisions should be made for less-developed countries to participate in development of these regions. This argument underlay Third World insistence on the creation of the international enterprise that would mine the deep seabed, as well as on the opportunity to become partners in the exploration of outer space.

Several of the major technologically advanced countries, led by the United States, have opposed this interpretation of the "common heritage of man," arguing that the principle simply provides that all countries are entitled to use a global commons as they have the means to do. Nevertheless, some concessions have been made to the Third World, such as the parallel system of national and international mining of the seabed and invitations to shared use of some of their satellites.

## Varying Vulnerabilities

The more vulnerable a country is to the adverse consequences of overuse or misuse of a global commons, the more likely it will strongly advocate regulations on its use. In the late 1960s, Sweden and Norway began pushing for international rules on transboundary air pollution after determining that the acidification afflicting their lakes and rivers was caused largely by pollutants originating in the heavily industrialized regions of the British Isles and the European continent. For many years, however, they encountered opposition from upwind states that were net exporters of air pollutants, in particular West Germany and the United Kingdom. Likewise, coastal states, seeing their offshore fisheries decimated by large fishing fleets based in distant countries, became the leading proponents of two-hundred-mile EEZs.

## Historical Uses

Negotiating rules for regulating global commons would be a simpler task were it not for historical patterns of use. Those who have taken advantage of them extensively in the past maintain that they have a right to continued use of them, especially if they have made substantial capital investments. Alternatively, those who have made little or no use of a commons may argue that it is now their turn to reap more of the benefits from the commons at the expense of the traditional users. This type of issue has arisen frequently over allocations of quotas for harvesting fisheries between the states that historically have taken most of the catch and those desiring a larger share in the future.

Less-developed countries have contested the first-come, first-served rule that has been applied to use of the airwaves and geostationary orbit, arguing that it enables the highly developed countries to monopolize key portions of these resources. Similarly, less-developed countries repeatedly call attention to the fact that the developed countries have helped themselves to a lion's share of the atmosphere's capacity to absorb the pollutants responsible for ozone depletion and global warming. Thus, they are reluctant to limit their emissions of these pollutants unless the developed countries drastically cut back on their levels.

## Previous Claims

Negotiations may also be complicated by a history of claims to a resource domain that states are reluctant to relinquish. One example is the unresolved territorial claims to Antarctica. Argentina and Chile continue to reassert their claims to the Antarctic Peninsula on the grounds that it is a natural continuation of the Andes mountain range. These territorial claims take on greater importance if it is presumed that they entitle the holder to a two-hundred-mile EEZ in adjacent ocean areas, which are rich in marine life. Another example is the extended territorial waters and fishery zones claimed unilaterally by numerous coastal states during the 1950s and 1960s. The 1982 Law of the Sea Treaty legitimated these claims of coastal states, although it has some provisions for sharing the resources located in them with other states, including adjacent landlocked ones.

## Previous National Restraints

International negotiations on controlling air pollutants typically focus on setting a deadline for a percentage reduction in emissions that would apply to all countries. It is hardly fair to expect states that have cut back significantly on air pollutants prior to the proposed base year, or that have never had a very high level of emissions, to make the same percentage reductions as heavily polluting countries that have not begun to address the problem. For example, in negotiations on limiting CFCs, the United States wanted credit for being well ahead of most European countries in banning use of the chemical in aerosol sprays.

However, in the case of $CO_2$ emissions that contribute to global warming, Europeans and Japanese, whose fuel consumption has been heavily taxed, question whether they should be expected to make further sacrifices while North Americans still consume nearly twice as much energy per capita as they do. Representatives of less-developed countries argue that they should be allowed to increase their $CO_2$ emissions as they modernize their economies, given that their per capita levels of energy use are a only a small fraction of those of the industrialized countries.

## ACHIEVEMENTS IN MANAGING GLOBAL COMMONS

Much has been accomplished in recent decades to establish a measure of international order over the global commons that conserves them as a resource and lessens or resolves conflict among the states that use them. These achievements can be observed not only in the general development of international environmental governance but also in what has been done to address specific problems.

### International Environmental Governance

The evolution of international governance for global commons is apparent in a spate of world conferences that drew attention to environmental problems, the growth of international environmental institutions, and the adoption of numerous environmental treaties and other international agreements.

**Conference Diplomacy.**    The United Nations Conference on the Human Environment held in Stockholm in 1972 ushered in an era of United Nations theme conferences, sometimes referred to as "global town meetings," which addressed world problems. Some conferences were more successful than others in focusing worldwide attention on the problems at hand and in setting forth action plans including new international institutions.

Several of these conferences addressed resource and environmental problems, such as population (1974, 1984), food (1974), human settlements (1976), water (1977), desertification (1977), and new and renewable sources of energy (1981). Others took up problems related specifically to the use of global commons, the most notable example being UNCLOS (1973–82), which drew up a new law of the sea. The ITU's World Administrative Radio Conference (1979), one of the largest international meetings ever held, adopted a new allocation scheme for the electromagnetic spectrum that will be in place for the remainder of the century. Issues pertaining to outer space were addressed at a conference in 1982. The World Meteorological Organization (WMO) sponsored major climate conferences in 1979 and 1990.

**Institutional Development.** The United Nations Environment Programme (UNEP), which was established in 1973 after being proposed at the Stockholm conference, has been very effective in using its limited staff and budget to coordinate and stimulate environmental action by national governments and other international agencies. One of UNEP's major accomplishments is establishment of the Global Environmental Monitoring System, which collects, compiles, and reports data on numerous environmental variables, including air pollutants, on a systematic and global basis. UNEP has facilitated the adoption of several major international environmental agreements, including the Med Plan for cleaning up the Mediterranean Sea, which became the prototype for its more extensive Regional Seas Programme.

Numerous other international institutions have strengthened their capacity for managing international commons. A notable example is WMO, which has undertaken several highly successful projects including the World Weather Watch in the 1960s, the Global Atmospheric Research Program in the 1970s, and the World Climate Programme in the 1980s. The World Bank has been developing the means for assessing the environmental impact of projects under consideration for funding. The bank shares responsibility with UNEP and the United Nations Development Programme for overseeing the Global Environment Facility, which was created in 1990 with $1 billion in funding to provide interest free loans for environmental projects in less developed countries. On a regional basis, the European Community has become increasingly involved in environmental issues such as uniform standards for air pollution and management of marine fisheries off the coasts of its members.

**Environmental Treaties.** A UNEP publication lists 152 environmental treaties in existence in 1990, two-thirds of which were adopted during the 1970s and 1980s. The 1982 Law of the Sea Treaty is one of approximately 60 treaties that address problems related to the oceans, such as the conservation of fisheries, the preservation of marine habitats, ocean dumping, safety, and vessel-source pollution. The atmosphere is a relatively underdeveloped realm of treaty law, but significant progress has been made on addressing the problem of long-range transboundary air pollution that causes acidification and the depletion of the ozone layer. The Antarctic environment is further protected by two treaties adopted during the 1980s, the Convention on the Conservation of Antarctic Marine Living Resources (1980) and the Convention on the Regulation of Antarctic Mineral Resource Activities (1988).

## Specific Accomplishments

The following are but a few examples of successful international efforts to regulate the use of international commons.

**Law of the Sea.**   By the 1950s, a wave of unilateral declarations of extended national jurisdiction by coastal states was seriously undermining the customary law of the sea, which was based on the centuries old doctrines of the "freedom of the sea" and the "three-mile limit." United Nations Conferences on the Law of the Sea held in 1958 and 1960 (UNCLOS I and II) failed to agree on the breadth of territorial waters and the rights of coastal states to resources off their shores. A third conference (UNCLOS III), which was periodically in session from 1973 to 1982, took up the challenge of negotiating a comprehensive ocean law. With an agenda including more than one hundred issues in twenty-five areas of marine policy, UNCLOS is arguably the most ambitious set of international negotiations ever undertaken.

UNCLOS III succeeded in adopting a comprehensive package of ocean law that addresses most marine activities, but not by the hoped for consensus. The United States, which has neither signed nor ratified the new Law of the Sea Treaty, has objected to the arrangements it would establish on mining the deep seas. Otherwise, the ratification process for the new ocean law has been slow, which is not uncommon for international treaties. However, within a few years, it is likely to have been formally accepted by the sixty states necessary to come into force. There is a broad-based international consensus on most of the treaty, and efforts are being made to negotiate a compromise on the seabed mining section that will be acceptable to the United States.

**The Antarctic Regime.** The international regime based on the Antarctic Treaty (1959) is generally regarded a successful arrangement for managing a global commons. Without the treaty, it is likely that national claims would have proliferated, laying the seeds for numerous international conflicts. Freezing existing claims, opening the entire continent to scientific research, and banning military activities has kept the peace among the growing number of countries with interests in Antarctica.

Some countries maintain that decisions about the continent's future should be transferred from the exclusive Antarctic Treaty Consultative Parties (ATCP) to the more inclusive United Nations General Assembly on grounds that the region belongs to the entire world community. There are advantages, however, to having the active users of a global commons be the ones who manage it. The ATCP have succeeded, where a larger group may not have, in negotiating treaties to conserve the marine resources of the region and to protect the pristine environment of Antarctica from the potential onslaught of mining activities.

**Regulation of the Airwaves and Geostationary Orbit.** A long tradition of international cooperation in the field of telecommunications dates back to the mid-nineteenth century. The first international rules on the use of radio waves were published in 1906 and since then have been revised periodically, most notably at major World Administrative Radio Conferences convened by the ITU in 1959 and 1979. Other ITU conferences have allocated locations on the geostationary orbit and frequencies for satellite communications to the countries that requested them, regardless of whether they would be able to make immediate use of them. Thus, the two global commons critical to telecommunications are subject to comprehensive management schemes that enable the resources to be used efficiently without interference.

The ITU has had a long-standing reputation for making decisions based on technical rationality without the intrusion of international politics. The situation changed somewhat during the 1970s, however, when less-developed countries became more assertive in demanding international reforms on a variety of fronts, including requests for a "new world information and communication order." One issue was the fairness of the "first-come, first served" rule on the use of frequencies and slots in the geostationary orbit. Compromises on allocations were struck within the ITU that satisfied the anxieties of less-developed countries about whether they would have access to the spectrum and the geostationary orbit as they needed them, while reassuring technologically advanced countries that these limited resources be used efficiently.

**Reducing Ozone Depletion.**   A recent series of international agreements on the problem of depletion of the ozone layer is especially remarkable for being a comprehensive response to scientific warnings of an environmental problem whose harmful consequences are not yet manifest. In 1974 Sherwood Rowland and Mario Molina, scientists from the University of California at Irvine, first hypothesized that CFCs rising through the atmosphere posed a threat to the ozone layer that shields the earth from harmful ultraviolet radiation. It was not until the mid1980s, however, that scientific evidence began to mount that a general thinning of the ozone layer was already taking place. Then in 1985, a British team made the dramatic discovery that an "ozone hole" formed over Antarctica during the spring season, which further research confirmed was caused by human pollutants.

A series of increasingly strong international agreements addresses the problem of ozone depletion. The first, the Convention for the Protection of the Ozone Layer, adopted in Vienna in 1985, is a typical framework treaty that simply calls upon states to take "appropriate measures" to protect the ozone layer as well as to cooperate on monitoring and research. Further negotiations spurred on by more ominous scientific warnings led to the Montreal Protocol of 1987, which commits its ratifiers to reduce production of CFCs by 20 percent by 1993 and 50 percent by 1998, using 1986 as a base year. The London Amendments to the Montreal Protocol, which were adopted in 1990 by ninety-three countries, mandate a phasing out of all major ozone-depleting substances by 2000. Less-developed countries were given a ten-year grace period and a fund was established to assist them in adopting substitutes for the banned substances. An agreement was reached in 1992 to move up the timetable for the phaseout to 1995.

## THE FUTURE OF THE APPROACH

Resolving conflicts over the use of global commons will become an increasingly serious challenge as the world's population continues to mushroom and aspires to higher standard of living. Global commons will be used more intensively as a sink for pollutants and a source of resources to supplement those that are available within the terrestrial boundaries of states. In the next decade, the most formidable challenge will be to build upon the framework climate change treaty that was adopted at the 1992 Earth Summit by negotiating protocols that specify reductions in emissions of $CO_2$ and other greenhouse gases.

In recent years, the United States has obstructed key international efforts to establish strong rules for regulating the use of the global commons, its opposition to the new law of the sea and mandated reductions of $CO_2$ being notable examples. Indications are that the Clinton administration will significantly alter the position the United States takes on international environmental matters. With leadership—rather than opposition—from the United States, there is the possibility of significant international progress being made to preserve the global environment and to resolve conflicts over the use of common resources.

Humanity is entering a critical era in which international cooperation on a historically unprecedented scale will be needed if upwards of ten billion people are to live in peace and have their basic needs met. Without such a commitment, humanity will continue on a relentless course toward a global "tragedy of the commons" in which international tensions will escalate and future generations will be left with a seriously degraded environment. The accomplishments of the past several decades in managing global commons are reason for hope, but are by no means a guarantee, that a world community dominated by sovereign states can work together constructively to avert an environmental tragedy and achieve a more desirable future.

## ANNOTATED BIBLIOGRAPHY

Benedict, Richard E. *Ozone Diplomacy: New Directions in Safeguarding the Planet.* Cambridge: Harvard University Press, 1991.
A historical review and analysis of international negotiations on protecting the ozone layer through the London Amendments of 1990, written by the chief United States negotiator.

Caldwell, Lynton Keith. *International Environmental Policy.* 2nd Edition, Durham: Duke University Press, 1990.

A comprehensive overview of the development of international environmental policy since the 1972 Stockholm conference. Contains a chapter on international commons including the atmosphere, outer space, oceans, and Antarctica.

Gore, Albert. *Earth in the Balance: Ecology and the Human Spirit.* Boston: Houghton Mifflin Co., 1992.

A thoughtful analysis of threats to the global environmental and the dysfunctional aspects of modern civilization that have brought about this crisis. Proposes a Global Marshall Plan for mobilizing the commitment necessary to preserve the environment.

Hardin, Garrett, and John Baden, eds. *Managing the Commons.* San Francisco: W. H. Freeman and Co., 1977.

A collection of essays that critically analyze the "tragedy of the commons" from a variety of perspectives. Includes Hardin's original article as well as his later article presenting the controversial theory of "lifeboat ethics."

McCormick, John. *Reclaiming Paradise: The Global Environmental Movement.* Bloomington: Indiana University Press, 1989.

A readable overview of the contributions of preservationists and conservationists to international efforts to address global environmental problems. Highlights different perspectives of developed and less-developed countries.

Meadows, Donnella, Dennis L. Meadows, and Jørgen Randers. *Beyond the Limits.* Post Mills, VT: Chelsea Green, 1992.

A thorough revision of Dennis Meadows' famous study *The Limits to Growth* (1972) on the basis of twenty additional years of human experience. A computer simulation model is used to plot the tendency for humanity to overshoot its resource base and to identify the steps that would be necessary to avoid a global environmental catastrophe.

Ophuls, William, and A. Stephen Boyan. *Ecology and the Politics of Scarcity Revisited.* New York: W. H. Freeman and Co., 1992.

A thorough revision of Ophuls 1977 classic on the need for a modern day Leviathan to restrain human greed in exploiting natural resources. Chapter 3 presents an especially thought provoking case for curbing individual freedom in order to achieve a sustainable, steady-state civilization.

Ostrom, Elinor. *Governing the Commons: The Evolution of Institutions for Collective Action.* New York: Cambridge University Press, 1991.

An analysis of various approaches to the governance of common-pool resources. Summarizes numerous case studies of how commons have been managed at local or substate levels.

Soroos, Marvin S. *Beyond Sovereignty: the Challenge of Global Policy.* Columbia: University of South Carolina Press, 1986

> An overview of the processes through which global policy is made and implemented in a world in which nation-states are still the dominant actors. Includes six case studies on pollution, regulation of the oceans, and the electromagnetic spectrum and geostationary orbit.

Warner, William. *Distant Water: The Fate of the North Atlantic Fisherman.* Boston: Little, Brown and Co., 1983.

> A fascinating, eyewitness account of how distant water fleets and gigantic stern trawlers decimated North Atlantic fisheries by an author who traveled aboard the fishing vessels from several countries.

# APPENDIX

# Resources for Teaching About International Conflict and Peace

## Yasemin Alptekin-Oguzertem

### ORGANIZATIONS

The American Forum on Global Education
120 Wall Street, Suite 200
New York, NY 10005 Phone (212) 732–8606; fax (212) 791–4132

A newsletter, a variety of instructional materials and resources, and an annual conference on global education.

American Friends Service Committee
1501 Cherry St.
Philadelphia, PA 19102
Phone (215) 241–7000; fax (215) 864–0104

Occasional papers, other publications.

American Mid-East Training Service, Inc. (AMIDEAST)
1100 17th St., NW
Washington, DC 20036
Phone (202) 785–0022; fax (202) 822–6563

Videos, instructional materials, student and teacher abroad programs, conferences.

Bread for the World
802 Rhode Island Avenue, NE
Washington, DC 20018
Phone (202) 269–0200

Leadership training programs and seminars, publications.

Catholic Relief Services
Global Education Office
209 West Fayette St.
Baltimore, MD 21201
Phone (301) 625–2220

Publications and curriculum development.

Center for Education for Justice and Peace
Fordham University
113 West 60th Street, Room 1024
New York, NY 10023
Phone (212) 757–7516

Consultations, workshops, leadership training, curriculum development.

Center for Foreign Policy Development
Brown University
Box 1948
Providence, RI 02912
Phone (401) 863–3155

"Choices in the 21st Century Education Project," curriculum development, teacher education.

Center for Peace and Conflict Studies
Wayne State University
5165 Gullen Mall, Room 100
Detroit, MI 48202
Phone (313) 577–3453 or 577–3468

Preservice and inservice workshops, conferences, community programs.

Center for Public Education in International Affairs
School of International Relations
University of Southern California
Los Angeles, CA 900/89–0043
Phone (213) 740–2135

Courses, resources, consultancies.

Center for Teaching International Relations
University of Denver
University Park
Denver, CO 80208
Phone (303) 871–3106

Curriculum development, graduate course, teacher workshops.

Center for War/Peace Studies
218 East 18th St.
New York, NY 10003
Phone (212) 475–1077; fax (212) 260–6384

A quarterly newsletter.

Church World Service
Office on Global Education
2115 N. Charles St.
Baltimore, MD 21218
Phone (301)727–6106; fax (301) 727–6108

Publications, curriculum development, and audio-visuals.

Consortium on Peace Research, Education and Development
c/o Center for Conflict Resolution
George Mason University
4400 University Drive
Fairfax, VA 22030
Phone (703) 993–3639

Workshops, an annual conference, publications, and curriculum
development.

Educators for Social Responsibility
23 Garden St.
Cambridge, MA 02138
Phone (617) 492–1764; fax (617) 864–5164

Workshops, speakers, instructional materials and other publications.

Foreign Policy Association
729 Seventh Avenue
New York, NY 10019
Phone (212) 764–4050; fax (212) 302–6123

Scholarly works on foreign policy issues, the annual *Great Decisions* book with the *Teacher Activity Book*, teacher inservices.

International Association of Educators for World Peace
P.O. Box 3282,
Blue Springs Station
Huntsville, AL 35810
Phone (205) 534–5501; fax (205) 851–9157

Workshops, conferences, publications, consultations, and curriculum development.

Maryknoll Fathers and Brothers
Pinesbridge Road
Maryknoll, NY 10545
Phone (914) 941–7590; fax (914) 945–0670

Newsletter, instructional materials and resources, speakers.

Mershon Center
Citizenship Development for a Global Age Program (CDGA)
1501 Neil Avenue
The Ohio State University
Columbus, OH 43201
Phone (614) 292–1681; fax (614) 292–2407

Curriculum development, other publications, inservice education.

Peace Corps of the United States
World Wise Schools Program

1990 K St., NW
Washington, DC 20526
Phone (202) 606–3970

Program linking Peace Corps volunteers with grades 3–12 in U.S. schools. Instructional materials and speakers.

The Peace Education Commission (PEC)
International Peace Research Association
School of Education
Box 23501
S-200 45 Malmo
Sweden
Fax 46—40 32 02 10

Project Icons (International Communication and Negotiation Simulations)
Department of Government and Political Science
Room 1127E
Tydings Hall
University of Maryland
College Park, MD 20742
Phone (301) 405–4172; fax (301) 314–9690

Multisite computer-assisted foreign policy simulations, professional development programs for teachers.

Social Science Education Consortium (SSEC)
3300 Mitchell Lane, Suite 240
Boulder, CO 80301–2272
Phone (303) 492–8154

Curriculum development, teacher inservices, consultation, and study tours.

Stanford Program on International and Cross-Cultural Education
Institute for International Studies
Littlefield Center Room 14
Stanford University
Stanford, CA 94305–5013
Phone (415) 723–1114; fax (415) 723–6784

Teacher workshops, summer institutes, study tours, curriculum development and other publications.

United Nations Association of The USA
485 Fifth Avenue
New York, NY 10017
Phone (212) 697–3232; fax (212) 682–9185

Model U.N. program,, speakers, publications, and curriculum development. UNA-USA chapters are in many cities across the country.

U.S. Institute of Peace (USIP)
1550 M Street NW, Suite 700
Washington, DC 20005
Phone (202) 457–1700; fax (202) 429–6063

National Peace Essay Contest, monthly journal, resource library, grants and fellowships for graduate students and educators, and teacher workshops.

The World Bank
1818 H Street, NW
Washington, DC 20433

Annual *World Development Report,* instructional materials and publications.

World Game Institute
University Science Center
3508 Market St.
Philadelphia, PA 19104
Phone (215) 387–0220; fax (215) 387–3009

Publications, instructional materials, speakers, conferences, and the simulation "World Game Workshops."

Worldwatch Institute
1776 Massachusetts Ave., NW
Washington, DC 20036–1904

The annual *State of the World,* other publications.

## INSTRUCTIONAL MATERIALS AND RESOURCES

*The Anatomy of Conflict.* Stanford, CA: Stanford Program on International and Cross-Cultural Education, 1988.

General introduction to conflict, its resolution, and management of conflict on personal, group, and world levels. Students analyze the characteristics and mechanisms of conflict. Includes reproducible handouts and slides, which assist students in writing definitions of "conflict." 10 slides. For grades 7–12. 52 pages.

*The Arms Trade.* Bernard Harbor, and Chris Smith. Rourke, 1988.

This publication is part of Rourke's World Issues Series. The authors discuss issues related to the political and economic causes of arms trade and describe the attempts to control it. Reading level, 6th grade. For grades 5–12. 48 pages. Available through Social Studies School Service, 10200 Jefferson Blvd, Culver City, CA 90232–0802. Phone (800) 421–4246.

*BaFa BaFa.* Simile II.

This high school simulation and its middle school version, *RaFa RaFa*, help students and teachers learn to recognize and deal with cross-cultural misunderstandings, prejudice, and fear of people who are different. Contact: Simile II, PO Box 90, Del Mar, CA 92014.

*Barnga: A Simulation Game on Cultural Clashes.* Intercultural Press, 1990.

Simulation booklet promoting an understanding of how even the most subtle of differences can lead to confusion among cultures and peoples. This challenging card game asks people to compete in a tournament called "Five Tricks." Grades 9 and up. 31 pages. PO Box 700, Yarmouth, ME 04096. Phone (207) 846-5168; fax (207) 846-5181.

*Blue Helmets—The Story of United Nations Peacekeeping.* Brooklyn: Pacific St. Film Projects.

Examines the role of the United Nations in promoting international peace and conflict resolution through its peacekeeping operations around the world. Focuses on efforts to maintain peace through the use of soldiers drawn from member nations. Includes interviews with U.N. personnel, diplomats, and scholars. Contact: Pacific St. Film Projects, 333 Sackett Street, Brooklyn, NY 11231. Phone (718) 875–9722.

*Choices in International Conflict.* Stanford, CA: Stanford Program on International and Cross-Cultural Education, 1988.

An introduction to the causes and consequences of war and non-violent means of conflict resolution and management uses case studies of the Falklands/Malvinas crisis and the Camp David accords, and introduces the ideas of Gandhi. For teachers of social studies and language arts, grade: 7 through junior college. 98 pages.

*Conflict Activity Cards.* Jacquelyn Johnson. Denver: Center for Teaching International Relations, 1980.

The book contains activity cards for teaching students how to identify, define, analyze and resolve conflict. The unit comes with teacher instructions as well as a pre-test and post-test for evaluating student's progress. Includes 54 activities. For grades 6–12.

*Cooperative Learning. Cooperative Lives: A Sourcebook of Learning Activities for Building a Peaceful World.* Nancy Schniedewind and Ellen Davidson. Dubuque, IA: Wm. C. Brown, 1987.

Activity book with more than 100 lessons with reproducible handouts. Topics include "cooperative learning," Central America, arms race, family life, product boycotts. Includes a bibliography. For middle grades and up. Contact: Wm. C. Brown Company Publishers, 2450 Kerper Blvd., Box 539, Dubuque, IA 52001. Phone (800) 922–7696.

*Earthalert: The Active Environmental Game.* 1990.

This simulation draws upon students' knowledge of recycling, tropical rain forests, global warming, wildlife, pollution, and the ozone layer to raise awareness about the earth and to illustrate how they can make a difference in ensuring its future. Grades 7 and up.

*Educating for Global Responsibility: Teacher-Designed Curricula for Peace Education K-12.* Edited by Betty A. Reardon. New York, NY: Teachers College Press, 1988.

Designed to furnish practical peace education material and to demonstrate the wide range of possibilities for integrating peace education into all subject areas for all grades. Specific topics include conflict, world hunger, multicultural understanding, and art for peace. Contact: Teachers College Press, P.O. Box 939, Wolfeboro, NH 03694–0939. Phone (800) 356–0409; fax (207) 324–0349.

*The Environment: Decisions, Decisions.* Tom Snyder. Computer software simulation. Apple (5.25″) IBM (5.25″ and 3.5″), and MacIntosh format. 1990.

This simulation combines science and social studies as students address crucial environmental questions. From the perspective of a town mayor, students consider the roles of individuals and communities in both local and global environmental problems. Grades 5–12.

*Evolution of the Methods and Rules of War.* Stanford, CA: Stanford Program on International and Cross-Cultural Education, 1989.

Materials on the technical, organizational, legal, historical, and ethical issues related to war. Students work in groups to discuss the characteristics of war and society during the Stone Age, ancient Greece, the early and late middle ages, the Mongol empire, World War I and II, and My Lai. Topics include rules of war and kinds of warfare from guerilla warfare to mechanized, global warfare. For grade levels 7—community college. 130 pages.

*Fish Banks, Ltd.* Computer software simulation. Fish Banks Ltd.

This simulation is about management of natural resources, economics, and group problem solving. Contact: Fish Banks, Ltd., IPSSR—Hood House, University of New Hampshire, Durham, NC 03824. Phone (603) 862–2186.

*Global Summit: The Peace Game.* Pittsburgh, PA: Borderland Games, 1989.

Card game for 1–6 players. Players represent nations using economic, political, and social resources to resolve threats to world peace. Everyone wins if peace is maintained; presumably everyone loses if these threats are not resolved within the prescribed 30 minutes (or less) of play. Ages 10 and up. Contact: Borderland Games, 2316 Forest Drive, Pittsburgh, PA 15235, (412) 371–3232.

*Guns or Butter.* Salt Lake City: Creative Enterprises, 1988.

A revised version of the famous simulation of the 1970s written by William Nesbitt. Provides a simple and short introduction to the issue of limited national resource that can be used for purposes of defending a nation and improving the social welfare of its citizens. For as few as 15 students in secondary and college classrooms; teaching guide and a packet of student materials available. Contact: Creative Enterprises, 4066 Diana Way, Salt Lake City, UT 84124. Phone (801) 277–8974.

The Headline Series. New York, NY: Foreign Policy Association.

The Headline Series includes such publications as *Conventional Arms Control and Europe's Future* (1989), *Strategic Defense Initiative: Splendid Defense or Pipe Dream?* (1985). Excellent resource for libraries, teachers, and advanced high school students. Four issues published per year. 64–72 pages.

*The Individual and the State.* Stanford, CA: Stanford Program on International and Cross-Cultural Education, 1989.

Provides a focus on the individual citizen's responsibility in society, and terrorist warfare using the script "The Firebugs," an example of a learning play. Students consider how plays are different from other genres. For grade levels 9 through junior college. 165 pages.

International Human Rights. VHS videocassette, guide. Close-up Foundation, 1986.

The executive director of Amnesty International USA, John G. Healy answers questions from a group of social studies teachers about the state of human rights in general and the work of Amnesty International in particular. Originally produced for telecast over C-Span. Color. 60 min.

*Introduction to Peace Studies.* D. P. Barash. Belmont, CA: Wadsworth Publishing Company. 1991.

The first general purpose, integrated introductory text on peace studies by a single author. Designed for college-level use, it is also useful to secondary educators. Includes sections titled "The Promise of Peace, The Problem of War," "The Causes of War," Building 'Negative Peace,'" and "Building Positive Peace."

*Managing Conflict.* Edited by Karen Mingst and Angene Wilson.

Two looseleaf books of lesson plans, simulations, resources, and teaching units on negotiation, management of conflict, and decision making on related issues for middle school and high school students. Volume 1 focuses on international conflict, and volume 2 on managing conflict on an interpersonal or community level. Volume 2 includes the Red-Green simulation described in chapter 2. Available through the Office of International Affairs, 215 Bradley Hall, University of Kentucky, Lexington, KY 40506–0058.

*Nuclear Escape Conflict Resolution and Arms Control.* Minneapolis: Nuclear Escape, 1987.

This interactive board game takes a holistic approach to the nuclear arms dilemma by including all of the variables and dynamics of the nuclear weapons dilemma: arms reduction, escalation, proliferation, verification, ratification, and Star Wars, as well as trust, deceit, communication, and negotiation. *Nuclear Escape* can be purchased in either a table top version (2–16 students) or a magnetic version (up to 40 students). Both come with a teacher's guide and a nuclear weapons information booklet (eight chapters, three levels to choose from: Jr. High, Sr. High, or Advanced Sr. High and college edition). Contact: J. Leon Boler, Nuclear Escape, 1401 East River Road, Minneapolis, MN 55414. Phone (612) 872–0816.

Opposing Viewpoints (a series). San Diego: Greenhaven Press.

The series includes five student booklets on nuclear war, including topics such as civil defense, space weapons, survival, and how it would begin; and five titles concerned with war and human nature, including topics such as the causes of war, peace movements, and can war be eliminated? Each booklet includes attention to critical thinking skills. A teacher's guide is available. Contact: Greenhaven Press, Inc., P.O. Box 289009, San Diego, CA 92128–9009. Phone (619) 485–7424, (800) 231–5163; fax (619) 485–9549.

Peace and World Order Studies: A Curriculum Guide. Edited by D. C. Thomas and M. T. Klare. 5th ed. New York, NY: World Policy Institute, 1989.

Designed for college-level use but also useful to secondary educators. Essays and syllabi covering a broad range of world order concerns from general introductory courses to more topically focused ones on war and peace, economic development, human rights, and ecological stability. 736 pages. Contact: World Policy Institute, 777 U.N. Plaza, New York, NY 10017. Phone (212)490–0010.

*Pollution Control.* Computer software/role-playing simulation. Apple (5.25")and IBM (5.25" and 3.5") formats. Focus Media, 1989.

This simulation demonstrates the complexity of nature and the interaction of its elements, helping students learn the causes and effects of pollution, as well as the economic and business/employment associated costs of pollution control, as well as the economic and business/employment associated costs of pollution control. Grades 7–12.

*Social Issues Resources Series.*
Includes three volumes on *Defense,* which contain 80 to 100 reprinted articles representing a wide spectrum of opinion and complexity. Three annual supplements reflect new developments and changes since 1986. SIRS can be found in over 60 percent of U.S. schools and libraries. Contact: P.O. Box 2348, Boca Raton, FL 33427 Phone (800) 232-SIRS or (407) 994–0079; fax (407) 994–4704.

*Starpower.* Simile II.

The simulation teaches about inequalities in the global system. Different groups compete in a game that is stacked against some and benefits others. Contact: Simile II, PO Box 90, Del Mar, CA 92014.

*The State of the Earth Atlas.* Edited by Joni Seager. New York: Simon and Schuster, 1990.

Excellent atlas of global issues on such topics as water, rainforests, population, sewage, energy, biodiversity, and air quality. Some maps have proportional shapes that intrigue students.

*Survival and Dominance.* Milton Kleg. Denver: Center for Teaching International Relations, 1988.

This simulation game involves players in international diplomacy involving conflict situations. Includes game board, instructions, and all game pieces. Grades 9–12.

*Teaching About Human Rights: Issues of Justice in a Global Age.* David Shiman. Center for Teaching International Relations, 1987.

Activity book with reproducible handouts. The activities focus on political, civil, social, and economic rights. Reproducible student worksheets include "Comparing Political Freedom Across Cultures," "Crossword Justice," and "Equal Pay for Equal Work." Grades 7-12.

*Teaching about Peace and Conflict Resolution: Lessons for High School Social Studies.* Edited by M. Denham, B. Welling Hall, and J. E. Harf, 1993. Contact the Mershon Center, 1501 Neil Avenue, The Ohio State University, Columbus, OH 43201. Phone (614) 292–1681.

A book of 29 lessons designed to help teachers infuse particular peace/conflict resolution content into the regular curriculum. Includes case studies, sets of data, and other useful information.

*Teaching about Peace and Nuclear War: A Balanced Approach.* John Zola, and Jaye Zola. Denver: Center for Teaching International Relations and Social Science Education Consortium, 1986.

This is a teachers' handbook for teaching about peace and nuclear war. The authors provide a rationale and definition for peace and nuclear war education, examine how teachers can responsibly teach about controversial issues, and suggest topics and strategies suitable for teaching about peace and nuclear war at various grade, levels. A system for evaluating related curriculum materials is provided. Strategies for implementing curriculum change in schools are discussed. Grades 7–12. 109 pages.

*War and Human Nature: Opposing Viewpoints.* Edited by D. L. Bender and B. Leone, St. Paul, MN: Greenhaven Press, 1983.

Presents opposing viewpoints through essays on various issues under the chapter headings "Are Humans Aggressive by Nature?" "What Causes War?" "Is Nuclear War Justifiable?" "What Is a War Crime?" "Are Peace Movements Effective?" and "Can War Be Eliminated?"

*Why War?* Stanford, CA: Stanford Program on International and Cross-Cultural Education, 1988.

Leads students to an understanding and appreciation of poetry on war and peace. Poems by such authors as Herbert Asquith, Rupert Brook, R.N. Currey, Peter Porter, Cart Sandberg, and Sigfried Sassoon are set in chronological sequence and are treated as historical fiction. Students examine war in the middle ages, technical advances in warfare, and perceptions of war. For grade levels 9 through junior college. 120 pages.

*World Military and Social Expenditures.* Ruth Leger Sivard. Washington, DC, World Priorities, 1989.

Includes time-lines of military and medical breakthroughs since World War II, the state of the world arms race, the state of world health, military control and repression, the nuclear world, wars and war-related deaths since 1945, and comparative government expenditures on military and health sectors.

## ELECTRONIC NETWORKS

The PeaceNet, ConflictNet, and EcoNet databases described below are located at the Institute for Global Communications, 18 De Boom Street, San Francisco, CA 94107; Phone (415) 442–0220. **PeaceNet:** Helps the peace, social justice, and human rights communities throughout the world communicate and cooperate more effectively.

**ConflictNet:** A network of people dedicated to promoting the constructive resolution of conflict. ConflictNet enhances the work of groups and individuals involved in conflict resolution and links users to the worldwide conflict resolution community.

**EcoNet:** Serves organizations and individuals working for environmental preservation and sustainability. It is a community of persons using the network for information sharing and collaboration in order to enhance the effectiveness of all environmentally-oriented programs and activities.

**CompuServe:** A commercial online service. Established in 1979, CompuServe provides its worldwide membership of 1.1 million with more than 1,700 databases and services. It can be accessed by any modem-equipped personal computer utilizing the CompuServe Information Manager graphical interface or general communication software. For membership call (800) 524–3388.

**EnviroNet:** A free computer network featuring conferences on environmental subjects, daily Greenpeace press releases, and environmental newsletters, as well as realtime e-mail. To gain access and establish an account, set modem to call 1–415–512–9108 (1200 or 2400 baud). For further information, call (415) 512–9025.

## ARTICLES AND MATERIALS AVAILABLE THROUGH ERIC

The Educational Resources Information Center (ERIC) is the world's largest single source of education information. For information on any of the materials below, contact the ERIC Clearinghouse for Social Studies/Social Science Education, Indiana University, 2805 East 10th St., Suite 120, Bloomington, IN 47408–2698. Phone (812) 855–3838; fax (812) 855–7901.

Bjerstedt, Ake. "Young People and Peace: Prerequisites for Peace-Oriented Instruction." *School Research Newsletter* (Swedish National Board of Education) no. 1 (April 1987). ED288762.

Helping children and youth learn through school experiences to deal constructively with questions of peace, war, and ways to promote peace preparedness is the purpose of this four-year peace education project. The principal goals of the project include: (1) an inventory and analysis of experiences and related peace education projects in various countries, (2) studies of young people's concepts of war, peace, or the enemy, (3) explorations of viewpoints concerning schools' roles in pursuit of peace preparedness, (4) studies of various ways that schools teach war and peace concepts, and (5) the collection of related project reports, bibliographies, analyses, research, models, and teacher guides.

Bode, Robert A. An Intercultural Paradigm of Nonviolence. 1987. ED285239.

Much of the rhetoric used by world leaders is one of violence, based on destructive myths and images, which increases the probability of war. Tenets of the paradigm include: (1) adopting a spatial view of the world, which sees humans as world citizens, (2) a willingness to abstain from physical or psychological violence, (3) social and political responsibility, (4) shared values, (5) creating new ethics, (6) long-term, future, macro-orientation; and (7) interaction among the paradigm's tenets. Such a paradigm, if it is adhered to, can create a more cooperative climate in which cultural and political interaction can occur.

Carson, Terrance R. "Relating Peace Education and Social Studies in an Age of Insecurity." History and Social Science Teacher, vol. 20, no. 3–4 (Spring 1984): 8–10 EJ320403.

In the theme of insecurity there is a potential for peace education to address social education. Insecurity underpins the arms race and lies at the root of the growing cycle of violence. Peace education must help students understand the forms of structural injustices that preserve inequities and breed violence.

Carson, Terrance R., and Gideonse, Hendrik D., eds. Peace Education and the Task for Peace Educators. A World Council for Curriculum and Instruction Monograph. 1987. ED289795.

The development of informed citizens who are dedicated to maintaining the public good through wise action is the goal of peace education. Ten articles in this document discuss the various issues surrounding peace education. The first two articles, by Ken Os borne and Nigel Young, set an historical and conceptual framework for the field of peace education. Robin Burns speaks of the challenge that peace education presents for conventional school organizations and curriculum. Virginia Cawagas writes of the recent events in the Philippines and of the role played by educators in bringing about political change. Jaime Diaz analyzes peace education in the context of both direct and structural violence. Birgit Brock-Utne directs the reader's attention to the historical and contemporary problems of structural violence experienced by women. Two articles by Mildred Masheder and Lennart Vriens focus on the world of children, and encourages parents and elementary school teachers to focus on peace education from the child's perspective. The final two articles, by John Hurst and Peter Scott, seek to develop a pedagogy for university peace education programs.

Charnofsky, Norene M., comp. "Conflict Resolution Bibliography." 1987. (ED287770)

Various theories and approaches to conflict resolution and peace education are presented in the 31 resources listed in this annotated bibliography. It is divided into two sections. Section 1 contains materials designed to help adults become more effective role models for the peaceful resolution of conflict. Topics include parent/child conflicts, negotiation, control, mediation, power, interpersonal relationships, and peace strategies. Section 2 describes resources useful in establishing a positive environment and teaching conflict resolution skills. Included are a variety of books, curriculum guides, and materials to help establish a school-based mediation program and to teach conflict resolution and peace education.

"Controlling Conflict." *Update on Law Related Education* vol. 15, no. 2 (spring–summer 1991): 11–12. (EJ445204)

Presents a lesson plan for teaching students basic conflict resolution techniques. Calls upon students to identify issues that can lead to interpersonal confrontation, use active listening techniques, and analyze and select alternatives to conflict. Includes handouts, discussion topics, and an explanation of methods of conflict resolution.

Deutsch, Morton. *Educating beyond Hate*. "Preparedness for Peace." Peace Education Miniprints, no. 23. Malmo, Sweden: Lund University, School of Education, 1991. ED 351215.

In recent years, it increasingly has been recognized that schools must change in basic ways if children are to be educated so that they are prepared to live in a peaceful world. This recognition has been expressed in a number of interrelated movements: "cooperative learning," "conflict resolution," and "education for peace." This paper discusses four key components in these overlapping movements: cooperative learning, conflict resolution training, the constructive use of controversy in teaching subject-matter, and the creation of dispute resolution centers in schools. The basic view is that students need to have continuing experiences of constructive conflict resolution as they learn different subjects as well as immersion in a school environment that provides daily experiences of cooperative relations.

Hicks, David. "The Centre for Peace Studies: 1980–89." *Westminster Studies in Education* vol. 14 (1991): 37–49. EJ446524.

Reports the nine-year history of the Centre for Peace Studies. Identifies the aims of the project. Discusses the extent of interest in, and reactions to, the center. Describes "World Studies 8–13," a curriculum program of the center that continued under the direction of the World Studies Trust after the center ceased to exist.

London, Katherine. "Global Peace Begins in Our Classrooms." *Louisiana Social Studies Journal* vol. 15, no. 1 (fall 1988): 22–25 EJ424982.

Recommends incorporating the study of peace into the established curriculum in language, literature, and social studies. Suggests teaching concepts of peace and conflict resolution by relating such concepts to students' own lives and expanding these concepts. Includes class activities such as brainstorming, experiencing conflict resolution, and creating drawings from unrelated composite parts.

Maas, Jeanette P., and Stewart, Robert A. C., eds. *Toward a World of Peace: People Create Alternatives*. Proceedings of the First International Conference on Conflict Resolution and Peace Studies in the United Nations Year of Peace, Suva, Fiji, August 1986. ED282800.

This book is a review of the 1986 United Nations International Year of Peace conducted at an international conference in Fiji. The theme of the conference was "People Create Alternatives," and the issues of conflict resolution and avoiding global destruction were addressed. Specific topics discussed were: (1) "Theories and Techniques of Conflict Resolution", (2) "Nationalism vs. the World as Expanded Community", (3) "Economic Factors in Relationship to Conflict", (4) "Confronting the Nuclear Crisis", (5) "Human Rights in the Developing World and Everywhere Else", (6) "Peace Studies and Research"; and (7) "Super Power Rivalry in the Pacific Basin." Also included are proceedings from the following symposia: (1) "The Rotary Center for World Understanding and Peace", (2) "Globalizing Teacher Education: A Vehicle for Peace", (3) "Developing Curricula for Peace Education in Secondary Schools", (4) "Awakening the Sleeping Dragons"; and (5) "International Physicians for the Prevention of Nuclear War."

Roderick, Tom. *Stop and Think! Dialogue, Critical Thinking Skills and Creative Conflict Resolution in Peace Education,* interview by Ate Bjerstedt. "Preparedness for Peace." Peace Education Miniprints, no. 5. Malmo, Sweden: Lund University, School of Education, 1990. ED 351281.

An interview on peace education with Tom Roderick of Educators for Social Responsibility is presented in this document. Educators for Social Responsibility is a national teachers' organization in the United States that offers programs and curricula that are intended to help young people become engaged in the world. Tom Roderick discusses his background, the activities of Educators for Social Responsibility, and his thoughts on a number of areas that concern peace education.

Stoloff, David L. "Peace Education and Educational Technology. 1992. ED349945.

This overview of the use of educational technology in peace education discusses three questions: (1) how educational technology may be applied to increase world understanding and reduce intergroup tensions; (2) what strategies, within what contexts, have proven effective in integrating the study of peace across the curriculum; and (3) how motivated individuals might make use of leading edge technologies to enhance their voices in the global conversation on the future. Terms are defined and ten strategies for using technology in peace education are presented. These strategies address the following topics: (1) simulations to practice conflict resolution, (2) teaming across curriculum through technology, (3) incorporating information technologies to study peace, (4) developing databases on global themes, (5) creating software on peace through cooperative learning, (6) initiating local electronic conferences and support groups, (7) linking students to national and international classrooms, (8) participating in a *Kids-92 Newsletter*'s global conference, (9) supplementing software to widen perspectives, and (10) projecting twenty-first century curriculum themes.

Thompson, Kenneth W. "A Realist Response to the Appeal for Pacifism." *Perspectives on Political Science* vol. 20, no. 2 (Spring 1991): 73–77. EJ438468.

Defines war as symptom rather than cause. Identifies the root cause of the Middle East crisis as destruction of the regional balance of power through foreign augmentation of Iraqi power. Criticizes the tendency to see world problems as a fight between good and evil. Defines realism as the ability to see political realities as a balance of power.

Woodward, Ted. "Breaking Barriers through Adventure Based Citizen Diplomacy." *Journal of Experiential Education* vol. 14, no. 1 (May 1991): 14–19. EJ430418.

Traces the development of peace-oriented experiential philosophy in both its western and Soviet contexts, suggesting that adventure-based citizen diplomacy is a valuable means to build bridges between them. Adventure Based Citizen Diplomacy projects are working to decrease the cultural, sociopolitical, and psychological barriers that remain in the Soviet Union and the West.

Wulf, Christoph. *Education for Peace.* "Preparedness for Peace." Peace Education Miniprints, no. 28. Malmo, Sweden: Lund University, School of Education, 1992. ED 351254.

Education for peace is a process that must begin in the childhood of students and continue for the rest of their lives. Education for peace also is concerned with addressing the conditions that nurture violence and war and with seeking ways to change those conditions. Among the major themes of current peace education efforts are the aftermath of the Cold War, including the still existing threat of nuclear war; the North-South issue, including the southern hemisphere's deepening impoverishment; the problems posed by pollution and destruction of the environment; and the obstacles to the spread of human rights and social justice. Peace education also can be understood as a social learning process, including the development of individual skills such as empathy, and competence in communication.

# GLOSSARY

**aggression.** Wrongful first use of force by one state against another.

**air space.** The area between the earth's surface and outer space. States have legal jurisdiction over aircraft flying in the air space above their territories.

**alien.** A foreign national when within another state's territory.

**alliance.** Countries banding together, each promising assistance against an attack from their common enemy.

**anarchic.** Lack of supranational authority or government that can effectively regulate relations among countries by punishing aggression, enforcing promises, and protecting innocent parties.

**Antarctic Treaty Consultative Parties (ATCP).** The officially recognized group of states that meets periodically to adopt agreements pertaining to the Antarctic region. The criteria for membership are ratification of the Antarctic Treaty (1959) and maintenance of a permanent research station in the area.

**appeasement.** Giving a potential adversary a little of what he wants in the hopes of satisfying him, therby avoiding further conflict.

**arbitration.** The process whereby a third party makes a decision in hopes of resolving a dispute; in binding arbitration, the contending parties pledge to accept the arbitrator's ruling.

**arms control.** Specific limitations on certain aspects of the military competition, whether of weapons or behavior.

**authority.** The legal right to do something; to act; to command; the U.S. Congress has the authority to declare war; the U.N. Security Council has the authority to command states to apply economic sanctions.

**balance of payments.**   Systematic record of all economic transactions, including movement of goods, services, interest, gifts, investments, currency; country having receipts for items sold to rest of world larger than payments is in surplus; country having receipts from rest of world which are smaller than its payments to rest of world has a balance of payments deficit.

**balkanization.**   Breakup into small national or ethnic units, either through secessions or political decisions, as it threatened in the Balkans (the region of southern Europe from Serbia in the north to the southern tip of Greece).

**Balkans.**   Area of south-central Europe encompassed mostly by the former greater Yugoslavia.

**charter.**   An agreement; can mean the same as a treaty, as in "the U.N. Charter."

**collective security.**   Requires that all countries agree to come to the defense of any victim of aggression; an attack on one is an attack on all.

**colonialism.**   The formal, legal control by one state of all the affairs of the people(s) of a foreign territory.

**common heritage of mankind.**   Doctrine that a resource domain, such as the seabed or outer space, is owned by the entire international community. All states have a right to participate in making the rules that apply to the domain and to share in the benefits from its use.

**common market.**   A group of states that have decided to eliminate internal barriers to trade among participating units and establish uniform external barriers.

**commons.**   An area or resource domain that multiple users are entitled to exploit for their individual profit.

**communist states.**   States endorsing some type of Marxism as official ideology; they claim to be in the process of creating a classless society.

**concert (of nations).**   Participants agree to maintain a balance power among the principal members, promising to come to the aid of any individual great power if under attack from another great power.

**conditionality.**    Stipulations put on loans to developing countries by both bilateral and multilateral donors.

**condominium (of great power).**    A concert variant in which the key countries agree not to fight each other in order to free their hands to dominate the other states in the international system.

**con-federation** (or confederation, confederal system).    Federal arrangement in which some authority and power is transferred *from* the composing units *to* a political center.

**conference diplomacy.**    United Nations practice of convening world conferences to focus attention on specific problems, as well as to adopt plans of action for addressing them. The United Nations Conference on the Human Environment held in Stockholm in 1972 ushered in an era of conference diplomacy.

**conflict resolution.**    A general term for the ending of disputes short of violence.

**convention.**    A multilateral treaty.

**cooperation.**    States acting in a conscious way to adjust or change policy in keeping with what they believe is in the national interest.

**Council of Europe.**    Grouping of almost thirty states to deal collectively with social questions like human rights and migration.

**country.**    Used interchangeably with the term *state*.

**Covenant.**    An agreement between nations such as the Covenant of the League of Nations.

**CSCE process.**    Grouping of more than fifty states to deal with security, economic, and social issues among European and North American states; produced the 1975 Helsinki Accord.

**declaration.**    A special resolution of the U.N. General Assembly.

**Declaration on a New International Economic Order (NIEO).**    A 1974 declaration of the U.N. General Assembly proclaiming "our united determination to work urgently for" an international economic order to redress existing injustices, eliminate the widening gap between developing and developed countries, and "ensure steadily accelerating economic and social development in peace and justice."

**democracy.**  The practice of civil and political rights emphasizing free and fair elections; a system of governing in which the average citizen has relatively great influence in public affairs; different from dictatorship and oligarchy and other forms of authoritarianism.

**deterrence.**  Using threats to discourage another state from doing something.

**deterrence by threats of denial.**  The defending state threatens to defeat the attack of the aggressor state, thereby denying the aggressor any gain. Involves destroying the enemy army on the battlefield.

**deterrence by threats of punishment.**  Defending state threatens to strike back against the aggressor, destroying targets the aggressor holds dear in order to persuade the aggressor the prize is not worth the pain. Involves striking targets in the enemy's homeland.

**diplomacy.**  The practice of resolving disputes between states by communications between the trained, official representatives of governments.

**direct violence.**  Efforts to kill, incapacitate, or maim an enemy.

**disappeared persons.**  Person detained by government agents, who deny that the person is in custody. Ill treatment and summary execution frequently follow.

**disarmament.**  Complete eradication of weapons of war; at the very least, the transference of all such weapons to a single authority (the global sheriff).

**electromagnetic spectrum.**  The range of frequencies used for wireless transmission of various forms of telecommunications; otherwise known as "air waves" or "radio waves." International regulations pertaining to this resource are made at conferences of the International Telecommunications Union.

**ethnic cleansing.**  The driving out of other groups from a territory in pursuit of ethnic purity; practiced by Serbs against Croats and Bosnians, for example, in the Balkans.

**ethnic group.**  A group of human beings *whose members* consider themselves to be a distinct unit on the basis of a common ancestry, and/or common language, culture, and often shared religion and historical memories.

**European Economic Community.** Grouping of twelve states, soon to be expanded, to deal collectively with economic and social questions. Also called the "Common Market."

**exchange rates.** Prices of one currency in terms of another bought and sold on foreign exchange markets; rates may be fixed by agreement or may fluctuate according to market conditions.

**exclusive economic zone (EEZ).** The region of the seas between twelve and two hundred nautical miles from coastlines, as defined in the 1982 Law of the Sea Treaty. Within this area, adjacent coastal states have the first right to exploit the living and nonliving resources of the ocean waters and seabed.

**federalism.** A method of organization in which political authority is divided among different units with one unit having overarching authority.

**federation or federal system.** Federal arrangement in which some authority and power is transferred *from* a political center *to* the composing units.

**first-come, first-served rule.** Presumption that the first user of a part of a commons has a continuing right to its exclusive use. This rule has traditionally governed use of the electromagnetic spectrum and the geostationary orbit.

**freedom of the seas.** A long-standing doctrine of international law elaborated in the writings of Hugo Grotius; it provides that all states have the right to make use of the oceans as long as they do not interfere with other users.

**functionalism.** Theory that states that peace is achieved by eliminating economic disparity; economic disparity can be eliminated by cooperation among technical experts from different countries.

**General Assembly.** United Nations body in which all states are represented; can only suggest to member states what their policies should be.

**geostationary orbit.** The orbit arc 22,300 miles above the equator. Satellites moving in the direction of the earth's rotation at this altitude travel at a velocity that keeps them over the same location on the planet.

**global commons.** Areas outside the legal jurisdiction of any nation-state that are open to use by all states. The principal examples are the oceans and seabed, outer space, Antarctica, the atmosphere, and the electromagnetic spectrum.

**group of 77.**   A caucusing group that includes most less developed countries that began meeting in the United Nations in 1964. The group has grown to approximately 130 members.

**Helsinki Accord.**   The 1975 agreement among more than thirty states to, among other things, advance human rights; generated considerable pressure on European communists for human rights reform.

**human dignity.**   A worthy life; a life worth living.

**human rights.**   A means to human dignity; a claim that public authority must do something, or refrain from doing something, to protect or advance human dignity.

**Human Rights Commission.**   U.N. agency made up of elected states; it is the center of U.N. diplomacy on human rights.

**identity.**   An answer to the question: Who are you? The answer may be personal or collective and may pertain to a name, and/or language, religion, country, continent, etc.

**imperialism.**   Establishment of political and economic control by a state or empire over foreign territories.

**independence.**   Sovereignty of a political entity, such as a state.

**indigenous people.**   People native to an area prior to arrival of foreign settlers.

**International Bill of Rights.**   Human rights as set forth in the Universal Declaration of Human Rights, the Covenant on Civil-Political Rights; the Covenant on Economic-Social-Cultural Rights.

**international customary law.**   Distinct from treaty law; derived from international practice, that becomes legally binding; one of two main sources of international law.

**international organizations.**   Organizations having members from different states joined together by a common purpose; when members are governments, the organizations are intergovernmental (IGOs); when members are either interest groups or individuals, then organizations are nongovernmental organizations (NGOs).

**International Telecommunications Union (ITU).** A United Nations specialized agency that facilitates and regulates applications of various information gathering and transmitting technologies. It convenes World Administrative Radio Conferences, which allocates portions of the electromagnetic spectrum to specific types of uses, and assigns positions in the geostationary orbit to specific countries.

**irredenta (irredentism).** A government claiming (usually historical) rights over the territory of a neighboring state, or part of it.

**Islamic fundamentalism.** A version of the Islamic religion featuring strict enforcement of the Sharia, a harsh and puritanical social code; for example, under the Sharia, there is gender discrimination and there is amputation for common crime.

**jurisdiction.** The scope or range of authority; the jurisdiction of the United States is mostly limited to its territory.

**Kurds.** Refers to Kurdish people, an ethnic group found mostly in Iran, Iraq, and Turkey.

**Law of the Sea Treaty.** Completed in December 1982 after ten years of negotiation. The treaty provides a comprehensive regime for law of the sea, covering territorial limits, retrieval of gas and oil, fisheries, mining the ocean bed, maritime and naval traffic, pollution and scientific research. Also provides for a new International Sea-Bed Authority and mandatory procedures for settling disputes.

**liberal international economic order.** The desired outcome for those who believe that economic growth is best achieved if goods and services are allowed to flow across national borders without governmental restrictions; the theory suggests that economic growth occurs for the collectivity.

**long-range transboundary air pollution (LRTAP).** Refers primarily to pollutants that cause acid deposition in regions beyond the boundaries of the state in which they originate. The 1979 LRTAP Convention and supplemental protocols on emissions of sulphur and nitrogen oxides and volatile organic compounds regulate transboundary pollution in the European region.

**macro-economic.** Forces affecting the economy as a whole.

**Mandate (system).** Created by the League of Nations, in which territories formerly belonging to the defeated countries in the First World War were entrusted to various "advanced nations" having responsibility for their development through gradual introduction of self-government, toward eventual independence under League supervision.

**market incentives.** Strategies such as resource taxes and tradeable permits that encourage or discourage use of a commons by altering the calculation of profits by its exploiters.

**mediation.** Attempts by a third party to assist contending sides in reaching a peaceful agreement, often by suggesting possible solutions.

**multinational corporations.** Companies that have production facilities and sales in several different countries.

**nation-state.** A state that includes only one nation.

**negative peace.** Stopping the violence.

**negotiation.** Process of discussing or bargaining to reach agreement on subject of common interest.

**neofunctionalism.** A reinterpretation of functionalism that suggests that technical cooperation will not automatically or inevitably occur; specific political activity needs to be taken to push the process.

**New International Economic Order.** A list of demands made in the 1970s by the Group of 77 developing countries advocating changes in the structure of North-South economic relations.

**New International Information and Communications Order (NIICO).** A United Nations Educational Scientific and Cultural Organization (UNESCO) General Conference resolution adopted in 1980 calling for elimination of imbalances and inequalities in international communication such that all people can participate actively in communication and have access to information and such that there is "respect for each people's cultural identity and for the right of each nation to inform the world about its interests, its aspirations and its social and cultural values."

**nonforcible sanctions.**   Punishments such as economic embargoes that do not entail military force.

**nongovernmental organizations (NGO).**   Often applied to an organization involved in international issues; particularly applied to organizations involved in political activity in U.N. organizations.

**operational arms control.**   Limits the arms race, and its ecological consequences, throguh restrictions on key activities like nuclear testing.

**outer space.**   The region beyond national air space in which satellites orbit the earth. No specific altitude is officially recognized as the boundary between air space and outer space.

**parallel system.**   Arrangement for mining the deep seabed contained in the 1982 Law of the Sea Treaty. Deep-sea mining may be undertaken both by an international enterprise and by state-based mining companies.

**peace.**   Conditions under which human beings can fulfill their physical and mental potential without significant curtailment by factors that the society in which they live has the capacity to overcome.

**peacelessness.**   The absence of peace, which may be caused by war, extreme poverty, severe deprivation of human rights, or ecological disasters.

**people's organizations (PO).**   Sometimes used as a synonym for NGO, but often refers to an organization that is somewhat more informal and grassroots, as compared to the often more formally organized NGO that generally has more extensive geographic reach.

**plebiscite.**   Ascertaining the will of people in regard to their political status or affiliation.

**policy coordination.**   States agree to make adjustments in respective policies in order to satisfy mutual interests.

**positive peace.**   A condition in which society is organized so as not to create conditions that lead to violence or acrimonious conflict.

**power.**   The capacity to do, act, command.

**precautionary principle.**   Practice of taking the first steps to avert a potentially serious problem even before the problem has been verified conclusively by scientific evidence.

**preferential access.**   A guarantee of special access to the markets of another country.

**public goods.**   Something of value to everyone; clean air is a public good.

**public monopoly.**   Strategy for preventing a "tragedy of the commons" that gives a publicly owned enterprise the exclusive rights to use a resource domain.

**qualitative arms control.**   Eliminating certain categories of weapons.

**quantitative arms control.**   Limiting the numbers of certain types of weapon systems either through restrictions on growth or cutbacks in the arsenal.

**realist/realism.**   The political theory that views humans as flawed and power seeking and believes international relations is a struggle among nations for power in a hostile environment.

**Realpolitik.**   The conduct of political affairs according to calculations of power and gain, as opposed to ethics or morality.

**regime (international).**   Set of norms or rules of behavior, usually based on international agreement, governing particular issues in world politics.

**regional integration.**   Process by which states attempt to combine separate national economies into larger economic units.

**secession** or **separatism.**   Breaking away from a state.

**Security Council.**   Highest and most important body of the United Nations; composed of fifteen states, five of which are permanent and can block action with a single veto; can make law commanding states to do something.

**security dilemma.**   One state's efforts to improve its own security tend to make another state feel more insecure.

**self-government.**   Self-rule or autonomy, short of independence.

**sovereignty.** Supreme legal authority within a territorial political community; the legal right to have the last say on what should be policy within a state.

**state.** A political entity that includes a territory and population. Not to be used interchangeably with the term *government,* g.v.

**state of nature.** A state of war of all against all; states may place their trust in others for a time, but ultimately each must look after its own interests.

**structural violence.** Diminution of the physical and mental capacities of people by factors, such as deprivation of human rights, malnutrition, pollution, and lack of basic medical care, that are a result of the way societies are organized (structured).

**summit meetings,** or **summitry.** Formal meetings between the leaders of major political groups.

**supranationalism.** Subordination of the state in favor of a jurisdiction "above" the state, referring to an international body.

**terms of trade.** The balance of payments in foreign trade; terms of trade can be favorable or unfavorable depending on whether the value of one's exports exceeds that of imports or vice versa.

**territorial waters.** The offshore area in which coastal states may exercise most prerogatives of sovereignty that apply to land areas. The 1982 Law of the Sea Treaty increased the internationally recognized width from three to twelve nautical miles.

**Tiananmen Square massacre.** Massacre in The People's Republic of China, June 1989, by government troops of peacefully protesting student demonstrators.

**track II diplomacy.** Structured interactions between groups of people who represent contending viewpoints; such people typically are not diplomats or national leaders, and their meetings generally take place over a relatively prolonged time period.

**tragedy of the commons.** Tendency for resources subject to the commons arrangement to be overused to the point of their destruction, as elaborated in the writings of biologist Garrett Hardin.

**treaty.** A formal agreement, sometimes referred to as a "convention," between two or more sovereign states that spells out rights and obligations and is a form of international law. States are legally bound to comply with the provisions of treaties they ratify.

**Trusteeship (system).** Officially: International Trusteeship System, established by the United Nations at its founding for "territories held under mandates," "territories which may be detached from enemy states as a result of the Second World War," and "territories voluntarily placed under the system by states responsible for their administration"(See Chapter 12 of the U.N. Charter).

**United Nations Conference on Environment and Development (Earth Summit).** A major conference, held in Rio de Janeiro in June 1992, which was attended by more than one hundred heads of state. It addressed a wide range of global environmental problems, including climate change, biodiversity, and deforestation, in relation to economic problems of the developing countries and the goal of "sustainable development."

**United Nations Conference on the Law of the Sea (UNCLOS).** Conferences convened in 1958, 1960, and 1973–82 by the United Nations to adopt treaties that would spell out rules for the use of the oceans, including the rights of coastal states in off-shore areas. The third UNCLOS adopted a comprehensive Law of the Sea Treaty.

**United Nations Environment Programme (UNEP).** An international body that has responsibility for coordinating, facilitating, and stimulating international environmental programs in partnership with a number of United Nations agencies, national governments, and nongovernmental organizations. It has established the Global Environmental Monitoring System and has sponsored negotiations on environmental treaties.

**Universal Declaration on Human Rights.** Adopted by the U.N. General Assembly in 1948, covering civil, political, economic, social and cultural rights. Provided the basis for drafting a treaty on Civil and Political Rights and a treaty on Economic, Social and Cultural Rights, in 1966.

**universal jurisdiction.** The right of a state to arrest and try a violator of international law, without regard to nationality of criminal or place of crime.

**verification.** Making sure the other side honors its obligations in arms control.

**voluntary restraint.**    Users of a commons take responsibility on their own to limit their use in the interests of conserving the resource.

**war crime.**    A violation of the laws of war.

**weighted voting scheme.**    System of voting in some international organizations where large contributors have a greater voice in the decisionmaking process, in contrast to one country/one vote system where all countries theoretically have the same voting.

**World Meteorological Organization (WMO).**    A United Nations specialized agency that facilitates weather forecasting on a global basis through its sponsorship of the World Weather Watch. It also organizes international research projects on the atmosphere, weather, and climate change.

# CONTRIBUTORS

Chadwick F. Alger is Mershon Professor of Political Science and Public Policy, The Ohio State University. He has developed and taught two peace studies courses at The Ohio State University: "Introduction to Peace Studies," for freshmen and sophomores, and "Quest for Peace," for advanced undergraduate students and graduate students. He has published widely on the United Nations system based on first-hand observation and extensive interviews with diplomats and members of U.N. Secretariats in New York, Geneva, and Paris. He is coeditor of *A Just Peace through Transformation: Cultural, Economics and Political Foundations for Change* (1988) and of *Conflict and Crisis of International Order: New Tasks for Peace Research* (1985). He is past president of the International Studies Association (1978–79) and former secretary general of the International Peace Research Association (1982–86). Professor Alger has directed much of his research and teaching toward enhancement of citizen competence in world affairs. Toward this end he developed the "Columbus in the World: the World in Columbus" project, a study of the ways in which the everyday lives of people, and organizations in which they are involved (business, political, educational, arts, philanthropic, etc.), are linked to world processes and institutions.

David P. Barash is Professor of psychology at the University of Washington. He received his Ph.D. from the University of Wisconsin in 1970, and taught at the State University of New York before joining the University of Washington in 1973. His teaching includes courses in "psychosocial aspects of nuclear war," and "the psychology of peace." He is cofounder and codirector of the UW's Peace and Strategic Studies program, and is a Fellow of the American Association for the Advancement of Science. He has also served as a Fellow at the Center for Advanced Study in the Behavioral Sciences (Stanford) and the Rockefeller Foundation's Study and Conference Center (Bellagio, Italy). He has written about 165 technical articles, numerous magazine and Op-Ed pieces, and twelve books, including *The L Word: An Unapologetic, Thoroughly Biased, Long Overdue Explication and Celebration of Liberalism* (William Morrow, 1991), and the textbooks *The Arms Race and Nuclear War* (Wadsworth, 1986) and *Introduction to Peace Studies* (Wadsworth, 1991).

**Peter D. Feaver** is Assistant Professor Political Science at Duke University. His doctorate in political science is from Harvard University. Dr. Feaver teaches courses in international relations, national security, and international ethics. He has held postdoctoral fellowships at the Olin Institute at Harvard University and the Mershon Center at Ohio State University. His research focus is civil-military relations and nuclear weapons, especially with reference to the United States. He also has interests in nuclear proliferation, defense reform, and gender and war studies. He is a term member of the Council on Foreign Relations, and he consults on various research projects commissioned by agencies in the Department of Defense. His books include: *Guarding the Guardians: Civilian Control of Nuclear Weapons, Assuring Control of Nuclear Weapons: The Evolution of Permissive Action Links* (coauthored with Peter Stein), and *Battlefield Nuclear Weapons: Issues and Options* (coedited with Stephen Biddle). Recent articles and book chapters include: "Command and Control in Emerging Nuclear Nations," and "Key West Revisited: The Service Roles and Missions Debate." He has also penned several shorter pieces on foreign policy, the Gulf War, and just war doctrine for the *Los Angeles Times* and the *Christian Science Monitor*. Dr. Feaver is currently working on a book-length project on American civil-military relations and the decision to use force in international conflicts.

**David P. Forsythe** is Professor and Graduate Chair of the Political Science Department at the University of Nebraska-Lincoln. Dr. Forsythe received his Ph.D. from Princeton University and has been a consultant to the International Red Cross as well as serving as president of the Human Rights Committee of the International Political Science Association, and president of the International Organization Section of the International Studies Association. Some of his books include *Human Rights and Peace*, as well as *Human Rights in the New Europe*, both in press. Already published are other books such as *The Internationalization of Human Rights, Human Rights and Development, Human Rights and World Politics, Human Rights and US Foreign Policy,* and *Humanitarian Politics*. Among his approximately fifty journal articles and book chapters are "Human Rights in the Post-Cold War World" (1991) and "Human Rights and the International Committee of the Red Cross" (1993). He is currently cooperating on a book about the United Nations and will be publishing two articles on the question of humanitarian intervention.

**Merry M. Merryfield** is Associate Professor of Social Studies and Global Education at The Ohio State University. Her doctorate in social studies education, African Studies and educational inquiry is from Indiana University. Dr. Merryfield has taught high school social studies and

Latin in Atlanta, and geography and African literature in Sierra Leone. She has researched the role of education in African development through studies with the Bureau of Educational Research at Kenyatta University in Kenya, the Centre for Social Research at Chancellor College in Malawi, the University of Ife in Nigeria, and the Ministry of Education of Botswana. Her research in global education has documented exemplary programs in teacher education and the contexts of teacher decision making. She is presently serving as chair of the Research Committee for the National Council for the Social Studies (NCSS), member of the Board of Directors for the Alliance for Education in Global and International Studies (AEGIS) and is coeditor of *Theory into Practice*. Her publications include *Lessons From Africa, Teaching about Francophone Africa, Teaching about the World: Teacher Education Programs with a Global Perspective,* and *Responding to the Gulf War: A Study of Teacher Decision-Making*. Dr. Merryfield is currently working with classroom teachers to restructure teacher education through the development of professional development school in social studies and global education.

**Karen A. Mingst** is Professor of Political Science and Director of Graduate Studies at the University of Kentucky. She has published work on international organization and law, international political economy, and African politics in such journals as *International Organization, International Studies Quarterly, Journal of Common Market Studies, Review of International Studies, Journal of Peace Research, African Studies Review, Africa Today,* and *East European Quarterly*. She is the coeditor and author (with Margaret P. Karns) of *The United States and Multilateral Institutions: Patterns of Changing Instrumentality and Influence* (Unwin Hyman, 1990) and the author of *Politics and the African Development Bank* (University Press of Kentucky, 1990). Dr. Mingst has received financial support from the Carnegie Endowment, United States Institute of Peace, Ford Foundation, and the Fulbright Program for research in Europe and Africa. She is active in the International Studies Association and in 1990 served as vice-president of the organization.

**Yasemin Alptekin-Oguzertem** Born in Istanbul, Turkey, holds degrees in English from the Marmara University, English Literature and Languages from the Bosphorus University, Istanbul, and a M.S. in Instructional Systems Technology from Indiana University. From 1990 to 1992 Ms. Oguzertem served as the Associate Director at the National Clearinghouse for the U.S.-Japan Studies at the Social Studies Development Center at Indiana University where she developed a database for teaching about Japan for precollegiate educators. She has translated *The African Stories* by Doris Lessing into Turkish and co-translated *Traditional Turk-*

ish Art Today by Henry Glassie. She is the co-author of a chapter on the Teachers' Resource Centers in *Internationalizing the U.S. Classroom: Japan as a Model* published by the ERIC/CheSS in Bloomington-Indiana. Currently she is a doctoral student in social studies and global education and a Graduate Research Associate and interpreter for the National Education and Training for Employment (CETE) at the Ohio State University.

**Richard C. Remy**, Ph.D., is Associate Director of the Mershon Center at The Ohio State University and an Associate Professor in the College of Education. He received his Ph.D. in political science from Northwestern University and has taught in the Chicago public schools. His books include *Approaches to World Studies, Teaching About National Security, American Government and National Security, Civics for Americans, Lessons on the Constitution, Citizenship Decision Making,* and *United States Government.* Dr. Remy currently co-directs a project with the Polish Ministry of National Education to develop new civic education programs for Polish students, teachers, and teacher educators. He serves as a consultant on civic education to the governments of Albania, Bulgaria, and Lithuania as well as to the United States Information Agency and the National Endowment for Democracy. He serves on national advisory boards for the American Bar Association, the U.S. Education Department's project on national standards for civics and government education, and the National Science Foundation's Longitudinal Study of American Youth.

**Dov Ronen** is Associate Professor of Harvard's Center for International Affairs, Affiliate of Harvard's Center for European Studies, and Lecturer in Psychology in the Department of Psychiatry, Harvard Medical School. He received his B.A. in Political Science and Sociology at the Hebrew University Jerusalem, M.A. and Ph.D. degrees in Political Science at Indiana University. Dr. Ronen has taught at the Hebrew University, Jerusalem, as well as at Tufts and Brandeis Universities, and Wellesley College. He has taught at the Harvard University Extension since 1978, has chaired for several years seminar series on nationalism, ethnic conflict and self-determination at the Center for International Affairs, and served as director of its Africa Research Program. For six years he was chairman of the Politics and Ethnicity Research Committee of the International Political Science Association. His books include: *Dahomey: between Tradition and Modernity; The Quest for Self-Determination* (also appeared in Japanese translation); *Democracy and Pluralism in Africa;* and, with Dennis Thompson, *Ethnicity, Politics, and Development.* Dr. Ronen is currently the Principal Investigator of a research project of the Institute of Conflict Research, Vienna, Austria, on ethnic conflict in central Europe.

Steve Shapiro is a social studies teacher at Reynoldsburg High School, Reynoldsburg, Ohio. He currently teaches global studies as part of an interdisciplinary team called World Connections. Mr. Shapiro earned his B.A. from the University of Michigan, where he was recognized by the Michigan Association of Teacher Educators as Michigan's Student Teacher of the Year. He is currently completing his Master's degree in Social Studies and Global Education at The Ohio State University. His teaching and curriculum development in global education have benefited from his extensive cross-cultural study, work, and travel in more than twenty countries on four different continents. Mr. Shapiro is a field professor at Ohio State, where he collaborates with professors and other social studies teachers in six school districts in the restructuring and teaching of globally oriented social studies methods classes for preservice teachers. Reynoldsburg High School is engaging in a major restructuring effort as part of the Coalition of Essential Schools. As part of the "scouting party" in the reform effort, Mr. Shapiro helped design and implement an interdisciplinary team structure. As a result of its reform efforts, Reynoldsburg High School was honored as an A+: Break the Mold School in 1992 by Lamar Alexander, U.S. Secretary of Education. Mr. Shapiro is also a consultant on performance-based and authentic assessment.

Marvin S. Soroos is Professor and Head of the Department of Political Science and Public Administration at North Carolina State University. He received a doctorate in political science from Northwestern University. An active member of the International Studies Association, he has served as president of its Southern Section and chair of its Environmental Studies Section. Dr. Soroos has participated in Fulbright seminars in India, Japan, and Peru and been a guest researcher at the International Peace Research Institute in Oslo. He has lectured on international environmental policy in numerous countries, been a visiting instructor on the same subject at the University of Tampere (Finland), and participated in international workshops of the Human Dimensions of Global Environmental Change programme sponsored by the International Social Science Council. His books include: *Beyond Sovereignty: The Challenge of Global Policy; Environment and the Global Arena: Actors, Values, Policies, and Futures;* and *The Global Predicament: Ecological Perspectives on World Order.* He edits a series of books on managing global commons for the University of South Carolina Press. His current research involves transboundary air pollution and the management of the atmosphere as a common pool resource.

# NAME INDEX

# SUBJECT INDEX